When I Was a Dynamiter!

Or, How a Nice Catholic Boy Became a Merry Prankster, a Pornographer, and a Bridegroom Seven Times

Fables Without Morals:

Memoirs of a Primary Source

By

Lee Quarnstrom

Punk Hostage Press

When I Was a Dynamiter *Or, How a Nice Catholic Boy Became a Merry Prankster, a Pornographer, and a Bridegroom Seven Times.* Lee Quarnstrom

© Lee Quarnstrom 2014

When I Was a Dynamiter *Or, How a Nice Catholic Boy Became a Merry Prankster, a Pornographer, and a Bridegroom Seven Times*, Copyright 2014 by Lee Quarnstrom. All rights reserved. Printed in the United States of America. No part of this text may be used or reproduced in any manner whatsoever without written permission from the author or publisher except in the case of brief quotations embodied in critical articles and reviews. For information address Punk Hostage Press, Los Angeles, California.

Punk Hostage Press
P.O. Box 1869 Hollywood CA 90078
punkhostagepress.com

ISBN-13: 978-1-940213-98-9
ISBN-10: 1-940213-98-3

Associate Editor: Iris Berry

Introduction: John Riley

Cover Design: Geoff Melville

Cover photo from left to right: Deputy Sheriff Russell Gropp, Ken Kesey, author Lee Quarnstrom, and Neal Cassady, Beat Generation hero of Jack Kerouac's *On the Road* and driver of the Pranksters' famous psychedelic bus, *Further*.

"*After a raid by state, federal and local narcotics agents on the remote mountain home of Ken Kesey on April 24, 1965, the well-known writer and 13 of his fellow 'Merry Pranksters' were taken in handcuffs to the San Mateo County jail. Note the 'crop marks' indicating where a newspaper copy editor trimmed Cassady's likeness from the photo as it appeared on one Bay Area newspaper's front page the morning after the bust.*"

For Chris, who read my "dailies" with actual joy.

"Everybody's doing what he wants to be doing." – Ken Kesey

INTRODUCTION

If I were writing a screenplay about the life of the author of this book I would start it in a particularly dreary part of Sweden or Norway or Ireland, three dreary places from whence his ancestors came. My bio-pic would run for several hours, flipping through cold winters and through many generations until the fruit of all its suffering showed up at New Trier Township High School in Winnetka, Illinois. He was tall. He was skinny. Above all he was bright.

Lee Quarnstrom was my pied piper. My father wanted me to join the family business, which would have meant trying to prosper in the world of electric light-fixture sales. But Lee knew better: He led me downtown to the Loop, to the Chicago City News Bureau, where he had begun at age nineteen as a copy boy. Since that early start, Lee had been sent out to be reporter of police news—various sorts of mayhem ranging from apartment fires to floaters in the Chicago River to cheap murders over a pint of Richard's Wild Irish Rose Peppermint Wine. It sounded good to me. I signed on as a copy boy.

One night when I was running copy on the night shift, Lee was on the South Side covering a race riot. He called his editor to report that he had been chain-whipped by a gang of local youngsters and needed a ride to a hospital.

I was dispatched by the night city editor to some tiny South Side hospital to make sure Lee got some medical attention. The editor drove me to the hospital and I waited for the healthcare profession to perform its magic on the beaten street reporter. But nothing was happening. Injuries apparently more serious than his were being treated in the emergency room and Lee continued to wait. One particularly interesting case shunted ahead of him was the wife of a professional knife thrower who was brought in with a dagger lodged firmly between her shoulder blades. Was this a professional slipup or a marital spat? No one knew except the participants and they weren't talking.

I called in the details of the errant knife-tosser to City News just as the editor was arriving back at his desk. It was my first of thousands of news stories at City News and, later, the *Chicago American*. I will always be grateful to Lee for suffering that beating!

My editor asked when the doctors planned to deal with Quarnstrom's trauma, which included a broken nose, a concussion, and extensive facial battering. I suggested I extract him and drive him to Wesley, a North Side hospital of more proven reputation. I did so and Lee's wounds were attended to before I drove him homeward though the city.

At one intersection a non-hostile group of youths strolled past the car and Lee became hysterical, thinking they were his attackers come to finish him off. He grabbed the wheel and tried to take control. I was left with only once choice, a hard one. Just like in the movies, a slight punch, a tap, really, on the jaw put him out until I deposited him at his parents' house in the lily-white suburbs.

This was what old-time reporters used to call a war story. But reporters also function in peacetime. They fall in love and occasionally marry. Lee Quarnstrom had only one marriage at which I was not a witness, although I knew the bride. But I was present at six subsequent nuptials. I carefully worked my way up the Quarnstrom marriage bureaucracy. I started out as a simple guest dancing in San Francisco at the old Fillmore Auditorium as he married "Space Daisy," proceeded to champagne bottle-opener in Santa Cruz, and at one wedding danced with his mother. Finally, at Lee's seventh, and last, he swears, I served as Best Man when he married our New Trier High School Class of 1958 classmate, the former Christine Hultman.

Looking back, I can see that although our lives began intersecting in our hometown high school as well as at our Chicago journalism jobs, we continued to stay in touch as our choices led us to wander far apart, at least on a map. Lee lived for a while in Spanish Harlem and worked in a Greenwich Village bookstore. I covered the Nation's Capital for *Time Magazine*'s Washington bureau. Lee sojourned in Mexico City, then worked for the AP in Seattle. I learned Russian in Monterey, California, while in the Army while Lee and the Merry Pranksters lived across the bay near Santa Cruz.

I remember my twenty-third birthday, about as far from my familiar, everyday world as one could be. I was alone among my fellow recruits at Fort Leonard Wood, Missouri. I learned not long thereafter that Lee's son, Eric, was born that same day. And I remember the day eighteen years later when I learned Eric had been shot to death on a street in San Francisco. The last time I had seen Eric I gave him a twenty-dollar bill. Wish I could give him one today. His passing was a deep low point in Lee's life. Lee was closer by when I suffered a loss by death of a love of my own while attending Northwestern and working at City News.

In the eighties, Lee and I tried writing screenplays as a team. Our similar senses of humor led to an excess of zaniness that never conquered the marketplace. We tried to write in Santa Cruz and in my office in Beverly Hills. We had almost too much fun. We became big fans of an elderly piano bar *artiste* in Beverly Hills known as "the incomparable Rita Marlow." Lee went on to work for Larry Flynt and return to daily journalism for the *Watsonville Register-Pajaronian* and the *San Jose Mercury News*. I kept going as a screenwriter solo act and became enmeshed in Writers Guild politics after a six-month strike in 1988.

I knew Lee Quarnstrom before, during, and after the time he was among the merriest of Ken Kesey's Pranksters. While I was a Los Angeles correspondent for *Life Magazine* I rendezvoused with the two of them and Mountain Girl and rode around town in the bus of many colors.

When you have finished this fine book you will know him, too. Not as well as I do but well enough, as I have, to really enjoy the ride.

John Riley

Los Angeles 2014

Former journalist and *Los Angeles Times* Sunday columnist John Riley is a screenwriter, bon vivant, and raconteur.

CONTENTS

PREFACE 17

Ooooops 21

Introibo Ad Altare Dei 23

A Call in the Night 27

Eric 35

PART I. BOYHOOD 43

Pearl Harbor 45

When FDR Died 47

Why I Was A Skinny Kid 51

The Folks 57

PART II. YOUTH 71

LeeBoy 73

Sport 83

Fire In The Hole 89

Why I Left College and Became a Copy Boy 97

PART III. MERRY PRANKSTER 101

La Honda 103

The Bust At Kesey's Place 119

State of Grace **113**

The Great Duck Storm/Further Indeed **139**

On the Bus or Off the Bus **147**

Adios, La Honda, Aloha, Santa Cruz **153**

What Does "Psychedelic" Mean? **161**

Can You Pass The Acid Test? **163**

Electric Kool-Aid **177**

South of the Border **189**

A Wink, *El Norte* and The Summer of Love **199**

Dope, An Aside **219**

PART IV. ON THE ROAD, OFF THE ROAD 229

Existencialista **231**

I'll Take Manhattan **241**

When I Was a Mailman **249**

PART V. PORNOGRAPHER 255

The Realist **257**

Flights Of Fancy: Larry Flynt and Las Vegas **267**

The Wedding Gift **281**

Ethics, Smut, and TV **285**

The Ginger Man **299**

PART VI. NEWSPAPERMAN 307

Hail To The Chief 309

City News Kid 313

Julius 321

Police Reporter 325

Politicians 343

PART VII. BRIDEGROOM: THE SEVENTH TIME IS THE BEST 355

Songbird, Or Another Fable Without A Moral? 357

Crush 363

In-Laws 367

Weddings and More About Thomas Pynchon 371

PART VIII. SO IT'S COME TO THIS? 385

A Gun, Buddha, and *La Virgen De Guadalupe* 387

My Mother Goes Crazy and Dies and I Discover That I Have A Little Sister 395

What Have I Learned? Anything? 403

In the final paragraph of his Mexico City-based novel, *Tristessa*,

Jack Kerouac wrote:

"I'll go light candles to the Madonna, I'll paint the Madonna, and eat ice cream, benny and bread—'Dope and saltpork,' as Bhikku Booboo said—I'll go to the South of Sicily in the winter, and paint memories of Arles—I'll buy a piano and Mozart me that—I'll write long sad tales about people in the legend of my life—This part is my part of the movie, let's hear yours."

This part is mine.

PREFACE

In the mid- to late-1980s, the editor of the Sunday magazine supplement of the newspaper that employed me as a reporter assigned me to look for Thomas Pynchon. When I'd proposed the piece to that editor I was hoping for a great adventure: I'd foreseen visions of knocking on strange doors in odd parts of the world, of following false leads, of tracking down odd characters with phony names, and of rendezvous with assorted eccentrics sporting fake beards and prevaricating in bizarre accents, miscreants who would point me in wrong directions and suggest that I ask bogus questions that would never lead me to the great and famously shy author.

I had read of a would-be Pynchon interviewer who'd knocked on a door in Mexico City, in a neighborhood not far from the *Colonia Florida* district where I'd spent half a year when I was twenty, and had been told by the man who answered his knock to come back in a few hours when *Señor* Pynchon would be home. Of course, upon his return, the eager beaver found the gate unlocked, the door open, the *casa* empty and the friendly fellow, obviously Pynchon himself, vanished.

What fun I anticipated.

Before I started ringing strangers' doorbells, though, I asked a policeman I knew if he'd check with the DMV to see if any Thomas Pynchon held a California driver's license. My friendly cop stepped to his computer, put in the name, waited a second, then read me Pynchon's address. Not only did the reclusive Pynchon live in California, he was registered in rural Aptos, not ten miles or fifteen minutes from my house in Santa Cruz, not five minutes from the home of my closest local friend, Bill Kelsay. I could be there and back before lunch.

Instead of heading out to Aptos, I went back to the Sunday supplement editor's office and told him, "Sorry, I found Pynchon. I can't do the article."

"Why not?" he wondered.

Because, I explained, I had proposed *looking for* Pynchon, not *finding* him. I'd had no intention of actually tracking him down.

17

I'd never considered, nor wanted to, interview the famous writer. I just wanted to look for him. The editor didn't exactly savvy what I was talking about but he did reluctantly agree to cancel the assignment.

That reminded me of the time my friend Paul Krassner told me he was going to write to Pynchon and say he planned to interview the bashful novelist in *The Realist,* Paul's pioneering progenitor of America's alternative press. Paul said he was going to write Pynchon to say there were two ways to do the interview: actually and speciously, with Paul, in that latter case, not only asking the questions but making up the answers. Paul had, of course, done some "creative journalism" in the past, including his "expose" of LBJ's "abuse" of President Kennedy's corpse on the flight back to the Nation's Capital from Dallas. I was looking forward to his "interview" with Thomas Pynchon. I don't think, though, that Paul actually made that proposal—or threat—to Pynchon.

I thought about all that in the middle of a recent night after I'd been lost in a dream, lost and unable to find my way home. I could not, in that dream, remember where I lived. My address eluded me. And I'd realized that the only way to discover where I lived would be to wake up and think about it. I knew I was asleep and that I was sleeping in my house, no matter where the house was located. Were I awake, I understood, I'd be able to figure out where I was and thusly where I lived.

I did wake up sufficiently to go through that process. Then I began to consider the difference between looking for someone and actually finding them, actually tracking a person down to a specific address. They are indeed two separate things.

The time spent in my dream not knowing where I lived was both frightening, for obvious reasons, and exhilarating, because adventure loomed and suddenly and unfamiliarly I was, as Bob Dylan put it, on my own "with no direction home/a complete unknown/just like a rolling stone."

(When I moved to San Francisco in 1964, I found adventure by smoking a joint, getting stoned, driving up some hill such as Twin Peaks, making random turns, getting lost, then trying to find my way back my pad.)

So, not knowing where I lived and where I was, I sat up in bed for a while, wondering whether some fearful dementia was sneaking up on me, and if it were, whether it would confine itself to my dreams. Could some encroaching forgetfulness put the kibosh on finishing these memoirs, which are, after all, just another search for another writer? I wondered, would pawing over seven decades-plus of memories provide nearly as much excitement as I'd hoped for when I'd motored up Twin Peaks in fogs both literal and mental—or when I'd proposed the Looking for Pynchon quest, a story I'd hoped would lead along a trail of mirages, false scents, characters with fake eyeglasses and funny noses and bad toupees, silly pseudonyms, and just plain lying eyes?

I've been fascinated—who hasn't been?—by Arthur Rimbaud's brief but elegant autobiographical note:

"'I' is someone else." ("*Je est un autre.*")

It's one of those things that many of us wish we'd have said ourselves—or, at least, wish that we could put into our own prose. But only one guy, one outlaw poet, can get away with confining his autobiographical account into those four words. For me it takes many, many more. Plus, "I" is not someone else.

At this point, I think I still have most of my marbles, although a few aggies might have gone missing, perhaps a few puries, maybe a glassie or two. The ball bearings my Uncle George gave me when I was a boy—we called them "steelies"—actually have gone missing. I still have enough marbles to get this project on the road. So, here goes, while the quarry is still afoot. I am not someone else. I am,

Lee Quarnstrom
La Habra, CA 2014

OOOOOPS!

Ken Kesey once wrote a sort of apologia for exercising the true art of the raconteur: enhancing or exaggerating details here and there to improve a good yarn into a great story:

"If I'm saddled with having to tell the truth about all these people, I can't go explore the areas that are interesting to me. Facts are dull. Stories are interesting."

Even though I agree with Kesey about storytelling, my many years as a newspaperman helped me focus on reporting things as they actually happened, or, at least, as I recall them happening. Kesey, of course, believed that "journalists are like seismographs, novelists are like lightning rods." Again, I agree. This memoir is a seismograph, a record of actual events. I'm hoping to record the squiggly lines marking the tremors and upheavals that describe one life in the latter half of the Twentieth Century.

I've done my best to report events and to describe people and places as I best remember them. Memories fade, I've learned, and the mind can play tricks on those of us trying to recall some conversation or Monopoly game or drug-fueled rock-and-roll jamboree that happened a half-century or more ago. Certainly readers may find a mistake in the paragraph in which I describe their scene in what I think of as *my* movie. If you do find an error or a misstatement or a story that you believe is just plain untrue, I didn't do it on purpose. I merely did my best to dredge things up from a part of my mind that is used as a filing cabinet, I guess, and may be just a little bit rusty.

Introibo Ad Altare Dei

After the third or fourth kid in a row spoke to the packed church hall crowd early on that rainy 1982 Berkeley afternoon, I got up and walked out to the lobby, then out into the drizzle. I was tired of hearing "sincere" teenage boys who were unfamiliar with sincerity testify that my son's shooting death a few days earlier had changed their lives. I was tired of hearing them testify that they'd learned a lesson they'd never forget, that they were going to straighten up and fly right and tow the line and walk the walk as well as talk the talk and keep their noses clean and to the grindstone. I was tired of hearing them say they were forever going to keep Eric, my son, foremost in their minds as they made important decisions in their still-young lives. I was tired of the bullshit, in other words, even though I knew that the young men, and a few young Berkeley women—most of them Eric's schoolmates from grade school through high school, most of them around my son's age, eighteen, none of them students at the local University of California campus, many of them waiters or busboys or dishwashers at restaurants where college students and their instructors dined—believed that they were being sincere. They thought they were telling the truth when they bore witness to my son's death by promising, essentially, to be good boys and girls from now on.

I understood and was not even bothered, really, by my realization that they were all hoodwinking themselves and that they'd forget Eric, or at least forget how he had died or why he had died, within a few weeks. I wasn't bothered by the inauthentic soul-baring of those young people; I just didn't want to listen to any more of it.

Standing just outside the building, thinking about Eric and about the fact that had I not quit smoking a couple of years earlier this would have been the perfect time to light up, I thought about my boy and I continued the weeping that I'd put on hold during

*(I Shall Go Unto the Altar of God)

the drive up from Santa Cruz. I looked back inside and saw Eric's mom, Judy, my first wife, and her husband Larry, Eric's stepfather, sitting upright at the front of the crowd. Judy was dying of cancer and Larry, a sweet but feckless man who'd been my friend and fellow journalist in Seattle eighteen years earlier when Eric was born, was trying to be the pillar of strength that he thought he should be at this time of family tragedy. Eric's older sister Susan and younger brother Michael—each, like Eric, the child of different fathers—sat sharing the sadness with Larry and Judy.

Sensing that I wasn't alone I looked around and noticed a lovely young woman standing near me in front of the church-hall entrance. She seemed to know who I was and introduced herself. She said her name was Zia and that she had been Eric's girlfriend. She was not the same girlfriend Eric had brought to Santa Cruz a few weeks or months earlier. She seemed sweeter, brighter, deeper, than the other pretty girl who'd taken off her clothes and joined me in my brother Dean's hot tub as my brother and my son stood nearby talking. I had seen that other young woman in the church but I'd avoided her eyes; despite myself I'd made a value judgment that day at Dean's home, thinking to myself that having a girlfriend who'd climb nude into a tub with her boyfriend's father the first time they'd met was just a bit too … forward, I guess, is the term. Forward? Man, talk about sounding square!

Zia, who'd been crying, told me she and the other young lady had both been Eric's girlfriends. But, she continued, as we strolled away from the memorial service and walked around the block through the light rain, she and Eric had been in love and were planning to get married. Zia told me she thought she was pregnant and that my son had been happy at the prospect of fatherhood and that she still hoped she was pregnant even though the baby's father was dead and cremated and would never have a chance to meet his child.

Zia was so sweet and so bright and clearly so loving of my boy that I told her I hoped, too, that she would have Eric's baby. It hadn't occurred to me yet that my son's death meant that my genes had run into an unsurpassable roadblock, a dead-end, and would never be replicated, as intended by nature; all I thought on that rainy walk was that there was the chance, were Zia pregnant, that I might after all have a connection to my boy, that perhaps I would be a grandfather. I believed Zia would be a fine mother, a fine mother for my grandchild.

Zia and I saw one another a few times over the next year or so until she returned to New York, where her father, an esoteric rabbi, as she called him, lived among his bohemian friends on Manhattan's Lower East Side. Before she left for the East Coast she and I would drive up a road north of Berkeley and stop in the tiny town of Kensington, where Eric's ashes were buried in a churchyard that looked out, on the western horizon, over the Golden Gate. On one visit we saw that a wild iris had grown above the spot where the ash and hunks of bone that had been my son lay buried.

Zia called me ten days or so after the memorial service. She was crying: She wasn't pregnant after all. I felt a stab of regret but knew that was just a selfish bit of pain. But I felt relief, too, I guess, for Zia. She wouldn't have to spend her young womanhood as a single mother, changing the diapers and trying to feed a daily reminder of a murdered love.

Zia Ziprin and I have remained close over the three-plus decades since we lost Eric. I think of her today as my daughter-in-law and I think that Zia, particularly since her father died a few years ago, somehow honors that same relationship. We saw each other on a sultry day in 2011, for the first time since she left Berkeley and returned to New York. In the interim she had been married, divorced, and had a beautiful daughter, now in her early twenties, who shares her life on the Lower East Side. Zia designs shoes and owns a "shoe archive," as she calls it—a collection of exotic and/or period footwear available for rental to stylists for fashion photo shoots, films, and television shows.

After Zia and I have had one of our not-quite-cathartic but often weepy talks, it always occurs to me that neither of us has any way to know, had Eric lived, whether he and she would have stayed together over all the intervening years since they were eighteen. Lord knows: I've been married seven times! On the other hand, Eric didn't know I was his father. He thought I was a family friend or some sort of uncle, I guess, until he was about twelve. And, while I saw him regularly, I was not around enough to have been much of a role model. Maybe he and Zia would have survived as a loving couple. I like to think so and hope so and Zia knows it would have been that way.

One bright thing Zia and I share is that our Eric, the one we've carried in our hearts for so many years, is a tall and slender and wonderfully beautiful boy, a self-assured eighteen-year-old young man with a touch of mystery, a bit of compassion, and a sense of adventure in his eyes. He remains that way forever.

*The first words of the Latin or Tridentine Mass, said by priests until changed to vernacular languages in the 1960s. Altar boys, like me when I was eight or nine, replied, *"Ad Deum qui laetificat juventutem meum,"* or, "For God is the joy of my youth."

A CALL IN THE NIGHT

At night for years I dreamed my son was still alive. He was still tall and slender and cocky and beautiful. He was so handsome—in my dreams as well as in his brief young life—that women friends of mine told me frequently that they wanted to help him "learn the ropes." But Eric was eighteen and he already knew the ropes, all the ropes, all except the one about not taking a gun to town. Zia, the beautiful woman Eric said he intended to marry, pleaded with him not to carry the gun; he promised he'd return it to its owner, a "friend" who'd loaned it to him. Nonetheless, Zia, a woman who believes in premonitions and omens and auras and the like, saw something worrisome, something dark and frightening, in Eric's eyes when he left her place in Berkeley for the last time that March evening in 1982, when she and my son were both young. But at least, she says, he'd made that promise and at least he wouldn't be carrying that damned pistol.

Yet, there was Eric, dead with a bullet through his eighteen-year-old heart, on a 2 a.m. San Francisco sidewalk close by the familiar North Beach bars where I'd drunk with friends until closing time when I was only three or four years older. That had been when I lived in San Francisco and enjoyed hanging out in bars—and dancing and fighting and playing eight-ball pool for beers, drinking sweet port in dark doorways with pals when we had no cash, and wandering or staggering up and down those old beatnik streets and alleys smoking pot and eating, and occasionally shooting meth, methamphetamine, speed, and, in the words of so many social critics and novelists and journalists a half-century ago, "looking for kicks." All young people look for kicks.

Pretty much everything in my life changed forever when the phone rang in Santa Cruz in the middle of that March 1982 night and Larry, my first wife's third and final husband and the adoptive father of my son, told me, "Lee, Eric's been shot in San Francisco and he's dead!" That is the worst thing to be told about anyone at any time and it is so much, much more terrible when it is your own child who is dead, your own and only child whom you love to an almost-impossible degree and whom you're never going to see again, your own son whom you are now going to outlive. Forever.

It is wrong in so many ways when a child dies. It's not supposed to happen that way. We're supposed to pass away before our children do and they are supposed to look after us when we're too old to do it ourselves and to mourn us when we die and to bury us. Our children are supposed to give us grandkids and to make certain that our genes have new leases on life and that there is some child, or several, to whom we can leave our names, perhaps, and at least leave all that *stuff* that's hanging on the walls and cluttering up the closets and the far reaches of the attic and taking up space on bookshelves. None of that happens nor will it ever happen when one's only child lies dead on a closing-time sidewalk in San Francisco.

When Larry's call shook me from my last sound sleep for a decade or more, and after he had told me that he and Judy were already making plans to have the body cremated and buried in a churchyard in the Berkeley hills, I had no idea what to say other than to thank him for calling. I wanted to ask how it had happened, why it had happened, how the fuck could it have happened? "All I know," Larry reported, "is the police say that he got in a hassle with another young man and Eric had a gun and they say he took it out and the other boy grabbed it and shot him. Once. Through the heart. He died immediately."

Larry said he'd call again in a few hours with a time and place for the burial and a memorial service. I thanked him again and said I would drive up from Santa Cruz so I could be there when they buried Eric's "remains," surely a polite word inadequate to describe what is really buried when it's your child, even an eighteen-year-old grown child. And then I turned to my wife, Melody, and said I had to phone the editor at the San Jose Mercury, where I was supposed to show up for my new job in a few hours, for my first day of real employment since I'd left *Hustler* magazine and, later, a bad television "reality" show in Hollywood, a half-year earlier.

I began that new job as a *San Jose Mercury* reporter and writer a week later, one week after what was supposed to have been my first day on the job. I didn't understand it at the time but I realized long before I retired from that paper nineteen years later, when I was sixty-one and sick of what had happened to newspapers and especially to the *San Jose Mercury News*, that each time I showed up for work during the intervening years I was once again reminded, on some half-buried level of consciousness, of Larry's terrible 2 a.m. telephone call and the unfathomably permanent loss of my son.

It was not just reporting for work that brought back the feelings, if not always the actual memories, of that night and the sad, dismal days that followed. Even now, decades later, I can find myself weeping when I read a news story or see a television report that has anything at all to do with fathers and sons or even suggests that *any* child or even an animal, a pet, even a stray, has suffered any sort of sadness or pain. When I play now with our two beautiful Welsh corgis I can't help but consider mortality, theirs, mine, my son's, my wife's. Then, even *I* feel like telling myself to "Get over it!" But I can't. I can't control or limit or erase my feelings and I knew almost from the first, once I was able to think about Eric's death as well as cry about it, that I wouldn't want to harden myself to keep the pain and sadness in check, not then, not ever. I knew, too, that I would forever feel guilty that I was not a better father to Eric, that I had let my former wife's new husband adopt him when he was still a toddler and had even let them change his last name. (Judy assured me Eric would gradually be told, when he was older, that I was his real father. "Look on the bright side," she said on the phone one day when Eric was two or three, "you won't have to pay any more child support. And you can still visit him whenever you want.")

Some of the events I write about here happened before I met Judy and her daughter, Susan, my sweet stepdaughter. The rest occurred after that first of my seven marriages began to go belly-up, as did the subsequent five.

Writing these anecdotes and reports I've sought, and occasionally found, memories that remind me why I did what I did. But for the most part, I did things for fuck-all, for the hell of it. My youthful and callow reading of Camus, Sartre, et al. convinced me of two things: that we should try to act without fear, and that the consequences of my actions were no one's responsibility other than my own. But frankly, I never spent much time doing that kind of thinking when, for instance, I decided to get married during a rock-and-roll dance at the old Fillmore Auditorium in San Francisco or left a newspaper job to go work as a pornographer for Larry Flynt or when I left another reporting job in Chicago when I was twenty to move, penniless, to Mexico City.

As in myth, many, or most, of us set out upon adventures, often into unknown and dangerous territories. Some of us return having seen wondrous creatures and having escaped terrible monsters. Others, like a few friends and fellow acidheads of the 1960s, didn't really return at all. Some died when they were far too young. Some others were seduced by the wonders revealed to them by those same marvelous creatures, then felled by the monsters they often turned out actually to be.

Frankly, I've been lucky. I have been, over and over again, at the right place at the right time. I've been offered rare opportunities for adventure and, without truly conceiving of myself as an adventurer, have taken them. I have made love with far, far more beautiful and lovely and sexy women than I would consider my fair share. I've met remarkable people, fascinating men and women. I have shared the *darshan* of humans of high consciousness, yet I've learned that just because a man seems enlightened today doesn't mean he will be so tomorrow or remain that way forever. I particularly thank Ken Kesey for that, for teaching by example that we are all human and that even the seemingly most-enlightened of us still has feet grounded in, if not made of, clay. I learned, again from Kesey, as from others, that not everyone I have cared for has consistently been a particularly nice person. They helped me learn that the quality I most respect in a fellow being is not whether he or she is nice, or interesting, or politically progressive, or smart or high or beautiful, but whether that man or woman—or child—is a decent human being. I have met and loved, and do love, some men, women, and children who are all of those other things, too, perhaps. But they are indeed decent human beings.

I have been lucky. Except for losing my son.

I've believed for more than half my life that virtually *everything* a man does is done to get laid. I've also understood all along that, for the most part, men are assholes. Those are, no doubt, some of the reasons I've written about Eric in newspaper columns: glib self-therapy designed to garner sympathy—and to get laid. And I have fended off well-meaning calls from well-meaning readers urging me to join Parents of Murdered Children or some such organization. "It will help you get past this, Lee, it will help with the grieving." But I didn't want to get past it. I still don't. Who would want to get past grieving for their own son? Who the fuck would want to relegate him to the past?

I have so many memories of Eric, and more, and I have wanted to lay all of them out in front of me like a Solitaire player spreads a deck of cards, each face card a friend, each of the others a memory—except that it will never be possible to lay all those cards on the table: many of them that I'd held close to my vest until then, the face cards, the aces, the Jack of Hearts, vanished into the San Francisco night in March 1982.

But not all of them are gone. I still have so many memories:

I knew the day that Eric was born that it was, and forever would be, the happiest day of my life. I remember the maternity ward (no "birthing centers" then) nurse "presenting" my new son to me in the fathers' waiting room. Husbands never even dreamed of being in the room with wives and nurses at their childrens' births in 1963! The nurse made certain as she spread his fingers and then, as she unswaddled him, his toes, showing and not telling, as writing teachers teach, that his tiny hands and feet were perfect—as was all of my newborn baby boy.

I still recall clearly that I seemed to be floating above the ground as I walked home to be with my sweet step-daughter Susan and my not-so-sweet mother, who was visiting from

Chicago in what I knew would be a fruitless attempt to "help with the baby." I recall soaring across the spring sunrise-bright campus after reluctantly leaving my wife and my son in the University of Washington Medical Center maternity ward. It was far too early for anyone else to be up and about on campus—young people, students, didn't jog (or work out or stretch or powerwalk or pedal mountain bikes) in those days; the healthy, athletic look was not yet fashionable, thank God. The preferred look (by the kind of women who interested me) for young men in 1963 was perfect for someone tall and skinny like me: poetically thin, brooding, perhaps a bit sad, nonchalant, hungry, certainly not athletic in any way.

I felt as though I were the only person around as I crossed campus toward the bungalow where Judy and Susie and I—and now Eric—lived north of the U. I felt like the only man in a world of my own, like Gene Kelly kicking up his heels in a Paris downpour. Everything was clear, light, airy. And I was floating!

I didn't understand yet that "nothing lasts," as Ken Kesey later would frequently tell us, nor that all things that are put together will come apart, as the Buddha might have told me. That clear, light buoyancy that enveloped me ended when my son was about a month old and Judy, upset that I wasn't planning to dress up to take her to a campus flamenco concert, smacked me over the noggin with my guitar, leaving in the shiny brightwood back of the instrument a hole exactly the size of my gigantic Scandinavian head.

(I'd bought the handmade instrument for sixteen dollars from a craftsman on a little street of guitar-makers in Mexico City in 1960, when I was twenty. When I told Mexican friends I was returning to the U.S. after six months south of the border, *el maestro,* the elderly man who was my buddy Al's guitar teacher, looked at me in disbelief. He loved my guitar. "God," he prayed in *español,* "don't let him take the guitar!" He offered me five-hundred pesos, forty bucks, a lot of *dinero* for an impoverished music teacher. Wow, I thought to myself, seeing dollar signs, or at least peso signs, before my eyes. If it's worth forty dollars here, think what it'll be worth once I get back home. And I couldn't

32

even play the thing; I just thought it was beautiful. Of course, a guitar with a head-sized hole in the back was worth no dollars or pesos at all but it was a good indication that there was something terribly wrong with my marriage.)

However, strolling that May morning through (or, as it felt, above) the university campus I happened upon a hidden botany department herb garden I'd no idea even existed. I was tickled to see that one of the obscure plants growing there was identified by a small placard as "Cannabis Sativa." I recognized immediately that my new fatherhood made me so much higher than I'd ever been on any cannabis, even the potent Panama Red that found its way to Chicago when I was nineteen, a self-styled beatnik and reporter for the City News Bureau—a local wire service owned by the city's (then) four dailies and the training ground for almost every journalist in the Windy City. I was even higher than when I'd smoked the *mota de Michoacan* that was common on the artistic, bohemian scene in Mexico City. (An approximate ounce of marijuana, wrapped in a sheet of newspaper, cost twenty pesos, which, in 1960, was one dollar and sixty cents.) I'd bought one of those ounces late one night in a shadowy street near Plaza Garibaldi.

Memories. Memories of Eric …

ERIC

He was named after my *compadre* Eric List, a student at the National University of Mexico, where I'd studied *español* and Mexican history and had fallen in love for the first time—not only with a woman but also with a place: Mexico. My boy's middle name was James, after my Chicago actor pal Jim Deuter. Jim was the first gay friend to come out to me—I'd not understood until the day Jim, doing what may have been at that moment when we were both twenty-one the most-difficult thing he'd ever done, how supremely difficult it was to be gay in the very early 1960s.

And speaking of that marijuana growing unremarked in the University of Washington herb garden, I remember my son, then sixteen or seventeen, laughing with my boss Larry Flynt as he sat next to the *Hustler* publisher's gold-plated wheelchair: my handsome boy rolling joints for Larry and passing others around the room in a posh "cottage" at the Beverly Hills Hotel. Eric rolled Larry's dope into joints that I and other toilers in the porn empire of Larry and his wife, Althea, could smoke and get high on while we drank good champagne and ate caviar on crackers at the Flynt's wedding anniversary party. I knew Eric was not only smiling and laughing because he was having a good time joking with Larry, but because he was there with *me,* visiting in L.A. from his mother and stepfather's home in Berkeley. Eric seemed proud, I thought, that his dad was executive editor of *Hustler*, then, in 1980, the most-outrageous, most-notorious men's (i.e., smut) magazine in America—and he was *my* son, he was with *me!* I never saw him happier.

I was happy, too. I was out having a good time with my son, one of the few times, really, that we spent several days together. I was proud to be showing him off to my co-workers and to Larry and Althea Flynt.

I liked Althea. Some of my fellow editorial workers had little respect for Althea, a former dancer in one of Larry's early Hustler clubs in Ohio, the often hard-hearted woman who'd won his love, as well as a new chinchilla-lined Rolls Royce, by whipping up what he described to me as "the best sloppy joe I"—

which Larry pronounced "Ah"— "ever ate." Some of those editorial compatriots, particularly those who'd started with Larry back in Columbus, thought Althea was, let me put it this way, not as smart as they were. But she was! In fact, operating on instinct and a native canniness that she'd honed on the street, Althea Flynt was able, after an assassin tried to kill Larry in 1978, to save her husband's publishing empire from going broke. She nimbly beat back attacks from all directions by financial rats who saw the disabling gunshots, fired by a racist nut upset by *Hustler* photos of a black man and white woman engaged in staged sexual intercourse, as an opportunity to skip out on bills, to threaten liens and takeovers, or to gain financial and even editorial control of their magazines.

(For months Larry Flynt lay in an opiate haze, close to death, in a small hospital across the street from our plush Century City *Hustler* offices in West Los Angeles. Althea often "consulted" with her husband, who, gut-shot by the sniper with a high-powered rifle, came within an inch of dying and remains paralyzed from the waist down from his wounds. But actually, she pretty much saved Larry Flynt Publications on her own. By herself she made the decisions that counted and reported, not always truthfully, that Larry had agreed with her choices. When, in those days and as he recovered sufficiently to return to his office and resume titular control of things, Larry would frequently issue some outrageous, crazy directive that we knew he'd forget within minutes. We decided that Larry was often "confused." We'd tell one another that he'd been confused when, for instance, he'd order some impossible major rewrite or photo change after the upcoming issue had already been to the printer, whose presses were in Wisconsin.

(Larry was more than just confused; he was hurting badly. One day as I met with him to discuss some upcoming issue of *Hustler*, Larry politely apologized and told me he had to scream because of the excruciating pain. And he did. I remembered that scream years later when I first read the Buddha's Four Nobel Truths, the first of which is "All life is suffering." Larry Flynt suffered.

(I got to know Althea well and I was sad when she died a few years after I'd begun work at the *San Jose Mercury*. She might have been ignorant—she once tried to impress me and another *Hustler* editor with a French *"voila,"* only she said "viola," and when she thought a piece of *Hustler* fiction was sad she would tell me it was "poyg-nant" —but she was not dumb. She was sharp as a tack at judging character and as cunning as anyone I've ever known. I miss Althea and I miss the times we worked together. She and the staff and I put out *Hustlers* that we knew would make Larry proud.

(I'll say here for the record that the *Hustler* editors were the smartest group of people I ever worked with. Oddly, like myself, many were former Catholics. I say "oddly" but this probably isn't all that odd to psychiatrists.)

Althea penned a note to me when she heard of Eric's death:

> *As you know we felt close to you, beyond our professional relationship. I remember your bringing Eric to our anniversary party. Eric was a bright, handsome boy. If there is anything we can do for you please don't hesitate to call upon us.*
>
> *Sincerely,*
>
> *Althea Flynt*

There was nothing Althea or Larry could do for me. And later, when I wrote Althea's obituary for the *San Jose Mercury* newspaper, I remembered her moments of kindness with appreciation and even affection. She was a lot more than a country girl whose shotgun-toting daddy came home one night and blasted some of her siblings, then her mother, then himself, while young Althea hid under her bed. And I appreciated Larry's frankness when she died. He publicly revealed that Althea died of AIDS (which she could have contracted in *so* many ways!) at a time when having a family member or a loved one succumb to the new plague that was killing gay men was generally not mentioned but instead treated as something to be ashamed of.

In fact, when AIDS first exploded into the public's consciousness, the *Mercury*'s editor in charge of the front page, the cover of the A section, demanded daily stories about the new epidemic that was sweeping through the gay community in San Francisco and other cities. He figured that daily stories asking, *How is AIDS spread*? Would interest potential readers in San Francisco, located not far to the north. But at one editorial meeting, when I reported to the front-page editor that a university researcher had discovered how AIDS was apparently passed from man to man, he looked excited and asked, "How?"

"Butt-fucking," I reported.

"Put it inside the B Section," he ordered.

* * *

I wondered for years why my son was so fascinated with everything relating to President John Kennedy. Forty-eight years after Eric, his mother and half-sister Susie left me in Seattle and moved south to the Bay Area, his last love, Zia, visiting from New York, still had fond memories of Eric's collection of JFK memorabilia. I told Zia that the explanation for Eric's obsession came to me one sleepless night. The day Eric and Susie left our Seattle home with their mother for the Bay Area was the day President Kennedy was murdered in Dallas. The excruciating irony of infant Eric, who grew up fascinated by JFK, being taken from me that November 1963 day remained unclear to me for years. Eric died the same way as the late president whom he had so admired, by gunshot.

I stood one day with Ken Kesey in Wavy Gravy's Hog Farm commune kitchen in Berkeley. It was in 1990, when some of us quarter-century-older veterans of Kesey's Merry Band of Pranksters were taking a new and professionally painted version of his famous psychedelic bus—with "Further" or, from time-to-time, "Furthur," painted on the destination board—from Oregon to the Smithsonian Museum in the Nation's Capital.

(We didn't get there. Kesey never really intended to donate his bus for display. Unlike the original bus, which was then, in 1990, rusting and melting into a swampy thicket on Kesey's Oregon farm, this new bus was professionally decorated. The original bus, the one that took the first incarnation of the Merry Pranksters 'cross-country from La Honda, in the mountains above Palo Alto, to New York City and back, was indeed a colorful sight for sore eyes. We Pranksters constantly daubed and doodled on the old bus, painting and repainting and repainting it yet again. It was like a brilliantly colored molting reptile on speed, replacing skins with much psychedelic imagination, enthusiasm and vigor but, for the most part, amateurish illustrative skills. Aside from "Further" on the destination placard, a sign on the back of the bus read, "Caution—Weird Load." That was the bus we Merry Pranksters took on seemingly endless adventures in the Bay Area and elsewhere in California and, later, to L.A. and Mexico as we, with the Grateful Dead as the house band, put on the LSD-fueled Acid Tests that were brought to the world's attention with Tom Wolfe's fine—and, for the most part, fairly accurate— best-seller, *The Electric Kool-Aid Acid Test*.)

Anyway, there Kesey and I were in Wavy Gravy's kitchen. The newer model of Furthur was parked outside at the curb.

Kesey's younger son Jed, was a college wrestler like his dad, and attended Ken's alma mater, the University of Oregon. Jed was twenty when he was killed in 1984. A bus carrying the school's "grappling" team, as student newspaper headlines sometimes call those athletes, went over a cliff on a stormy Pacific Northwest night. (Afterwards, Kesey lobbied for years to force educational institutions in his beloved Oregon to put seatbelts on all school buses.)

The best writer I've ever known, Kentuckian Ed McClanahan, was along on that last (for me) bus trip. Ed described that 1990 Hog Farm kitchen moment in his collection of stories and essays, *I Just Hitched In From The Coast—The Ed McClanahan Reader*:

"I happened to be in the kitchen with Lee and Ken while the party roared in the other room. The two of them stood there by the kitchen sink in a broad beam of late-afternoon sunlight, the featured players in what was—and is—for me a deeply moving tableau.

" 'Up in the hills today,' Lee told Ken, 'we went past the church where my son's funeral was held.'

" 'You never get over it,' Ken said softly.

" 'Yeah,' Lee said. 'And you never want to.'

" 'Right,' said Ken. 'It's how you keep them with you.' "

"Compared to grief, I was beginning to discern," Ed reflected in his book, "dying is a breeze."*

It took a while, maybe months, maybe a year, after his death for my dream that Eric was still alive to begin its nightly visits. Then it came regularly, night after night, for year after year. It was a wonderful dream, a miraculous dream: Eric had not been shot at all, he had not been killed. He was still alive! Those were the happiest dreams a father could ever have.

But then morning would come and I'd be jolted quickly out of my dream and instantly I knew the truth. My son Eric had been killed and was dead and had left me forever. He had been killed yet once again.

Meanwhile, life goes on.

*Also with our Aging Band of Pranksters when we stopped at Wavy Gravy's Hog Farm commune in Berkeley was my pal Paul Krassner, founder of *The Realist* and so-called "Father of the Underground Press." (He demanded a paternity test, of course.) Paul also published his remembrance of that sad moment in the kitchen when Kesey and I remembered our dead sons: "*During the reunion bus trip, Quarnstrom and Kesey talked with each other about their mutual tragedy for the first time, in the kitchen at Wavy Gravy's house.*" Paul wrote that Kesey and I agreed that we thought about our lost sons daily and that we each believed keeping them in our memories was the right thing to do.

I.

BOYHOOD

PEARL HARBOR

The Japanese, and the fact that there was a larger world than I had suspected, entered my consciousness when Pearl Harbor was bombed less than a month after my second birthday. That December 7 is the first memory I have that I can pinpoint to a specific date. My parents and I drove from Longview up the fifty miles or so to Spirit Lake and Mount St. Helens for a Sunday picnic. I don't know if the lake's there any more; the mountain blew its top off in 1980 and for a while the lake, where as a young teenage boy I went to YMCA camp, was filled with ash and cinder and pumice and dead trees, thousands—millions—of dead trees. They say a new forest is regenerating atop the volcanic debris near the noticeably shorter peak; I hope the lake has also returned to reflect the mountain from the site of the rustic former Y camp.

That December 1941 day must have been, because I remember it so clearly, one of the sweetest of my young life. My dad, my mother and I had a happy lunch on a picnic table at the edge of the crystalline lake. I recall my delight at smelling for the first time the evergreen tang of the Douglas firs and red cedars. I remember seeing from our Plymouth, a green 1941 sedan, the snow-covered, volcanic St. Helens peak rising above the lake. And I can recall later, after we'd driven back to Longview, my dad having to rush off to work, even though it was a Sunday and even though it was the best day of my life so far.

"The Japs have bombed Pearl Harbor," he explained as he sped off to his job as city editor of the *Longview Daily News*. For many months I thought that he'd said "chaps" and was confused whenever I'd hear him refer to someone a "a nice chap."

Somewhere I have a front page of that Extra Edition the *Longview Daily News*, like every paper in America, hurried off the presses that first Sunday of November 1941:

Japs Bomb Pearl Harbor!

I must have thought that the chaps, the Chapanese, were terrible meanies for bombing Pearl Harbor on a Sunday, especially on a Sunday I'd enjoyed so much with my mom and dad. Frankly, I have few family memories of such pleasant, peaceful times as that day at the base of that shapely volcanic mountain, once compared favorably with Japan's Fuji, now, with its top blown to bits, squat and almost formless, no longer rising majestically on the horizon as seen from Longview or nearby Portland but, rather, just a lump above the treeline.

WHEN FDR DIED

Toward the end of the war I was standing with my dad in the garage he built, or, more likely, had someone else build, on the alley behind our house in Longview. Since we were in Southwest Washington state, on the Columbia River and not too far from the Pacific Ocean, we were probably in the garage to get out of the rain.

Out along the alley, buttercups grew at the margins. In those days I believed that if you held a buttercup beneath the chin of someone you loved and that person's chin reflected the yellow of the flower's petals, that man or woman or boy or girl loved butter. I cannot now remember why that insight was so important to us youngsters who played in that alley. Perhaps it was because we rarely saw or ate butter; our folks bought those one-pound sacks of oleomargarine, then colored it by pinching and breaking the tiny pellet of red pigment before working it through the oleo until the goop in the cellophane bag resembled butter.

My dad was at his garage workbench, although he was not a man who knew how to use tools, nor did he care to learn. In fact, Gordon Quarnstrom was one of the few fathers of boys in my neighborhood circle of friends who still had all ten fingers.

(Many of Longview's men had at one time worked in the lumber mills that, along with the pulp mill, were the town's main sources of income. And many of those men lost a finger, or two, or three, running logs and boards through the giant band-saws that sliced them up into smaller and smaller pieces until they became two-by-fours that, in those days, actually measured two-inches by four-inches. If you can find a two-by-four today, perhaps at the Home Depot, measure it and notice how much such a board has shrunk in the past few decades. I remember when the older brother of one of my neighborhood pals lost two fingers at the mill and how proud he was to have gone through that important rite of initiation into young-manhood as things stood in the logging and lumber-mill town of Longview, Washington.)

On that rainy day in 1945, I saw that my dad was weeping softly as he stood at his workbench, staring into the distance that would have been visible had we not been inside the garage. I saw my father cry only three times. The first time was that day, when I was a boy. The second time was many years later when my brother and I joined him at what had become our family home in a Chicago suburb after my mother had died. He was not crying not because he missed my mother; who would? He was crying because for the first time in decades his two sons were at home at the same time. He was relishing being paternal, experiencing with my brother and me the death of his not-beloved wife. The third time I saw my father cry was when I visited him in Texas. We thought he was dying and he tearfully asked me to shave the gray stubble from his chin. He had moved to Austin, after an almost-respectable mourning period for my mother, so he could be with his longtime girlfriend Connie. I was happy when he finally asked Connie, a pleasant, friendly Texas widow and fellow travel-writer to be his second wife.

But that day in 1945 in Longview, my dad, Gordon Martin Quarnstrom, son of a Swede, Gustav Frithiof Quarnstrom and a Norwegian, Jenny Martinson, was standing at that unused workbench, holding a screwdriver or a hammer or some tool that he rarely used but that he kept there with his sickle and the putty knife and the rasp file, in the garage with the dirt floor. I can still see him standing in the afternoon gloom, the large posters of Norman Rockwell's illustrations of the Four Freedoms—outlined in a recent speech by President Roosevelt—tacked to the wall above his tool-bench. (I have small versions of the Rockwell illustrations in my own garage, where they serve as a sort of memorial to my dad: "Freedom of Speech," an earnest fellow, a working stiff, stands to speak his mind at a public meeting in Rockwell's painting; "Freedom of Worship," a pastiche of men and women praying to each worshiper's god; "Freedom from Want," a Rockwell depiction of Grandma serving a turkey to her happy family while Grandpa watches benevolently; and "Freedom from Fear," a couple tucking their kids in for a restful night's sleep.)

"Why," I asked my dad, "are you crying?"

"Because," he told me, "President Roosevelt has died." This shocked me. I had never considered that Our President Franklin Delano Roosevelt might be subject to the same laws of life and death as the rest of us. I felt betrayed somehow. How could we survive without our president? Who was going to kill Hitler (who was, in fact, a suicide fewer than three weeks later) and who was going to kill the Japs? How could we go on?

"Was President Roosevelt the greatest man who ever lived?" I shyly wondered.

My father, not a religious man, a fallen-away Lutheran like most Scandinavians in the Pacific Northwest, looked down at me, tears standing in his usually inscrutable eyes.

"Was the president the greatest man who ever lived?" he repeated my question.

He looked at me for a moment and even then, at age five, I knew he was considering the beliefs of my mother, Lenore, who was a Catholic of an unwavering Irish stripe and who was seeing to it that my younger brother and I were being raised, with her husband's assent, in her Roman Catholic faith.

"No, son, no," my father finally said, wiping the tears from his eyes. "No, President Roosevelt was a great man but he wasn't the greatest man who ever lived.

"Who was?" I asked.

"Jesus was."

Even at my young age I could tell he didn't mean it.

WHY I WAS A SKINNY KID

My mother, Lenore Lee Quarnstrom—named by her father for a woman mentioned in the Edgar Allan Poe poem *The Raven*, specifically, the "rare and radiant maiden, whom the angels named Lenore"—was the worst cook I've ever known. No kidding. When I was young I thought you only ate so you didn't die.

Also, I thought everybody was Irish, or at least part Irish, just as I thought everyone sang "When Irish Eyes Are Smiling" on St. Patrick's Day. Every St. Paddy's Day, to mark the festive day, we gathered in some public hall to give cartons of Lucky Strikes to Father Mulligan, pastor and confessor. And we sang, "When Irish hearts are happy, all the world seems bright and gay/And When Irish Eyes Are Smiling, sure, they steal your heart away."

The Irish were not noted for their abilities in the kitchen. Neither was Mrs. Quarnstrom, nor her mother and grandmother before her. Nor, as far as I know, were my Scandinavian ancestors on my father's side of the family.

I was as ignorant of good food as I was of clean air: Longview's usually damp atmosphere was dominated by the stench from the local pulp mill where they made paper and cardboard. It was a sour odor that stunk of sulfur, of rotting garbage and seemingly of the skunk cabbage that grew near the sloughs that connected Lake Sacajawea, our municipal pond, with the Columbia River. I believed that God had somehow screwed up, that He had made the world green and beautiful but somehow He had forgotten the air and left it foul.

Similarly, I believed that because the food I was served three times daily tasted *so* bad it must be that all food tasted terrible. I concluded, as anyone would, that people ate merely to keep from starving to death. Had I died before I was eleven, it never would have occurred to me that people ate because they wanted to, because they actually enjoyed their meals.

My mother cooked what she called "nourishing" food that "sticks to your ribs." This was her way of identifying and justifying meals that included, as an example, canned peas overcooked until they were gray and mushy, low-grade hamburger that sizzled down from a nice-sized patty to something resembling in every way a salty hockey puck, eggs with yolks fried until they were hard and as dry as powder—all of it fried in the bacon grease she hoarded in the squat one-pound coffee cans that took up one of the cupboards above the stove. She even used the bacon grease from one of the old coffee cans to grease the pan when she fried bacon!

Sometimes, when there were tomatoes or ears of corn or peas or beans ready to harvest in our "Victory Garden" in the back yard we had fresh vegetables at the Quarnstrom house. But Lenore took much of the fresh stuff from our garden down to the local cannery, where she and many of the other ladies in town cooked all color and flavor out of their homegrown produce, then sealed it in tins for future use, when the previously fresh and tasty vegetables from household gardens could be served the way the kitchen gods of the 1940s had decreed it should be served: minus color, flavor, and texture. The cannery—filled with muggy clouds of steam billowing around sweaty Longview housewives standing on slatted floorboards above rivulets of running water and packing their homegrown peas and green beans into tin cans that would be sealed tightly somewhere back in the dark bowels of the building, someplace from which loud bangs and crashes and hisses noisily emanated—was a Fellini-esque version of Hades. I hated being dragged by my mother down to that hellish cannery, where my mother secured me to a table and a zinc sink, tied by a tiny leather harness, which I also had to wear when my mother took me when she went shopping downtown, to keep me from running for fresh air and freedom.

I assume my dad also cherished the day or two that we'd have fresh peas on the table instead of the soggy, greenish-gray mush that Mrs. Q served after she'd boiled away the flavor and color, then packed the unappetizing results in tin.

One day right after WWII ended, she brought home a steak, a big hunk of round steak the size and shape of first base, and fried it until it was dry and rubbery. It was my first steak, as well as my last, until I was old enough to drive over to my friend

John Riley's home, where his dad bought good hunks of meat and cooked them properly on the first backyard barbecue I ever encountered. By then I was seventeen years old.

The "rare and radiant" Lenore specialized in her special versions of what Army cooks used to call shit on a shingle. "Creamed" chipped beef on toast, or even worse, "creamed" canned, oily, fishy, tuna on toast. Just how that gray library paste-like crap came to assume the mantle of being "creamed" anything is beyond me. Mrs. Quarnstrom always served it, though, on toasted Wonder Bread, which in those days only built strong bodies eight ways, not the twelve ways touted in more-recent years.

I was, in fact, a very skinny kid.

Later, being tall and skinny kept me from being drafted and sent, possibly, to Vietnam, although I was about a year too old during much of that war to have actually been called up. When I took my required pre-induction Army physical when I was twenty-two, I was adjudged too underfed to serve my country. I was six-feet, four-inches tall and weighed one-hundred and forty-nine pounds, a kilo or two under the minimum for someone my height. (The sergeant optimistically told me, "Go home, kid, and eat nothing but bananas. Come back in ten days and you'll be able to pass. No sweat." I went home and for ten days ate nothing but Benzedrine. I weighed one-hundred and forty-three when I light-headedly stumbled into my return appointment.)

I realize that my mother was part of the first generation of American women to enjoy the convenience of buying almost any darned thing she wanted already canned and ready to open and toss on the stove. This convenience, of course, meant that many women of her generation really didn't have to learn to cook if they didn't want to—or if they lacked the talent—because they could open a couple of cans, turn on a burner on the stove, and **presto!** it was ready to serve.

Lenore was also among a generation of women who, for the most part, were housewives who cleaned and sewed and raised kids, none of which she excelled at, instead of joining the salaried workforce. It didn't take two breadwinners to make the house payment and car payment and cover life's necessities in those days, so many moms just acted like moms without, as far as I could tell, giving any other options much thought.

I remember the day that my mother's culinary activities took a distinctly new turn for the worse.

If you're old enough, you'll probably recall those framed illustrations that used to hang behind the counter at the local Rexall when drugstores were pharmacies instead of discount emporia. Every pharmacist displayed nicely framed prints of paintings depicting Great Moments in Medicine, such as Madame Curie Discovers Radium or Doctor Harvey Invents Blood or Louis Pasteur Discovers Bugs. The Great Scientist or Physician was always portrayed in that ubiquitous series of drugstore art at the AHA! instant of discovery, surrounded by awe-stricken colleagues gazing in wonder as they uncovered yet another key secret of medicine or pharmacology.

I have in my mind a tableau that could have belonged to that series of druggists' illustrations of famous men and women of science making their great discoveries: The tableau in my mind is of my father, my brother Dean and me standing in the kitchen in Longview watching Lenore in apparent awe as ...

Mrs. Quarnstrom Discovers the Fish Stick.

My friend John Riley, whom I met in high school and who has remained one of my close buddies for the intervening decades, recalls the first, and only, time he accepted my mother's invitation to dine at the Quarnstrom household. He remembers that I stood behind my mother as she asked him whether he'd like to stay for dinner. He says I was shaking my head no and trying to wave off the polite acceptance of her offer that I heard forming on his lips.

Later, Riley—whose dad had the barbecue and whose parents were both wonderful cooks who prepared tasty dishes from scratch—told me with some embarrassment it had been the first time he'd ever known that food could taste bad. Well, I had tried to warn him.

When my mother died in 1991 I wrote about her in my *San Jose Mercury News* newspaper column. I noted that she was not a great cook but that her potato salad recipe was fine and that I still use it to this day (lotsa mayo was her secret).

I mailed that obituary column to my dad, half-expecting him to take some sort of umbrage at this insult to his late wife's culinary skills. I'd never discussed her cooking with him since I'd complained once when I was a child that she'd somehow managed to ruin the Cream of Wheat. After my whining complaint he had angrily used some of the Swedish he'd picked up from his own father, sternly ordering *"Hold sheften,"* or Shut up!

He dropped me a note in reply to my column about my mother and her lack of cooking skills. His note read, simply:

"Her apple pie wasn't bad."

THE FOLKS

I recall no discussions, ever, with my parents about the meaning of life, the rules of the game, the difference between right and wrong, the nature of the universe, how to deal with the opposite sex, or anything else along those lines. My mother did ask, when I was in the eighth grade, to let her know when any "changes" started to occur in my body. I didn't. She also warned me against the use of Ouija boards, which, she was quite certain, channeled something diabolical, demonic, perhaps Satan himself.

When I was a few years older she told me that she feared that I'd go to hell, but offered little advice how to avoid the place other than to stop doing everything I liked, and was therefore doing, and to go to Mass every Sunday. My mother was no doubt more of an Irish Catholic than her Irish forebears, who generally seemed at least as interested in surviving the tribulations of life as with reaching Paradise.

My father told me only to respect my mother.

On my sixteenth birthday he also told me to get a job. Immediately. And to start contributing toward my room and board.

He never did tell me that I had a half-sister, but I didn't have one until I was a senior in high school, and by that time, I guess he thought there would really be nothing to gain by telling my brother and me about the birth of his love child. He must have believed (correctly) that there would be nothing but trouble in store if he spilled the beans to Mrs. Quarnstrom. My mother was already crazy and was sufficiently jealous of his unknown mistress or mistresses without a new and illegitimate, as she would have put it, addition to the Quarnstrom family tree.

I had no hint about my half-sister Tracey until I was almost seventy and she was in her late forties and living in New York City. She tracked me down after her birth mother, one of my dad's previously unknown girlfriends, died, giving Tracey access to some love letters in a locked drawer. Yes, Gordon Quarnstrom was a ladies' man.

Besides letting me know with his tears that he was human, when we learned of the death of President Franklin Delano Roosevelt, four other events involving Gordon Quarnstrom—or GQ, as his second wife referred to him—stick in my mind. In reverse order, they are:

4) Shaving, at his request, the gray stubble from his chin and neck as he lay not in his deathbed but in whatever you'd call his bed before his deathbed, in what would, in a few months, be his deathbed, at the home he shared in Texas with his second wife, Connie, a travel-writer like himself, a woman he had met on a travel-writers' junket to the grand opening of some hotel, I suppose, in some far-flung world capital. Scraping the gray bristles off his chin I understood suddenly all the implications of William Wordsworth's line, "The child is father of the man." A boy fathers himself in the sense that he creates what he becomes as a man—unless something goes haywire, like being shot through the heart at age eighteen. And, as a man declines into old age, his son, if he is lucky enough to have one, may take care of him as he himself had cared for that son when he was a boy.

3) On a quick round-trip in the spring of 1960 from Mexico to New York, Chicago and then back south, we—my Mexico City housemate Al Roth and Bob Gordon, a roué who lived in a downtown Mexican whorehouse—stopped for a day and night at my folks' home north of the Windy City. As my father and I stood at the top of the stairs a few minutes after we'd arrived, GQ looked with obvious disgust at my beard, my longish hair and my admittedly ratty clothes. "You're a horse's ass," he opined. "I wonder," I spat into my father's angry face, "whether it's environmental or hereditary?" He kicked me down the stairs.

2) I was with my dad at a dingy A&P supermarket in Silver Spring, Maryland. Used to the friendly folks at the Piggly Wiggly grocery market back home in Longview, my dad and I were shocked when we got to the front of the line at the Silver Spring A&P store, only to have the clerk put a chain across in front of us and tell us his cash register was closed. "Go to the next line," he ordered. Rather than follow that particular directive, which would have led to another stint standing in another queue,

my dad looked at me for a moment, then tipped the full-to-the-brim shopping cart on its side. Cartons of oatmeal and Kellogg's Pep, cans of peas and carrots and green beans, Campbell's Scotch Broth and packages of Lux and Boraxo, a box of Ivory Snow, and cartons of ice cream and bags of fresh lettuce and bananas spilled across the floor of the supermarket. "Come on, son," he said loudly, "let's find a store where they're not too busy to serve the customers." We walked out of the store. I was eleven years old and goggle-eyed, not the least embarrassed and suddenly proud of my dad and feeling very powerful.

Although my dad and I never spoke of the incident, even in the car as we looked for another grocery store, I've taken it as a life lesson from him: Don't take crap you don't have to take!

1) When I was very young, barely three, my mother was in the hospital with my new baby brother Dean, whom I'd not yet met. Hospital stays were as long as two weeks for new moms in those days and no one but the infant's father, who was required to dress in scrubs like a surgeon, was allowed into the maternity ward.

On the Sunday morning of the week my mother and Baby Dean were in the hospital, after my dad and I had read the comics in the *Oregon Journal,* he got a call from the cops in Kelso, then the small and generally shabby county seat across the Cowlitz River from Longview, where we lived. The cop reported a suicide.

Aside from his duties as city editor of the *Longview Daily News,* GQ was also the elected Cowlitz County coroner. He'd had no medical training but being coroner meant mainly he signed some papers after a doctor had declared a dead person dead.

We drove over to Kelso and my dad told me to wait in the car. He went inside one of the small cottages that made up the residential neighborhood near the string of taverns that constituted Kelso's downtown.

(I loved those loggers' taverns because, when I was a few years older, I'd buy ten copies of the *Longview Daily News* for two-and-one-half cents apiece and take them around the corner to

Commerce Avenue, where a drunk in a lumberjacks' tavern would buy them all for a half-a-buck because I was such a cute little newsboy! And that meant quarter's profit for five minutes worth of effort.)

No one questioned my dad leaving his three-year-old son in the car while he went into the little Kelso house to inspect the body. My dad didn't tell me, of course, what was going on inside the place, just that he had to talk to some policemen. In those days it was okay to leave a child in a car, even with the windows rolled up. I guess kids didn't fry or die of sunstroke in the early 1940s, particularly in a part of the country where the sun doesn't shine all that much. Also, automatic window buttons were off somewhere on the Cars of the Future that appeared regularly on the pages of *Popular Science Magazine*, so I could roll the windows up and down with a handle whenever I wanted or needed to do so for fresh air.

After a while I got bored watching serious-looking cops enter and leave the house and I was no doubt probably petulant and lonely as well and itching to see my dad. So I left the car and toddled into the bungalow.

I remember turning left into the living room and seeing my father and a pair of policemen gathered in front of the fireplace. A raggedy Christmas tree stood alone in a corner with a few ornaments and a handful of tinsel that helped the tree look even more desolate. There was a body, or most of a body, crumpled on the faded gray carpet just off the concrete hearth.

Before my father and one of the cops could hustle me out of there, I saw that the body was missing its head. It was unbelievable! A body and no head? How could that be?

The cop looked up as he strode across the room toward me, so I looked up, too. I saw the head, or some stuff that used to be a head, splattered on the ceiling and dripping onto the rug. What remained of the man's brains and bits of skull had exploded upward when the man had put his shotgun beneath his chin and, somehow, pulled the trigger.

Seven decades later, I'm still not sure what affect that scene had on me. It was not my first meeting with death. That had happened not long before when a game warden arrested a neighbor who'd shot and skinned some does and fawns somewhere near town. Ignorant or stupid, the hunter had brought the skinned deer carcasses home to butcher in his garage. Neighborhood kids had swarmed around the man's pickup truck and someone called the game warden. All of us children gagged but stared anyway through a fog of horseflies at a heap of bloody deer flesh, *sans* any recognizable bit of hair or skin or head or antler except their big brown eyes.

But this encounter with a suicide's body and his head on the ceiling was my first experience with a dead human being. I wouldn't see my second until I was a cub reporter in Chicago sixteen years later. I wonder to this day why I've never dreamed of the dead man or the pitiful Christmas tree or the brain goo and bits of bony stuff on that ceiling in Kelso. I feel pretty sure that the whole scene must have done more than stick benignly in my memory. But maybe that's all it did. After all, I feel no catharsis now as I write and as I remember it all—the lonely Christmas tree, the body and some brains on the ceiling, and my father, the county coroner, telling me never, ever to tell my mother what we'd seen while she was in the hospital with my new baby brother.

* * *

My father, Gordon Martin Quarnstrom, was born in Spirit Lake, Idaho, in Kootenai County, more recently a center of armed and dangerous right-wing "patriots" and religious nuts. But when he was born, in 1912, the remote Idaho panhandle and, in fact, the whole state of Idaho, was quite a different place. It was a center of radical labor activists, a place where the Western Federation of Miners and the Industrial Workers of the World found sympathetic ears at the smelters and in the silver mines and among the loggers in the forests.

My grandfather, Gustav Frithiof Quarnstrom, was born in Sweden and married Jenny Oliva Martinson, an immigrant from Norway. They met, naturally, in Minnesota, the main gathering place for Scandinavian immigrants seeking family, jobs, or mates.

Gustav was a master blacksmith—something like a tool-and-dye maker. Jenny raised kids, three sons, Reuben, George and Gordon, and a daughter, Hattie. Like so many other Swedes and Norwegians, the Quarnstroms moved west from Minnesota, following the damp and chilly climes along the border with Canada, staying on the flat prairies or in the dark forests that reminded them so much of home. And like so many other Swedes and Norwegians who headed west, some of the companions died along the way while others made it to Seattle.

When I was a boy in Longview the town had sizable Swedish and Norwegian populations and even some Finns, who must have been real bruisers because it seems other Scandinavians were wary of Finns. There was a Finnish hall for meetings, dances and other get-togethers just out of town near where my first friend, Ned Piper, moved with his family to be out "in the woods." There were Vasa and Sons of Norway halls closer in.

In about 1917, when my Uncle Reuben was at the right age to go off to the war that was beginning in Europe, my grandfather squirreled him away on a small farm in the Columbia River Gorge community of Underwood. Reuben, who was dead for twenty years before I was born a hundred miles down the Columbia River, died there, or across the Columbia in Hood River, Oregon. My dad tried, when he had grown to middle age, to find his brother's grave or, at least, a death certificate or newspaper obituary but he could find no trace of Reuben Quarnstrom on either side of the Columbia.

The middle brother, George, took the train to Detroit after he retired from the U.S. Navy Yard in Bremerton, across Puget Sound from Seattle. George bought a brand new Cadillac right off the assembly line, as one could do in those days, usually at a price much lower than West Coast dealers had to charge because they had to pay for transporting the new car for the intervening two thousand miles.

Uncle George drove his new DeVille from Detroit back to Bremerton but made an important stop in the Minnesota towns where he had spent his boyhood and where cousins still lived, Two Harbors and Brainerd (where the movie *Fargo* takes place). He made certain that all the cousins and all of his schoolmates and all of his boyhood neighbors and high school girlfriends saw the expensive new Caddy sedan. Then he drove it to Bremerton and sold it to a dealer, who put it in his used car lot at a higher price than General Motors had charged at the factory.

(I thought of my Uncle George and his brief time as a Cadillac owner when one of my former wives told me about her aunt, who had put on her fur coat before leaping to her death from a bridge in Providence, R.I. She wore the fur coat because she didn't want people to think she'd committed suicide because she was poor. Only she didn't die, so only the ambulance driver and a couple of nurses knew that she owned a mink coat.)

* * *

Margaret Lenore Lee, my mother, a pretty woman when she was young but a mean-spirited drinker and pill-popper in her later years, was born in Havre, Montana a couple of years after her future husband had debuted in Idaho. Her father, Ellis Lee, was a barber. He was also a drummer in a prairie jazz band, second baseman for a semi-pro baseball team and, for a while, after moving west from his home state of Michigan, the proprietor of a pool hall in Devon, a tiny frontier Montana burg where my grandmother, Mary Margaret, called Mayme, *May-mee,* Lee, was postmistress.

I suspect that Ellis was not much of a husband because Mayme took to living out of town with her three girls, my mother Lenore, her sisters Norma and Virginia, called Gee-Gee, and their brother Charlie, who died at age three of what Mayme told me was "the summer complaint," a polite if grim way of saying diarrhea. They lived in a sod dugout on the family's homestead. Out there, she told me, the "half-breeds" who lived up the road would get drunk and randomly shoot their guns and generally scare the hell out of everybody else.

One stormy night, hearing a heck of a racket outside the remote one-room house and certain it meant the half-breeds were on another rampage, Mayme unholstered her loaded pistol and told the girls and their sickly little brother to hide in a corner of the sod-covered hut.

This homestead was not all that far from the Little Big Horn and there was an old cowboy named Dick, my mother said, who helped with chores on some local ranches. The elderly cowpoke said he'd fought with Major Reno at the Battle of the Greasy Grass, as local tribes had called Little Big Horn, and was still able to frighten women and children with his yarns about the dangerous red Indians. So I'm not surprised that Mayme Lee, a tough and decisive woman all her life, gathered her son and daughters behind her and, holding her Colt .38-caliber revolver, went out into the windy night and emptied the weapon in the general direction of the loud noise she could still hear out near the road.

Come dawn, she told me, she went outside with the reloaded sidearm and half-expected to find some dead Blackfeet in the yard. Instead she saw a huge knot of tumbleweed that had been wedged by the strong prairie winds beneath a corrugated zinc washboard that was hanging from the clothesline. When the wind gusted, she noticed, the tumbleweed scraping and brushing against the metal washboard sounded like dangerous drunken rascal Indians up to no good.

There were five bullet holes through the tin washboard, Mayme, boasted, obviously proud of her own shooting prowess.

After Mayme and Ellis had taken their daughters to Seattle, and after my grandfather had either moved out or been kicked out (he told me that my grandmother could not abide the fact that he spent most of his spare time reading, so she booted him out), Mayme got a job. She spent the 1930s raising her daughters and working full time. She was a tough woman but a sweet and loving grandmother. She had a quirky side. On nights when my mother and brother and I traveled to Seattle to spend a week at Grandma's place I was fascinated that the last thing Mayme did before going to sleep would be, in order to prevent the sore throats and snoring that come with breathing through the mouth, to affix a strip of adhesive tape over her mouth. It was weird but it worked.

* * *

My dad knew little about his parents' families back in the old countries. Jenny Martinson had two sisters but neither shared my grandmother's last name. A genealogist told him that a majority of births in Norway at the turn of the Twentieth Century were illegitimate and that the different last names probably indicated different fathers for the girls. Jenny had been born in Moss, on the sound that terminates at Oslo, known in those years as Kristiania. Gordon could find no record of his mother's arrival at Ellis Island.

Nor could he turn up any immigration records for his father. He believed Gustav had left his home in Jämtland, in northern Sweden, as a teenager bound for Germany to apprentice himself to a master blacksmith. My dad visited the tiny municipality where Gustav was born but could find no civil or church records indicating that his father had been either birthed or baptized. (He did, however, hear stories of some "giants" who had come to town several centuries earlier and he was shown several massively oversized graves at the town's only cemetery, the only evidence that some overgrown men had once lived in the vicinity.) It was possible, my dad told me, that his father had apprenticed in Germany and emigrated from Bremen, not from a Swedish port at all. He hadn't checked the manifests on ships from Germany to Ellis Island.

From wedding-day portraits I have of Gus and Jenny, I can say that neither of my paternal grandparents descended from a race of giants. While my grandfather was a short, slender, dapper fellow—not yet the squat, fat, mustachioed man in a photograph taken shortly before his death—Jenny was more than "pleasantly plump" when she and Gustav tied the knot. Her husband outlived Jenny by more than a decade.

I have slightly more information, most of which I'll keep under my hat, about my mother's side of the family. My grandfather and his unpleasant sister, my great-aunt Mae, did some tracing of the family tree back in the 1940s, long before extensive records were available online. By the time those far-flung sources of genealogy had become easy to tap, both had died and no one since has been interested in the Lee-Ellis-Willard-Stiles family line.

On the other side, the Irish side, of my mother's family, a shirttail relative in Texas, researching his own family tree, happened upon mine and has shared much of that with other family members online.

Something I learned not from the Texas genealogist but from my mother, was that her grandfather, Mick Connolly, was either a brother or a cousin of James Connolly, a leader of the 1916 Rising of Irish patriots against the British. James Connolly, born in Scotland to Irish immigrant parents, became a martyr when, seriously wounded and unable to stand on his own, he was tied to a chair and executed by a British firing squad. He's the one mentioned by William Butler Yeats in his powerful poem to the martyrs of the Easter Rising, "Easter 1916":

> ...We know their dream; enough
>
> To know they dreamed and are dead;
>
> And what if excess of love
>
> Bewildered them till they died?
>
> I write it out in a verse—
>
> MacDonagh and MacBride
>
> And Connolly and Pearse
>
> Now and in time to be
>
> Wherever green is worn,
>
> Are changed, changed utterly:
>
> A terrible beauty is born.

As far as I know, my Great-Grandfather Mick Connolly was not political at all. He died not from being shot by a firing squad, like his brother or cousin, but much, much less gloriously, by being crushed between the gears and blades of a huge, mule-drawn threshing machine. Those giant specimens of farm apparatus, accompanied by gangs of farmworkers and mule drivers, mostly single men, moved from farm to farm across the Great Plains. They returned annually to every spread to harvest the endless fields of wheat that covered whole states on both sides of the border with Canada. Men like Mick, who owned part of a wheat ranch in Northeastern North Dakota, joined the itinerant threshers while the women, like my great-grandmother, cooked and put out huge spreads for the men at mid-day dinner and evening supper.

Mick's wife, my Great-Grandmother Connolly, possessed a clairvoyance that my mother, whose American version of Catholicism had been sieved and strained to remove any particles of mysticism that might have drifted over from Eire, abhorred and refused to recognize. My Grandmother Mayme, though, was not as skeptical as her daughter Lenore. Mayme told me that her mother several times knew at long distance when someone in the family had died. She knew that the final bell had tolled because at night she would see, out across the plains, the twinkling lights from the windows of passenger cars of a train that steamed across the prairie. But, Mayme told me, there *was* no train and *were* no tracks out there in the distance, far across the prairie. What her mother, my Great-Grandma Connolly, saw, Mayme whispered, was "a death train."

My Great-Grandmother Connolly saw that terrible train while she was driving the buckboard back from Grand Forks when Mayme was a little girl, she told me. And when her mother saw the lights from the death train moving through the dusk, out there across the flat Dakota landscape, she knew that one of her children, her baby boy she'd left back home on the farm near Larimore, had died.

When my Great-Grandmother saw those faraway lights from her porch one evening, as she stood and watched the phantom railroad train moving silently across the distant flatland, she turned to her daughters and sobbed: "Mick has died. Mick is dead." And Mick Connolly was indeed dead, crushed in the machinery of the mule-drawn threshing combine. Members of the crew that accompanied the thresher brought his body in later that night.

Eventually, Mary Margaret Connolly's daughter Mayme moved to Montana, where she met and married Ellis Lee, who fathered my mother, Lenore.

Ellis Lee, who'd traipsed out West from his family home on the Eastern shore of Lake Michigan, was a barber. But cowboys didn't have much call for barbers, so Ellis became a jack-of-all-trades so he could support his wife and growing family.

Cowboys cut their own hair, my Grandpa told me. Those young buckaroos really did put a mixing bowl over their heads and trim their hair around the edges, Ellis complained during one of my annual trips to his two-chair barbershop in Seattle. So, never needing haircuts, cowpokes only visited the barber when there was a Saturday night shindig like a dance in town and they needed a shave.

Ellis Lee, tired of losing money as a barber and finding no way to make a fortune with his jazz band or his pool table, packed Mayme and my mother and her two sisters into his Model T and drove to Seattle, leaving his son's body buried somewhere beneath the prairies of Montana. The Lee family had to back the Ford up the steeper hills, according to my mother, because they could make better time uphill in reverse gear than they could chugging up some of the steep grades in low.

It wasn't long before Ellis sort of wandered away from the new family home south of Seattle. He'd found himself a place closer to his new two-chair barbershop on Olive Way, right in downtown Seattle, a stone's throw from the old Frederick & Nelson department store. He put his prints of Charles Russell's Montana cowboy art on the walls and taped his autographed photo of Russell and Will Rogers to one of the facing mirrors that gave me, on those annual childhood visits to his tiny shop, my first vision of infinity.

My mother couldn't abide her dad, claiming he'd abandoned his family and caused innumerable hardships for us all. I never heard Mayme say a word about him, though. My mother would agree to have lunch with her father once a year, with haircuts for my brother and me. I still remember fondly those Manly Smells that permeated his shop: the perfumes of multicolored bottles of bay rum and Mennen After Shave and Jeris Tonic and Wildroot Crème Oil and Pinaud Lime and some violet-scented pomades that he kept handy behind his chair, the way bartenders in lawyers' bars now keep the single-malt scotches and expensive vodkas on mirrored shelves behind the stick.

Ellis told me when I was older that he'd left Mayme because she didn't care for all the reading that occupied his spare time between haircuts and most of his time at home. I still find that an unlikely reason to end a marriage. Ellis did read a lot, though, including, the last time I saw him, *Decline and Fall of the Roman Empire*. He had two sets of the Gibbons edition, one at home and one that he read sitting on the barber's stool when he had no customers.

Ellis imparted one piece of barbers' wisdom to me, his oldest grandchild:

"If you go to a two-chair shop to get your hair cut, Lee," he said, "and one of the barbers has a good haircut and the other has a bad haircut, always go to the one with the **bad** cut. Because *he* got *his* hair cut by the other barber and the other guy got *his* good haircut from the guy with the bad cut."

II.

YOUTH

LEEBOY

Unlike most other ex- (or "fallen-away, as the Church thinks of us) Catholic men who write about their lives, so it seems, I was not molested as a child or teenager, not by a priest, not by a scoutmaster. I served Mass as an altar boy at St. Rose's Catholic church in Longview but was never touched by any of the Irish priests hired to say the Mass and dispense the sacraments. I served at Mass a couple of days a week and at one of the Sunday services.

I memorized the whole kit and caboodle in Latin and the last time I attended Catholic services, perhaps twenty years ago with a woman I was seeing at the time, the "vernacular" or, in our case, English, version of the mystical-sounding dialogue between the priest and the altar boys and the congregation sounded suspiciously better-suited for a Protestant service. There was even talk of "the Good News," a roundup of liturgical news we'd never heard when we sat through the Mass in Latin.

One of the assistant priests who said Mass in Longview required altar boys, before we strode onto the altar, to fill the wine cruet to the brim. Unlike the other padres who took just a drop of the sweetish altar wine as they mystically changed it into the blood of Christ, this father wanted every last drop available to drink. He loved his wine. He *needed* his wine. When I mentioned this to my mother and one of her old Longview friends many years later, she accused me of "always looking for bad things to say about The Church." That may or may not have been true, but her friend interrupted to note that the priest in question had been sent to a "sanitarium to dry out" after we'd moved away from Longview. My mother was unhappy to hear that my remarks about the alcoholic priest were apparently spot on. She actually harrumphed!

* * *

Aside from the facts that the air stunk because of the local pulp mill and I rarely did more than nibble at my food because of my mother's inedible cooking, my boyhood was fairly normal. I walked to school, was a good student, was, according to the class photographs my dad saved in his attic, one of the tallest kids in class each year, and learned, in the second grade about the "brave sailors aboard the armored cruiser Potemkin" who mutinied in Odessa in 1905 against the oppressive regime of the czar. Why we learned about that harbinger of the revolution I do not know.

Of course, we also read the Dick and Jane books, the stories and list of characters getting longer and more exciting each year with the addition of Baby Sally, Spot the dog and other family members and neighborhood characters. I collected comic books that I stacked at the side of my bed. I swapped comics with school chum Donald Harrison and an older neighborhood boy who took me to the cleaners every time we traded, me getting the dregs of his collection and him essentially stealing some of my best ones.

My first brush with philosophy came from a half-page Mickey and Minnie shortie in a Disney comic book: Minnie, as usual, was back-seat driving and nagging Mickey to "Look both ways," "Be on the lookout for stop signs," etc., when she suddenly warns, "Watch for falling elephants!" I cannot explain it now, but that one comic strip panel changed my life—or, at least, it changed the way I thought about life. It never occurred to me that there really could be falling elephants, even if only in a comic book. Or nagging mice, for that matter. Or, by extrapolation tempered by growing older, such unbelievable, impossible things such as unpleasant Democrats, fallen-away Catholics who were not slaves of the devil or child-molesting priests or, gasp, no God!

I'd not yet considered the sources of the wonderful and amazing places in my head where Mickey and Minnie and the Riders of the Purple Sage and, as I grew older, *la virgen de Guadalupe* and Simon Girty, Nelson Algren, Quetzlcoatl, Chavela Vargas, Ken Kesey, Chief Seattle, Emiliano Zapata, Rimbaud, Bird, Iz and Gabby and Emma Veary and Madam Pele and their Hawaiian *aina,* homeland, Robinson Jeffers, Billy the Kid,

Puccini, Buddha, Camus, Coyote, Joaquin Murieta and a million other holy or hair-raising or high and heroic and even demonic men and women and gods could twirl like whirling dervishes on the head of my pin.

Our main goal at Kessler Elementary School was to make it from kindergarten all the way through eighth grade without being sent to the Ungraded Room. This dreaded classroom, at the distant, other end of the long hallway, far from my early education classrooms, was where students with "problems" were exiled and where they stayed, said the kids in the know, until they were old enough to get jobs at the local mill. Children who drooled or were morons or had harelips or wore eye-patches or stuttered or suffered palsies or heavy sweating or who wet their pants or caused mayhem in class or had one leg shorter than the other or smelled worse than the rest of us or who sassed the teacher or got caught a second time shooting marbles for keeps would disappear all the way down the hall to the other end of the building, it was whispered, to the Ungraded Room.

I remember one day when a classmate whom I'll call Arvid was absent. He was gone the next day and the day after—and we were not having any outbreaks of mumps, measles, chickenpox, or lice at the moment. Arvid was a nice boy. I don't believe that he wore shoes to school on an everyday basis; but he was generally clean, well-groomed, and always dressed in overalls. He didn't swear and smelled about as same as any boy who lived out in the woods and didn't have to take too many baths. He didn't smoke or spit or holler too loudly. Now, Arvid wasn't the brightest kid in the class, but he could read some of the earlier volumes of the Dick and Jane oeuvre.

I was baffled. Had Arvid moved out of town?

"Hey," I asked someone, "where's Arvid?"

"Oh," I was told in a soft voice with a tremor of fear in it, "they sent him to the Ungraded Room. He ain't never coming back!"

It turned out that Arvid had pissed his pants one time too many on the school bus on the way home out to Dead Finn Creek.

There were some kids at Kessler School who were having trouble with English, and not for the usual reason, which was stupidity. Rather, these kids—we called them DPs because we were told not to. DPs were "Displaced Persons" from war-ravaged Europe. They had names quite different than the usual Scandinavian or British Isles names most of us sported.

I can't recall the name of the boy whose family had fled from some central European nation that had been absorbed into Hitler's empire. But I do remember the annual health checkup in second grade when we were each given a half-pint cream bottle and told to go into the boys' room and return with "a specimen." This DP, whose English was negligible, came out and proudly presented to the horrified school nurse his little glass bottle, filled to the top and, to the nurse's dismay, neatly smoothed off, packed with a specimen—of his feces.

We got regular health checkups and lice and ringworm screenings at school and every year we were warned about polio and shown a film about tuberculosis. It shocks young people these days to realize that polio and TB were scourges that caused panic in American households. A polio vaccine was not readily available for children until 1952 and while a tuberculosis vaccine was on doctors' shelves there were soldiers and nurses coming back from parts of the world where TB was still a menace. I remember a second cousin whom I barely knew who was a nurse in a TB isolation ward and I think my godfather spent time in quarantine after he returned home from the war suffering from TB.

Displaced Persons were not the only new Europeans in Longview. During the war, a crew of POWs—I used to think they were German prisoners of war but it's more likely, so I've learned, that they were captured Italian soldiers—could be found daily mowing the lawn and trimming the hedges on the grounds of municipal edifices such as the Post Office, the library, city hall, Monticello Park, which featured a bust of town founder Robert A. Long, as well as several other public places needing the attention of gardeners. The labor shortage existed because most of the young men (my father was 4-F because of some sinus problem) had left town to go to war.

Some of those young soldiers and sailors and marines, of course, didn't come home. You could tell when a family's son, or young father, was not coming back from the war by the Gold Star pennants that poignantly proud families who'd lost a soldier boy in battle would hang in their front windows. Personally, I think the POWs who spent their war years mowing lawns in Longview's parks got the better of that deal.

We lived a couple of blocks from a house where a boy caught polio and, after his family moved elsewhere, one of the new tenants came down with the disease and then, with yet another set of new tenants, polio struck again. Naturally, we called it The Polio House and swore that we'd never let *our* families move into the cursed place.

We also worried that if Tom Dewey became president in 1948 he would make us go to school Saturdays. We worried, at my house, that Ike would turn out to be a Republican instead of a Democrat. Some of my dad's friends left the Democratic Party to vote for Henry Wallace in 1948 but Gordon Quarnstrom had political ambitions and stuck with the Democrats. (He was a liberal but never as progressive as my mother. Lenore had a running argument with her dad, who, after years of genealogical work, wanted her to join the Daughters of the American Revolution. He could never understand what the fuss was about when she told him she couldn't join the DAR because in 1939 the organization had refused to allow Marian Anderson to sing at Constitution Hall and the President and Mrs. Roosevelt stepped in to allow the talented black contralto to sing at the Lincoln Memorial.)

My mother may have been liberal but she was late. My mother was *always* late: for trains, for church, for the movies, for everything. Some of my worst moments, knowing even as a young boy what giant enterprises the railroads were, involved running from the Great Northern-Northern Pacific Railway station in Kelso, across the Cowlitz River from Longview, to plead with the conductor not to signal the engineer to get the big steam locomotive going quite yet: "My mommy is just buying the tickets," I'd whine while the black porter stood ready to lift the metal step-stool into the passenger car and the conductor, shiny steel Hamilton pocket watch in hand, stood glancing at his timepiece and shaking his head while I anxiously looked toward the station hoping that she would soon appear.

These days, in fact for the past six decades or so, I have been compulsively early for almost everything.

I was called "LeeBoy." I had a golden cocker spaniel called Tony. Tony kept running away, usually a few blocks away to the Post Office. (A few years later my brother Dean annually tried to run off with the circus, which pitched its tents on a huge lot behind the Post Office once a year. Fortunately, I guess, the circus hands were familiar with boys who wanted to hit the sawdust trail and would hold him for the police, who would call to let us know that Dean was again available for pickup down at the circus grounds.) After the dog ran away for the fourth or fifth time, my dad said it was time to find him "a nice home in the country." Oh, it was terrible, it was the first time I'd felt abandoned. I didn't want Tony to live in a nice home in the country. I wanted him to live in *my* home in the town.

And then I learned what "a nice home in the country meant: It mean curtains, The End. There was no nice home in the country. There wasn't even a bad home in the country. There was just the county stray animal pound.

I asked my dad when as he was old and ill and all but on his deathbed, whether, in fact, he'd actually sent Tony to a nice home in the country when I was a small boy or whether he'd taken the dog to the pound. Gordon, gaunt and gray, the light dimming in his eyes, suddenly looked away.

"Just tell me the truth," I said. "Did you find him a nice home in the country?"

"Yes, yes I did," he assured me. I knew he was lying.

I told him I'd considered finding an old, shabby business place, perhaps a Quonset hut, on the edge of town, a suspiciously small Quonset hut, and call it "A Nice Home In The Country" for unwanted dogs and cats. He didn't like the joke. He looked guilty as hell.

* * *

I ordered important survival tools that all boys should have by sending cereal boxtops and a quarter off to various breakfast-food companies. In return, these manufacturers of Post Toasties and Kellog's Corn Flakes and Wheaties and Kix and Cheerios (called, for a while, Cheerioats) would send me a Decoder Ring with a built-in ballpoint nib or a Tom Mix Arrowhead Tool with a magnifying glass, a secret compartment to hide coded notes in, another decoding device, a compass and, for dire emergencies that any boy might face, a shrill whistle. I drank Grapette in the soda's tiny bottles and Nehi and Nesbitt's orange sodas and Green River at the soda fountain, the neon-green syrup mixed nicely with sparking water. We could go to the movies for fifteen cents and see Randolph Scott western double-features and lots of cartoons and *The March of Time* newsreels and we could get Coke and popcorn for a nickel each. I saw the worst movie I've ever seen, *Curse of the Ubangi*, at the Columbia Theatre. It featured semi-naked African women with huge, flat lips and, although I don't think I was old enough to notice whether they were firm or floppy, breasts.

My dad took me to Optimists Field to watch local boy Eddie Feigner, pronounced Fay-nor, with his four-man virtuoso softball team, The King and His Court, when he returned each year from his national tour. He and cowboy star Bob Steele were, at that point and probably still, among the most-famous Longview boys to make it big. We said the Pledge of Allegiance this way: Holding our right hands over our hearts we would say in unison, "I pledge allegiance to *my* flag," and, raising our right arms and hands, palms up, toward the Stars and Strips (with forty-eight stars), we'd continue "and to *my* country for which it stands..." with no "under God," which wasn't added until Ike was president. We went to the Little Store to buy penny packs of Lik-M-Aid, a sweet-and-sour Kool-Aid-like powder that exploded with flavor once we'd poured it into our mouths. We bought some kind of red goo that went in a glob on the end of a red straw and, when you blew through the straw the stuff turned into balloon-like shapes or doughnut shapes but mostly it had some nice fumes that, when inhaled, got you high for a second or two, much like the Energine cleaning fluid that my mother used for its intended purpose and which I used for sniffing purposes. Then I learned I could get high with the "laughing gas" the inept dentist used when he was working on my teeth. God I hated those old belt-driven drills, the loud noise, and the slow, slow progress they made as they painfully ground out a cavity. But I loved the nitrous oxide.

My dad gave me a folding Buck knife the first time I went to the circus for any reason other than to corral and walk my brother home from his dream job in show business. He told me about Little Miss 1565, as of then still unidentified except by the number assigned to her at the Hartford, Connecticut morgue after the 1944 circus fire that took an estimated 168 lives. The knife, my dad told me, was to be used *only* to cut through the Big Top canvas, to escape if the tent collapsed during a blaze or any other disaster. Longview was a regular stop on some second-string circus circuit; the Clyde Beatty the Wild Animal Trainer who came to town one year wasn't the same guy identified as the famous circus owner and master of wild beasts who'd show up the following season. Ditto for the Harlem Globetrotters: they must have had a B-list team of players who went exclusively to tiny towns like Longview, Washington, to show the rubes what black people looked like.

I went with my mother to see the Tau Moe Family Hawaiian musical and dance troupe at the high school auditorium and another time saw a roving company of Shakespearean actors put on *Macbeth* at the same venue. Occasionally my mother took us to piano recitals or concerts by some itinerant symphony orchestra or appearances by opera singers or musical comedy stars who had never been east of the Mississippi.

I remember my mother's disappointment on one wedding anniversary in the late 1940s when my dad gave her a "mangle iron" to press his shirts and on another occasion when he gave her a jar of Nal-O-Nil ("Lanolin Spelled Backwards") for some reason, coaxing her to appreciate the cream, or "crème," by quoting its slogan, "Did you ever see a bald-headed sheep?"

One day my dad called from his office at the *Longview Daily News*—in those days there were newspapers in every small town and they were always located in the center of the downtown commercial district, not on cheap real estate out on a frontage road on the edge of nowhere.

"Come down here and see the strange fellow with the wheelbarrow," he urged my mother. "Bring the boys." We went down to Commerce Avenue, which would have been, in the street-layout scheme of things, 13th Avenue had town founder Mr. Robert A. Long not been superstitious. There we joined our fellow townspeople gaping at an old man with a white beard, looking much like Santa Claus in civvies, pushing a wheelbarrow down the main street. He had, my dad said, pushed that wheelbarrow all over the country and to some other countries as well. What an oddball. But there was something about the steely-eyed old wanderer that fascinated me. I guess it was the freedom and the lack of direction. He went where he wanted, when he wanted.

Years later, working for a newspaper in California, I interviewed one of that old man's footloose compatriots. Plenny Wingo was his name and walking backward was his game.

Wearing a tiny dentist's mirror affixed to his hat so he could see behind himself, Plenny Wingo strode backward into Watsonville, California, and, with a practiced nose, sniffed out the newspaper office. I was assigned to come up with something, caption material for a photo, at least. His story was much what you would expect of a man walking backward into a newspaper city room. He'd walked backward here and he'd walked backward there and, aboard a ship, he'd walked backward across the Atlantic Ocean twice. What had Mr. Wingo learned backward on the road? Not much. To walk backward *with* the traffic, for one thing—that way you could see cars bearing down on you. And to have a good, sturdy hat you could strap under your chin and to make sure to have good, sturdy shoes.

The last I saw of Plenny Wingo was on the edge of the Coast Highway south of Watsonville. Mr. Wingo was being questioned by a bewildered highway patrolman. The patrolmen had not met many men walking backward along this highway through the artichoke fields north of Castroville, which bills itself as "the Artichoke Capital of the World."

I'm sure Plenny Wingo had a good, sturdy story to tell the cops.

SPORT

I know it's supposed to be traditional that a boy's father takes him to his first big league baseball game, but that wasn't the way it happened in my case. I took myself. The game was at Griffith Stadium in Washington, D.C. The year was 1951.

We had just moved to Bethesda, at the northwest edge of the nation's capital. We moved because my dad found a job working for U.S. Senator Warren Magnuson, a Washington state Democrat. That was after my father's first of two unsuccessful attempts to get elected to the House of Representatives from the district that included my hometown, Longview.

I got a taste for politics during my dad's campaigns.

It was during his 1950 Congressional campaign that I met Estes Kefauver, the Tennessee senator who wanted to seek the 1952 Democratic presidential nomination. He was crisscrossing the country rounding up support while helping to get local Democrats elected to Congress. Estes, a nice guy who became famous for his crime-busting Senate hearings exposing the Mafia, gave me a coonskin cap, a classy one with a satin lining. I wish I still had it.

I guess it was understood that my dad's job with Senator Magnuson was for a year-and-a-half and then my dad would make another run for Congress in 1952. He did, and he lost again. After that, Gordon Quarnstrom stayed out of politics and stuck to the two things he did best: writing and courting pretty women, the latter something that Estes Kefauver was also quite adept at, it turns out.

While my mother never learned to drive around Washington, D.C., I quickly figured out the city's bizarre street system, including DuPont and other circles. That meant, unfortunately, that whenever my mom wanted to go downtown, which was not often, I had to go with her to keep her from getting lost. (Once, on a trip to Paris with my dad, she got lost and spent most of a day wandering in the Tuileries. I suspect my father left her there hoping she'd just wander away, never to be seen again.)

It also meant that I quickly figured out the quickest way for an eleven-year-old boy to get from our house to the ballpark.

The Quarnstroms spent a couple of months in Silver Springs, Maryland, before we moved to nearby Bethesda. I was never more happy to move from one place to another because leaving Silver Springs enabled me to leave St. John's Catholic School, perhaps the most repressive educational institution ever established in this country by whatever order of nuns ran the joint. Learning was by memorization; punishment actually involved a Bart Simpson-like detention, staying after school writing and rewriting slogans such as "I will never be late to class again" on a classroom blackboard two hundred or even five hundred times. My argument that staying after school would make me miss my bus fell on deaf nun ears. God (if you're listening) it was a nightmare!

A trolleycar to downtown Washington and the Capitol ran along Wisconsin Avenue, at the end of the block where we first lived in Bethesda. I boarded the streetcar right by the vacant lot where the Kaiser-Frazier dealer stored new models of the Henry J, America's first economy car. I can't remember if or how many times I transferred, but I was able to find my way to the dilapidated Griffith Stadium, home of the Washington Senators.

The Senators from that era, the team that the Griffith family later renamed as the Twins and moved to Minneapolis, was in the midst of a four-decade slump. They were so bad that sports wits noted gleefully that the hapless Senators were "First in war, first in peace, and last in the American League"—a takeoff on the eulogy in which Lighthorse Harry Lee described the late President George Washington as "First in war, first in peace, first in the hearts of his countrymen."

With a couple of bucks in my pocket for trolley fare, admission to the game and a hot dog and soda, I found my way to my first Major League baseball game. My introduction to professional baseball was on a Thursday, May 24, 1951. I remember not only the lopsided score but also the fact that one of baseball's all-time greats was pitching for the opposing team.

The Senators, whom I never learned to love quite the way I came to feel about the also-hapless Chicago Cubs, fielded such luminaries as Eddie Yost, Irv Noren, and Mickey Vernon, who batted cleanup that May 1951 day. Their opponents that sunny Thursday in May were the Cleveland Indians, who had some actual stars on the roster, including Larry Doby and Al Rosen and perhaps the best pitcher in the majors, Bobby Feller.

Doby homered, Feller was as great as he was supposed to be, and the Indians trounced my new home team, the Senators, 16-0. Feller pitched the whole game and gave up only two hits. He was brilliant. The Senators stank.

I took in several more Senators games, always by myself, during the two-plus years we lived in Bethesda. Since we spent much of each summer back in Longview—where we needed an established address so Gordon could run for office again—I wasn't in town enough to see all that many Senators' games. But when we were in Bethesda I saw some and I listened to the rest on the radio. Occasionally, games were broadcast on TV, but the Quarnstrom household didn't get one of the newfangled television sets until 1953, so it was the radio or nothing.

My dad did take me to my pro football game, played at Griffith Stadium, the Washington Redskins versus some other team I can't recall. What I do remember is the marching band, a group of happy fat white men with horns and drums and dressed like Indians, with long, trailing feather headdresses and tomahawks at their belts. Those guys, a thousand of those guys, couldn't have changed the outcome at the Little Big Horn.

After we'd moved to Chicago, so Gordon could ply his writing trade at something called the *Wood Preserving News*, I went with him to another professional football game, this one at Wrigley Field, the longtime venue of baseball's Cubs. At the time Wrigley was also the home field of the Chicago Bears. Now, you're probably wondering what Gordon Quarnstrom wrote about in the *Wood Preserving News*. He wrote about wood that had been treated with toxic chemicals, of course, to prevent bugs from boring and destroying whatever forest product had been dipped in that noxious crap. One article was about the use of chemically soaked wood in constructing huge roller-coasters.

Gordon didn't linger at the wood-preserving publication; there are only so many things you can write about preserved wood and he wrote them all. He got a job at the home office of the Allstate Insurance Co. in suburban Skokie as public relations director.

The Bears lost that 1953 home game at Wrigley Field to the San Francisco 49ers. George Blanda was quarterback of the Bears, some of whom appeared to still be wearing those old-timey leather helmets. The great Y.A. Tittle quarterbacked the 49ers.

My dad also took me to one of my first Cubs games. It was an easy trip on the elevated, the El—from Wilmette to Wrigley. We sat in the grandstands behind third base and watched the St. Louis Cardinals whip the Cubbies.

That was the last sporting event I attended with my father, but it certainly was not my last Cubs' game. If I could get down to the northern terminus of the El, in Wilmette, the North Shore suburb where we were living, it only took fifteen cents, I think, and about ten or fifteen minutes to get to Wrigley Field. I loved baseball. I grew to love Wrigley and how could anyone not love the Cubs, a team so bad for most of my life that they've been known as "those lovable losers"?

My personal athletic career was Cubs-like:

When I moved from Bethesda to the Chicago area, my baseball teammates at Our Lady of Lourdes Catholic School all signed a ball and gave it to me. One wrote, "To the best pitcher we ever had." But I wasn't and I knew the guy who wrote that knew I knew I wasn't the best pitcher anywhere, not even on that little team.

At St. Joseph's school in Wilmette, fortunately my final brush with Catholic education, I was tall so I was made an end on the football team that practiced every afternoon after school but played only two or three games that season. Our triumphal tie in the first game was followed by two incredibly embarrassing losses to other Catholic boys from other Catholic schools.

Aside from football practice, overseen by a pair of sadistic older brothers of a classmate who was embarrassed at his siblings' cruelty to his friends, St. Joe's was easy. I'd already spent three years in Catholic schools in Longview, Silver Spring, and Bethesda. That meant I could spell, diagram sentences, do the required math, remember historical dates, and sing Gregorian chant.

But I was not a well-rounded Catholic boy, nor were there many in my 8th grade class. The monsignor who ran the parish made certain that we all knew that we were living on the edge of damnation and that if we didn't change our ways, no matter what those ways might be, we were all doomed, doomed! So when I stumbled that year upon James Joyce's *Portrait of the Artist as a Young Man* parts of it seemed eerily familiar, particularly Father Arnall's grim sermon predicting "death, judgment, hell" to Stephen Dedalus and his schoolmates. It echoed Monsignor Neumann's frightening jeremiads to us St. Joe's boys.

Fortunately, my non-religious dad, who'd been raised as a Lutheran but had forgotten it all, agreed to send my brother and me to Catholic grade schools on the condition that my rabidly Irish-Catholic mother not complain when we attended public high schools. This occasioned debate as my graduation from an education provided by nuns and monsignors drew near, but my father prevailed. At last, the childhood rhyme made sense:

"No more pencils, no more books, no more Sister's dirty looks."

* * *

Nuns don't teach gym, so at New Trier High School in suburban Chicago, I had my first P.E. classes, which I disliked intensely. I did enjoy physical education classes on foggy days, though, when we were ordered to run around the school's half-mile track. The coach, stopwatch at the ready, would blow his whistle and we'd run like hell into the fog. Then most of us would stop and quietly circle around the coach, waiting a few yards from the finish line. After some real athlete or cross-country runner passed, we'd wait a few seconds, then jog onto the track and past the coach, who would look pleased at our performances as he checked his stopwatch.

Similarly, in the one gym class I had to take at the University of Washington,—badminton—I learned that if I was the first one down the steps from the racquet courts to the fieldhouse, where we ran laps before showering and changing back into street clothes, I could turn right into the tunnel to the locker room, shower and leave without running even one yard.

I am not now, nor was I ever, athletic.

FIRE IN THE HOLE!

I didn't get home until dawn the morning after our graduation dance at New Trier High School in Winnetka, a suburb north of Chicago. A couple of hours later I left for Midway Airport to catch a plane to Seattle so I could start my summer job in Olympic National Park on the other side of Puget Sound.

I reported for duty as the assistant dynamiter on a three-man trail crew dispatched up the Elwha River into the huge, and, in 1958, relatively isolated chunk of rugged mountain wilderness. Our trail crew's task was to clear the trail from a place called End of Road up across a remote mountain pass called the Low Divide, then down a fork of the Quinault River, which ran to the Pacific Ocean on the other side of the remote and magnificent park.

I didn't know it at the time, but looking back I realize that the many hours I spent alone during that summer—hiking to and from job sites, sitting in mountain meadows watching a herd of elk grazing, climbing up a steep granite ridge slippery with shale until I reached its sharp apex overlooking two huge and separate mountain watersheds—was my first taste of solitude. I was reminded constantly of the wonder I'd felt almost fifteen years earlier at Spirit Lake and Mount St. Helens on what turned out to be Pearl Harbor Day.

Perhaps that summer was my first opportunity to reflect on the topics that traditionally capture the imaginations of young people, the only humans, perhaps, who actually ponder deep and serious matters of the mind and of the spirit. That summer afforded me the time and place and quietude to consider, for instance, the meaning of life, the existence of God, the possibilities of love, and the impossibilities of life with no women and, especially, the importance of visual material (there was *none!*) for masturbation fantasies.

The contemplations of an eighteen-year-old kid don't amount to much and could at best be branded as callow beyond belief. But eighteen-year-old kids don't know that, so I found my ruminations satisfactorily deep and mind-expanding. If nothing else, that summer provided the opportunity to spend time sitting on boulders at the edge of tumbling mountain streams or on fallen firs or cedars and on decomposing stumps, staring at a ground-hugging microworld of brushy forest undergrowth or through verdant expanses of lacy ferns or up through the crowns of giant Douglas fir and red cedar and spruce and hemlocks or at the hidden life in remote forest ponds.

It's clear to me now that solitude is a thing of the past. I cannot imagine that my grandchildren—the sons and daughters of my stepchildren—will ever put away their smart phones and iPads and iPods and Kindles long enough to experience even one instant of silence, one minute without inane telephonic voice or text communication, one moment of quiet contemplation or fantasy. As far as I can tell there is no place in the world where you can't use your cell phone.

The three of us on that Olympic Park trail crew were Bob the Foreman, who did little or nothing all summer long, Tony Jacobson, an old Swede and Wobbly, meaning he a card-carrying member of the all-but-forgotten, far-left Industrial Workers of the World, and me. Tony, who was almost seventy, was the dynamiter; I was his assistant. Bob was "in charge."

Tony drank a lot during the winter off-season but remained sober for the summer, a condition necessitated by the absence of liquor stores in the forest primeval. He'd been blasting rocks and stumps in the woods around Puget Sound since boyhood. The front of his body was pitted with scars from nature's shrapnel, mostly from the old days before dynamiters used those classic little generators with the plunging handles, like you see in Road Runner cartoons, to detonate a charge. In the old days, Tony told me, when you lighted a fuse on a stick of dynamite and it didn't explode you were supposed to wait two hours before you went up to see what was wrong, to check whether it was a dud. In the real world, of course, with timber bosses wanting you to hop to it, you waited only a few minutes before going to check why the damned thing hadn't gone off.

Sometimes, he told me, the explosives were a dud; sometimes the fuse had stopped smoldering or the dynamite or the powder was wet; some of the time it was only a slow fuse and would explode just as he got there, shooting bits of rocks and slivers of tree stumps into his flesh.

No wonder he drank.

We saw only eleven other people that summer, ten of them hikers, only two, a grandmother and granddaughter, women. The other was Gordon Cooke, an old cowboy who'd rodeoed around the West before getting a job leading a pack train of horses and mules to carry supplies to the crews who, like us, were building and clearing trails in different quadrants of the national park. Gordon would show up about every ten days with a couple of horses and three or four mules to replenish our supplies and, in most cases, to help us move our camp a few miles up the trail. Besides our dynamite and tools we had a heavy cast-iron stove and two sturdy canvas tents for the mules to tote along the trail.

Mules don't actually follow trails. Once they went from one campsite to another a day up or down the trail, those incredibly smart animals swerved off the beaten pathway and disappeared into the forest, always to beat the horses and the rest of us to our next destination.

Our tools in 1958 did not include chainsaws, although we did a lot of work where we could have used one. Chainsaws in those days were huge, heavy, unreliable and dependent on gasoline, which would have been just one more item to be packed in—and one more particularly volatile substance to store there with our dynamite and blasting caps.

So we carried a ten-foot-long, double-handled buck saw when we hiked to our worksite. When a tree needed felling, Tony and I whacked away at it with our double-bitted axes until we cut out a bite where we could saw most of the way through the Douglas fir or cedar with that long, big-toothed bucksaw. Next, Tony, an artist when it came to bringing down tall timber, would put one of his steel wedges into the cut and pound it with the sledge-hammer we carried until the giant was about to tip. Then, usually with one final tap on the wedge, he dropped the tree just where we wanted it to fall—out of the way so we wouldn't have to saw or blast it again to get it off the trail.

Once we bucked those firs and cedars into sections and split them into lengths, we used some of them for puncheon, the crude, unfinished planks used for building bridges across streams and rivers. Those puncheon spans frequently disappeared during winter storms, when raging waters and rockslides picked them up and knocked them downstream.

Man, that was grueling work. It did have one exemplary effect, though, on this recent high school graduate: It made me realize that I was no longer a boy playing at working. I was authentically working. I came to know that I was doing a man's job. I was a man!

Every visit, Gordon freighted up the "portable" radio that was supposed to keep us in touch with the rangers down at park headquarters. Now, this radio was only portable in the sense that it had a handle on it, like a steamer trunk. A portable two-way radio in 1958 was as heavy as a Volkswagen engine.

The thing didn't work the first time he brought it, nor the second, so Gordon hauled it away for repairs back at headquarters. The third time he unpacked the radio from the back of one of the mules we turned it on. It worked.

We fiddled with the dials to get rid of the static and finally, when we could hear a voice on the Olympic Park channel, we realized that, at that very moment, the dispatcher down the mountain in Port Angeles was trying to contact us. He was trying to get us to respond so he could send us across a couple of steep mountain ridges to fight a small forest fire that had broken out in some other remote sector of Olympic National Park.

Explaining to me that there is nothing, *nothing!* worse than fighting a forest fire—because, he told me, the intense heat forces billions of flying bugs that live by burrowing into the bark of the trees to extricate themselves from their homes and buzz around in huge clouds of angry, biting pests—Bob the Foreman opened the back of the portable radio.

"Them goddamned bugs'll get right inside your clothes and bite the crap out of you," Bob said. "It is goddamned awful!" Bob made it clear that *he* was not going to lead us on any strenuous double-time trek across the mountain ridges to fight some damned distant fire as well as swarms of vicious biting bugs.

So, reaching into the guts of the radio, Bob unhooked a wire connecting some gizmo to some other important element. The chattering from park headquarters stopped instantly. Once again, the radio was dead. Bob shook his head and looked at Gordon.

"Take the goddamned thing back to headquarters," he told the cowboy. "It still don't work."

As we made our daily hikes between campsites and worksites, Tony Jacobsen taught me how to roll my own cigarettes using either tiny flakes of Bull Durham or longer strands of Sir Walter Raleigh pipe tobacco. In fact, he taught me how to roll a smoke one-handed so I could shoulder my tools with the other, a trick that came in handy during my pot-smoking years. Mostly, though, I'd stop to roll a smoke, putting down my axe and my tool called a Pulaski and the sledge-hammer or a heavy iron bar used for chipping holes in boulders that we could pack with wads of dynamite to move or to pulverize the huge rocks.

When he was working with the dynamite, Tony wouldn't smoke. He'd put a wad of what Scandinavians and other loggers call snus (pronounced "snoose")—smokeless tobacco like Copenhagen—between his lip and his gum to feed his nicotine habit.

Tony was also an artist with explosives. He would point at a boulder blocking a shallow ford across the middle of a creek, turn and point to a spot downstream, and say, "Lee, I'm gonna put him right down there." (He called all inanimate objects "him," the way some folks refer to a ship as "her.") After packing the charges around the base of the huge stone and sending me a hundred feet down the trail to warn any oncoming hikers of the impending danger—despite the absence of campers or anyone else on the trail nine days out of ten. And, as required by state law, Tony would go a hundred feet up the trail with his generator, hooked to the blasting cap by one hundred feet of wire, and shout, "Fire in the hole!!" Then he'd detonate the charge. Inevitably, the boulder flew into the air, travelled many yards down the stream gorge, and landed exactly where he'd pointed.

Although Tony eventually let me take the generator with me and let me push the plunger to set off the blasting cap stuck into the clay-like wads of dynamite, I never could get the hang of packing explosives around the base of a huge stone so it would fly just where I wanted it to. I could, however, blast a gigantic white cedar stump or a good-sized stone to smithereeens.

Like many people who work with explosives, so I'm told, I started to get headaches after several weeks spent blowing up things with dynamite. There was something about the faint fumes that lingered after an explosion, along with the almost palpable sense that the blast had re-animated some long dormant spirit or dryad or animus that lay decaying inside the ancient trees and granite boulders, something that started making me woozy, nauseous, and then brought on the headache pain. Tony was the first to tell me that my headaches were normal for dynamiters. He'd had them for years. That's why he drank, he said. Fortunately, mine lasted only for a few months after I left the woods. However, I continued to drink long after the headaches had passed.

Those headaches weren't as painful as what could have been the outcome the first time we exploded anything that summer.

Tony sent me a hundred feet down the trail after explaining that he would yell before he set off the charge. More than state law—common sense and blasting etiquette, too—call for the dynamiter to shout the warning, "Fire in the hole!" three times before setting off an explosion.

I was a hundred feet down the path and actually twice that distance from Tony, who had strung out one hundred feet of wire up the trail and around a bend from the blasting caps and the dynamite. But I couldn't hear him when he shouted his warning so I didn't know that the blast was imminent. I strained to hear but Tony was just too far away.

So I was standing there, sitting on a stump a hundred feet in the other direction from the dynamite, looking for hikers and seeing none, blithely picking my nose, when there was a huge and sudden explosion. The hillside rocked. I almost jammed my finger up through my sinuses into my brain.

Jesus, I thought as I jerked my finger from my nostril, how embarrassing to be found lobotomized in the wilds of the Olympic Peninsula with my finger three inches up my nose, fatally wedged into my medulla. I had finally learned something more important and far, far more practical than I'd picked up contemplating the nature of the universe.

WHY I LEFT COLLEGE
AND BECAME A COPY BOY

After my summer blowing up tiny portions of Olympic National Park I moved into a dormitory in Seattle for my first quarter at the University of Washington. That school had been my choice because it was a long way from home and because I could enroll as a state resident since my parents owned a small residential lot in Longview. I was listed as a journalism student but I never took any such classes after I left high school.

Higher education did not appeal to me. The dormitory was segregated—all men—which was discouraging. Also, I found a job as a copy boy at the *Seattle Post-Intelligencer*, which meant I had to be downtown at the P-I building at six in the morning and couldn't begin classes until one in the afternoon. I'd been working since my dad told me on my sixteenth birthday that I had to begin earning my room and board and I'd found a job hauling packages out to the parking lot in a department store in Evanston, the suburb between Chicago and our home in Wilmette.

The highlight of my quarter-and-a-half as a freshman at the University of Washington had nothing to do with class. It was noticing all the grad students and other professors in the English-Philosophy building shunning one elderly professor whenever he walked along the hallway. The faculty and older students actually faced the wall, turning away from the elderly instructor. It was baffling, at least until I learned that he had testified years before to some state legislative "un-American Activities Committee" investigating any campus Communist connections. He had named names and thereby got a few of his UW colleagues fired for their lefty political affiliations. I learned this from one of the fired professors, a man who'd crippled his hands and arms when he leaped from the top floor of a campus building in an unsuccessful attempt to take his own life. Now, with broken hands bent into claws, he spent a lot of time drinking beer in the Blue Moon Tavern, a hangout for campus artists, radicals, and beatniks. As far as an actual college education, however, I was learning nothing.

(I made another run at college a few years later when I moved back to Seattle from Chicago with the woman who would become my first wife. I enrolled in some classes but by then I was working full time as a writer for the Associated Press and saw no reason to get a degree that would help me get a job that I already had. The highlight of that second brief time as a U. of Washington student was that I could sit in the press box with the AP sports editor at Husky football games.)

My copy-boy job that first quarter at UW was not in the P-I editorial department with the writers and editors; instead, I worked in "dispatch," a hitherto unknown, to me, newspaper precinct connected to the display advertising department. Our job, as I understood it, was to rip so-called "tear sheets" of large display ads from the morning's first edition and deliver a set number of those ripped-out pages to the stores that had placed the advertisements. The stores had display cases at their entrances where they would exhibit the day's newspaper ads so customers could see what was on sale.

A guy with a three-wheeled motorcycle took the tear sheets to outlying advertisers. I delivered to the big department stores downtown, notably, in those days, the Bon Marché and Frederick & Nelson. And, it turns out, the main thing those big downtown department stores advertised in their full-page notices was women's lingerie.

I did not know it at the time, but my future as a newsman and a pornographer was even then being molded by my dispatch department copy boy circumstance and, of course, my instincts.

Meanwhile, back at the University of Washington, I had been compelled to enlist as a trainee in the ROTC, the Reserve Officers Training Corps. Like many public universities in those days, the UW was a so-called land grant college, meaning that all male students had to complete a certain number of hours in that training branch of military service. As an ROTC trainee, I had to wear, one day a week, an Army uniform that most-closely resembled not the outfit worn by pre-Vietnam War soldiers but the khaki outfits sported by the Boy Scouts. I was supposed to learn how to march, an activity that had already, at a youthful age, impelled me to drop out of the actual Boy Scouts of America. I did learn to fire some type of antiquated rifle only used, in the late 1950s, by ROTC units on American college campuses and by banana republic armed forces in Africa and Latin America. Oddly, to me, I was quite talented at target practice at the ROTC shooting range.

To make a slightly longer story suitably short, I hated walking around campus one day a week looking like an Eagle Scout. That self-conscious attitude became moot when I lost my ROTC official issue black necktie in the debris that had piled up in the middle of my dorm room. The ROTC wouldn't issue me a new black tie and I sure as hell wasn't going to pay for one.

So, having spent a couple of hours each weekday morning hanging around department store art departments watching lovely lingerie models in lacy brassieres and flimsy panties, I had no problem dropping out of the university. I moved out of the dorm and into an apartment with a fellow copy boy employed by the Seattle P-I dispatch department. I took, as a duck takes to water, to spending much of most mornings drinking coffee and shooting the breeze with scantily clad ladies' underwear models in their working outfits.

The newspaperman's life was clearly the life for me.

* * *

In early 1959, I left my job and Seattle and drove my souped-up 1950 Ford to San Francisco, en route back home to Chicago, where I wanted to find work as a real newspaper reporter. The Ford's transmission gave out, fortunately on the top of a San Francisco hill, and I was able to roll it downhill, the engine still running like a champ, to a used car lot, where I got two-hundred dollars for it.

I bought a train ticket back to the Windy City and within a few weeks I landed a job with the City News Bureau of Chicago. I was nineteen. I was making one dollar an hour. I was a reporter. I was very happy.

III.

MERRY PRANKSTER

LA HONDA

Yo-yoing, as Pynchon described pointless wanderings from here to there, from pillar to post, from coast to coast, found me back in Seattle after stops in Chicago, Mexico City, and Greenwich Village. I was working for the Associated Press and married to Judy, who had an infant daughter, Susie. In May 1963 we had our son Eric. Then Judy packed her suitcase and took the kids south to the Bay Area and her boyfriend Larry.

I wanted to be near my stepdaughter and my son, so I moved south from Seattle to San Francisco. I found work as a reporter at the *San Mateo Times*, a somewhat typical crappy suburban paper south of the city halfway to San Jose. I found an apartment in what would come to be known within a year as the Haight, or the Haight-Ashbury district near the Panhandle of Golden Gate Park.

The *Times* was like a thousand other mid-sized or small newspapers in 1964. The boss was a Republican, he was pro-business, he made clear his disdain for the reporters and editors who worked for him. Essentially, he treated us as though we were coal miners pick-axing anthracite in his subterranean mineshafts.

He loved money and he hated controversy. I left after a year when he refused to credit students at the local community college for expressing a mild interest in politics by supporting a faculty member who went to join Martin Luther King's march from Selma to Birmingham in March of 1965. By then I had moved from San Francisco to the mountain community of La Honda to live near Ken Kesey.

When I proposed to the city editor that I interview Kesey, our local San Mateo County author, already known locally as "a character," I expected the word would come down from above to let well enough alone. I was pleasantly surprised when City Editor Jack Russell, a great man toiling under oppressive journalistic conditions, gave me the nod right off the bat. He even agreed with my proposal to combine the interview with a review of Kesey's magnificent new book, his second novel, *Sometimes A Great Notion*.

Jack smirked, but affectionately, when I told him that as far as this twenty-four-year-old was concerned, *Sometimes a Great Notion* was a contender for the fabled title of The Great American Novel. I still believe it's in the running.

It's important to keep in mind that Kesey was known at the time not as a psychedelic Pied Piper but as a writer, albeit a writer who'd just led a cross-country expedition aboard his brightly painted old school bus. He and his close-knit Merry Pranksters were quite familiar with psychedelic drugs, but the world at large was not yet familiar with LSD and other psychotropic substances, nor about Kesey and the boat he was already beginning to rock.

After phoning Kesey to ask about interviewing him, I headed up into the redwood forest that covers much of the crest of the northern tip of the Santa Cruz Mountains that bisect San Mateo Peninsula. I met Ken at his rustic log cabin in La Honda, deep in the redwoods, a wide spot in a narrow road that linked Palo Alto and the Pacific Ocean beaches at the tiny community of San Gregorio. It was my first hit of coniferous forest since my dynamiting summer in Olympic National Park.

Kesey's vividly yet amateurishly painted bus, with FURTHER on its destination board, was parked, or, the more that I think about it, was broken down, in the mud in front of his house. No one, Kesey and the Pranksters included, could have known this particular bus, just back from its well-chronicled round-trip to New York City, would be the first and by far the most-famous, most-notorious member of a huge and unorganized fleet of crazily painted buses and VW buses and run-down vans and other vehicles that would be circling the nation (or sitting curbside or roadside awaiting either a tow truck or more gas for the tank) within a year. It was an impressive piece of motoring machinery and I was smacked in the head, or the brain, by the wild, yet intricate artwork decorating the old school bus inside and out.

Several men and women about my age, apparently immobilized and preoccupied in what seemed to me—having not yet experienced LSD—to be quiet contemplation. They stood, sat, or lounged around the yard at the edge of La Honda Creek. Kesey was inside and not, as far as I could tell, under the influence of anything.

As I proceeded with what I thought would be a standard interview, asking Kesey questions and taking a few notes, a fast-talking Neal Cassady, wearing a short-sleeve sportshirt and a narrow necktie, breezed in, greeted Kesey, calling him Chief. Neal shook my hand and yakked for half a minute. Suddenly he said goodbye and hurried back to the car he'd left running in the yard, a white 1957 DeSoto. Kesey bought the car for Neal after cashing a sizeable royalty check that had arrived from his publisher. (A few weeks later, after I moved to La Honda—to a cabin up a muddy road a half-mile west of Kesey's place—Neal arrived at Kesey's one morning riding with Ken's cousin Dale, a Kesey lookalike. To Neal's chagrin, his DeSoto had been stolen!

Talking slightly faster than is humanly possible and, as always, jumping seamlessly from one abstruse topic to another, Neal muttered, "...stole six-hundred cars by the time I was sixteen and dammit now somebody steals *my* car!" He seemed dumbfounded at this revolting irony.

* * *

Neal attired in a shirt and tie for some job he was trying to hold down at a tire-recapping joint down in Los Gatos was a far cry from the Neal Cassady I, like other Pranksters, came to know and love. In my mind's eye I see Neal at the wheel of a car, any car, one arm around girlfriend Annie Murphy at his right, another arm around his other girlfriend, a granny-glasses-wearing hippie girl named Sharon, on the other arm, smoking a joint and punching buttons on the car radio, his non-stop monologue punctuated with boasts about letting his subconscious direct which

105

radio button to push so he never, ever, heard any ads, any disk jockeys talking, nothing but music… "Don't ya know?" He'd look at Ann and at Sharon and at me and at anybody else in the car, yet somehow he stayed on the road without ever seeming to give it a glance.

Cassady included in his on-going, never-ending gabfest a timely report on just what he and the car were doing at that very moment—"…heading into a declining-radius right turn, hard on the accelerator like Juan Fangio at Le Mans, controlled slide, passing Stirling Moss on the inside, tapping the brakes…"

Neal seemed familiar with every instant in every sports car race that ever happened. And if he didn't know the details, he'd make up the story with such authority that you never believed he was talking through his hat:

"Fangio slides around Moss as they slip into the chicanes and avoid, just barely, the upside-down Maserati that's just burst into flames…"

And Neal would *still* be carrying on separate romantic mumbles or arguments with each of his women and *still* having a simultaneous conversation with the rest of his passengers. His multi-level, multi-layer chatter, punctuated by frequent puns, references to Greek myth, baroque music or Ottoman architecture or Shakespearean sonnets or you-name-it, was a work of verbal art that surpassed the complex mixes of rock, raga, symphonic, and folk music on the Beatles' finest albums, *Sgt. Pepper's Lonely Hearts Club Band* and *Rubber Soul*. Except that Neal's verbal symphony was composed on the fly, sometimes literally, as he sped up and down the Peninsula between San Francisco and La Honda and Palo Alto and down to San Jose. And if you were high enough and paid attention, it was all wise and funny and spectacularly erudite and it all made sense, to boot.

In a short tribute written after Cassady died, Kesey wrote—in "The Day After Superman Died," from his collection *Demon Box*—that Neal "was Lenny Bruce, Jonathan Winters and

Lord Buckley all together just for starters... [with] his hurtling, careening, corner-squealing commentary on the cosmos."

One day, with a carful of Pranksters, Neal was speeding home through the curves and corners and hills of La Honda Road, sliding, as usual, leaning, drifting around corners, drifting and sliding across both lanes of the twisting, narrow roadway, smoking a joint, gesticulating with both hands at once, running the radio and looking at each of us in the car when suddenly he took the rare step of tapping on the brakes and pulling over into the right-hand lane as we started around a U-shaped turn to the left. As we rounded the curve we realized that had he not slowed and pulled into the right-hand lane we would have smashed into the front end of a loaded logging truck chugging up the hill toward us. "Jesus, Neal," I asked in wonder, "how did you do that?"

And without breaking his smoking, radio button-punching, arm-waving, girl-hugging operation one bit he explained to me, "Lee, the seventh dimension, which, you understand, is the same as the fourth and we know that the fourth is time and the seventh, you see, implies that I am a moment or so faster than you, a step ahead in reaction time and, you understand, that in reality we were already *around* that corner only none of you knew it but I knew we were there because I had *perceived* it and you hadn't, you understand, and since my mind was already there and I saw the truck, you understand, I just used my body to pull over so we didn't hit it."

"Oh, yeah, I see." And you know what? I did.

It was on another La Honda Road corner that Neal gently rolled the car one afternoon. No one was hurt.

"Everybody out," he commanded. "Turn it right-side-up." And when the car was back on its four wheels Cassady started the engine and took off as though nothing had happened.

I guess none of us was ever surprised by traffic situations once we'd ridden just one time with Neal. And, of course, we were all familiar with Neal Cassady at the wheel: We'd already met him as Dean Moriarty in Jack Kerouac's *On the Road*—the

Beat Generation hero, the speedy sidekick who drove constantly, coast to coast and back again, always in a different car, always on the road.

In the Bay Area most of Neal's endless trips were from one place where he might pick up some bennies or uppers, amphetamine pills—to swallow (not to smoke or to inject or to snort) to another place where someone might have some illegal stimulants. Neal would drive to Palo Alto to get some pills to keep him awake to drive to San Francisco to get some pills to last him until he got to another source back in San Jose. Although La Honda was in a redwood forest atop a mountain ridge, Neal managed to make our Prankster community at Kesey's house a key stop on his Bay Area meanderings.

For a while Cassady had an understudy named Bradley Hodgman, a former tennis star at Stanford University, down the road adjacent to Palo Alto. Bradley was the only person I ever met who talked in exactly the same cadence and with the same seemingly disconnected sentence structure as Neal. One difference was that Neal always made sense to me and Bradley rarely did. Another was that Bradley, who seemed unable to handle enormous amounts of stimulants (Bennies, Dexadrine, Obitrol, methadrine, etc.) as well as Neal did, referred to himself in the third person. That only took but a few seconds to get used to, however.

I asked Bradley once when Neal was driving north to see some dope dealer in San Francisco whether he still played tennis.

"No," Bradley muttered.

"Why not?" I wondered. He looked at me for a moment, then explained:

"Bradley lost the ball!"

Neal did his best to handle Kesey's bus the same way he drove an automobile. In the middle of one long night on the road, with Neal at the wheel, a bunch of us cruised up the Coast Highway in Marin County toward the Mendocino Coast. As the bus dipsy-doodled up and down hills and in and out of tight switchback curves, I awoke, feeling something strange was going on, perhaps something wrong. The bus was drifting around corners like a Jaguar sports car! Then I heard Prankster Ken Babbs chiding Neal over the sound system that hooked speakers and microphones throughout and on top of the bus: "Cassady, I'm not asleep. I can tell what you're doing. Stop sliding the bus through these tight little turns."

"You got it, boss," came Neal's reply from the driver's seat. All was well with the world and I went back to sleep.

* * *

Two months or so after I'd moved from San Francisco to a cabin deep in the woods, down La Honda Road a half-mile or so from the Kesey place, Ken told me, as he complained about book reviewers, that he had enjoyed reading my combination interview-book review in the *San Mateo Times*. (I'd subsequently quit that paper after an argument, about something else, with the managing editor.)

Ken pointed to another writer's review of *Sometimes a Great Notion*. The reviewer compared the bond between two characters in his first novel, *One Flew Over the Cuckoo's Nest*, to the supposedly homoerotic relationships noted, or discovered, in an inexplicable exegesis by Leslie Fiedler in his essay, "Come Back to the Raft Ag'in, Huck Honey!")

Shaking his head at Fiedler's obscure notion about Kesey's own writing, Ken told me that my little piece in the *San Mateo Times* was "the only one I ever liked, Lee, in fact, the only one I understood." Now I didn't believe the latter half of the compliment—Kesey was much smarter and so much better-read than his put-on Oregon hick manner suggested. But I was tickled anyway.

It was inevitable as I left La Honda after that first meeting with Ken Kesey that I would move to be as close to him as possible. Not only was I bored with the beatnik drinking life I was leading in San Francisco, I had been fascinated by Kesey the raconteur and shaman and by the solitude and forest smells of La Honda. And I was fascinated by Kesey and his friends.

My shabby, fifty-dollar-a-month La Honda cabin, heated only by a fireplace that was far too much work to get going on cold mornings, was just up muddy Redwood Terrace from the house where one of Kesey's pals, author Ed McClanahan, lived with his first wife and their kids. Ed had an actual writing room, the first I'd ever seen, where he spent much of his time composing and then rewriting and then polishing and then perfecting his stories.

Besides Kesey and his wife Faye and their three kids, Zane, Shannon, and Jed, I got to know Cassady, Kesey's best friend Ken Babbs, and Gretchen Fetchin', Babbs' girlfriend. I became close friends with Zonker, from San Jose, and Hassler, just out of the Army down at Fort Ord. I met Ron Boise, a grizzled sculptor and, in time, Mountain Girl—who bore Kesey's daughter Sunshine and married Grateful Dead guitar-player Jerry Garcia—showed up. It seems like I made a new friend every day for the first few months I was living in La Honda.

Within weeks of my move south from Height-Ashbury in San Francisco, I discovered that Kesey had spent most of his royalties from *Notion* on the bus and on the New York Trip and on what was essentially a busload of movie-making equipment. My weekly unemployment checks became, after I took out enough to pay my own rent, one of the diverse sources of income for day-to-day living among the Pranksters. Babbs got a regular check for his duty in the Marine Corps—he'd wrecked his back when his helicopter crashed in Vietnam—and royalties from Kesey's two books would come in every now and then. One day a seven-thousand dollar royalty check for the Italian translation of *Cuckoo's Nest* arrived in Kesey's mailbox.

"I didn't even know there *was* an Italian edition," Kesey said as he beamed at the sudden windfall.

* * *

Another discovery was that I was in love with Faye, Kesey's wife. Unlike any woman I had met so far—unlike the beatnik girls I'd known in Chicago and San Francisco or the bar girls or the drug-addicted street girls I'd met everywhere, or the pretty college girls I knew or the *chicas* or *chamacas* I'd known in Mexico—Faye was sweet, nourishing, yielding, possessed of a deceptively soft and natural aikido that accepted almost everything as it was without surrendering her power as a woman and especially as a mother.

Faye was a fierce protector of her children. One dinnertime around the huge, round, carved-wood table where we ate and where we smoked dope and where Kesey told stories, Ken went to the kitchen during supper and returned with a half-full bottle of milk, which he gulped until the container was empty. This was a time when funds were low, almost non-existent, and the check had not yet arrived from Italy. Faye strode from the kitchen, angrily pointed out to her husband that the milk was intended for the kids and then beaned him with a skillet. After she'd gone back to the kitchen and Kesey had recovered his composure, he looked at us two or three Pranksters sitting around the table on this cold winter night. I could tell he had learned some sort of a lesson and now he was going to pass it on. "I think we should all thank Faye when she cooks dinner or does other stuff for us," he said, somewhat abashedly. We all nodded. Each of us was more than wiling to thank Faye for dinner, and to leave food that was meant for the kids, in order to avoid assault with a frying pan.

It was at that round table that I had my first inkling that Kesey was human, just like the rest of us, or, at least, that he wasn't perfect, as I'd begun to believe. One day he got a call from

Kurt Vonnegut. Did Ken want to add his name to a list of prominent American men and women of literature, music, and other arts protesting the escalating hostilities in Vietnam? The names would be on a full-page advertisement in the *New York Times* and would demand that President Johnson stop sending troops to fight in the so far little-known war that was brewing in Vietnam, in southeast Asia. Kesey, whose disinterest in politics was matched only by his aversion to joining fads, trends, or causes, declared that he would not sign the ad. "Why," he asked us, displaying his ignorance not only of geography but of world events, "would I want to protest fighting on some tiny little island out in the Pacific Ocean?"

By now I had fallen for Faye. Kesey was spending a lot of time with Mountain Girl in the so-called Back House out by the creek, supposedly editing the forty miles of film shot on the New York bus trip but actually, of course, screwing. Faye hadn't seemed to mind and had, in fact, established a relationship with George Walker, one of Kesey's old Oregon friends, a kind and gentle man always ready to lend a hand.

Mountain Girl, whose name before she arrived and signed on as a Merry Prankster was Carolyn Adams, was only eighteen the first time she came to La Honda. Her arrival, the constant attention from Ken, and the fact that George Walker seemed to have found another romantic interest—none of that was on my mind the first time I took LSD. Kesey and a few other Pranksters drove up to see someone in San Francisco and I stayed home and took a tab of acid, not really knowing what to expect.

I spent part of the evening, until it got too complicated, putting LPs on the turntable, some choral music by Gabrielli and Mahler's Fourth Symphony. I sat in Kesey's large front room, with lacquered redwood paneling and a high, open ceiling, sitting in front of the fireplace watching flames, then embers, listening to the music and watching Faye, who was busy in the kitchen but would occasionally stop and sit with me.

I had a fine first trip, gentle, pleasant, encompassing universal truths and insights and heavenly views of infinity as well as microcosmic visions of...of *everything*...in a single pore on one arm. I lay out on a log at the edge of La Honda Creek and watched the constellations, crystal clear in the dark La Honda sky, and saw some shooting stars and the twinkling lights of distant airplanes and satellites and occasional vast clouds of energy that I concluded had to be from another world, even from another cosmos. I went inside to the Keseys' timbered living room and played some Gabrielli church music and a Mahler symphony and fell in love with Faye Kesey.

I couldn't tell her that night—I was too entranced with light and vision and enlightenment and all the wondrous infinity of things that can be noticed on a good LSD trip. She came and sat by me for a while and smiled. She was very kind and brought me a glass of water that turned into a boundless ocean before I drank it down. Faye seemed angelic. I seemed angelic myself. She spoke in music, it seemed, and in the untranslatable poetry of archangels.

In the days that followed I found ways to spend time with Faye and to whisper one day while Bob Dylan was singing "Mr. Tambourine Man" on the hi-fi in the other room that I loved her. And she squeezed my hand and later, after we made love in one of the bunk beds in the rear of the house, beds generally occupied by whichever Prankster got there first and claimed it for the night, she told me that she thought she was pregnant. For one egotistical moment I believed that she was telling me some hippie-girl premonition following our love-making. Then she explained that she had experienced a few miscarriages and that she thought she was pregnant again and that this time, she hoped, this baby would live. And I told her I hoped it would, too. But it was Ken's baby, of course.

A few weeks later she told me she'd lost that baby, too.

* * *

The first time I saw Mountain Girl she was leaning hard into a right-hand curve as she sped a motorcycle through one of the treacherous corners on La Honda Road, headed up from Palo Alto to Kesey's for her first meeting with Ken and the rest of us. With her wit, her intelligence, and her beauty, she obviously made an immediate impression on Kesey. Before a week had passed she and Ken were hanging out together much of the time in the Back House—and Faye and George were occasionally mooning, but less freqently, over one another in the main house.

Faye—who married author and old Kesey friend and colleague from the Stanford writing program Larry McMurtry in 2011, a decade after Kesey's death—took care of all of the practical parts of running a household as well as caring for our gang of acid heads. She paid bills, kept receipts for the tax man, cooked, soothed those who needed it, and raised her three beautiful children. She did it, I noticed, while talking to herself, keeping track of what she was doing and what needed to be done and what Kesey needed to do by constantly and softly reminding herself of what I would have put on a "to do" list, had there been anything I felt I must or should be doing. Kesey told me one day that without this verbal "keeping tabs" on herself she might just, as she had as a little girl, wander away and discover that she was lost and unable to know what to do next. So, often I would walk into the kitchen, where Faye was usually doing something that one of the rest of us could have done, but didn't do, and I would stand and listen to her whisper, almost, directions to herself about what task she was doing and what she would do next. Then I would caress her cheek with the back of my hand, the most-sensitive surface of my hand, and she would smile and turn into me and kiss me and then tell me what she was doing and what she would be doing next.

Looking back it is clear that the feminism that entered society's consciousness at the end of the 1960s, and was in the news for much of the 1970s, had not yet made itself known in La Honda. Male bohemian culture in general—from beatniks to artists to writers to musicians—was as unaware of the concept of "freeing our sisters" and thusly "freeing ourselves" as was the country-club culture we all hated and parodied. Maybe our lingo was not quite as demeaning as the cigar-chomping Republicans or the guys drinking shooters in the tavern after work—I mean, we beatniks, long-hairs, hippies, whatever we were called, didn't refer to women as bimbos, but we did refer to them as "chicks" and we said a girlfriend was our "old lady" and expected the old ladies to make dinner, take care of the kids, and keep the place neat if not exactly clean. We didn't do the dishes but we did, usually, bring home the bacon and create the art and fix the car when necessary. After all, that's what men did. We also drank, got in occasional bar fights, argued about writing and politics, puked, got high, made excuses when we couldn't find work, cheated (if we were found out) or didn't get home until the next morning. In fact, there's a whole school of criticism on the writings of Jack Kerouac—by women who knew him but mostly by women who didn't—that focuses on the male-dominated ethos of the Beat Generation. Since Kerouac was such a major influence in both his writing and his lifestyle, that had he opined that men and women were social equals, the so-called liberation, which was actually an evolution, would have occurred much sooner and with the help of people of my gender.

By 1975, when Kesey called a statewide referendum in Oregon on nuclear power and other critical political and ethical matters, women were conscious and organized and their issues were in the forefront of lefty political thinking. "Free our sisters, free ourselves" really was the keystone of our politics in those days.

When Kesey organized the famed Bend in the River conference, in the mountainous central Oregon city of Bend, a surprising variety of delegates and speakers showed up. I'd been assigned by *Rolling Stone* magazine to do a piece about the get-together and Annie Liebovitz was there to shoot for Jan Wenner's publication. (The article never ran in *Rolling Stone*.)

Kesey's idea was for conferees to come up with alternative and far-sighted options to create a better statewide community. Among those presenting their visions were maverick former U.S. Senator Wayne Morse, new age Dr. Andy Weil, erstwhile Prankster and publisher of *The Realist* Paul Krassner and radical Italian architect Paolo Solari. In Kesey's mind, environmental issues were paramount: pollution, over-use of natural resources such as water and timber, urban problems caused by over-crowding and, to a lesser degree, I think, what were called "women's issues."

At one point during the conference, women delegates gathered on the lawn outside the resort in chilly Bend to demand that the conference endorse abortion rights. Clearly, at least then, Kesey found the idea of abortion abhorrent. He tried to argue the women into dropping their demand. He said he worried the issue would split rather than unite the state. Then, to everyone's surprise and especially to his wife's, he made an outrageous promise to the women:

"Alright, any one of you who gets pregnant and doesn't want to keep their child, I swear to you now that I'll take the children and raise them on our farm!" I was sitting next to Faye, who spent years raising not only her three kids but mothering a drug-addled Prankster frat house scene in La Honda and then, on the family's Oregon farm. I looked at Faye as she listened to her husband's grandiose promise. She blanched.

* * *

Although I'd sniffed fumes from various cleaning products a child, I took my first illegal drug when I was nineteen. I purchased a five milligram Benzadrine tablet for a dime from a guy in the tiny bathroom at the Cellar Boheme, as two young, gay black men called their Chicago basement apartment when it was open for partying on weekends. They played jazz and rhythm 'n' blues, sold beer for ten cents a glass, and encouraged the beatniks and hipsters in their Hyde Park neighborhood on the South Side near the University of Chicago to break as many laws as necessary to relax and have a good time. That was the first of many, many bennies and other stimulants that I ate or cooked and injected over the next decade or so.

I knew the moment the amphetamine began to kick in that I was going to like these "bennies."

By the time five years later that I met Kesey and the Merry Pranksters I'd used a nice variety of illegal drugs—including pot, of course—as well as all available amphetamines, including injectable methadrine, as well as heroin, morphine, barbiturates, and cocaine. But I'd not yet taken any psychedelics. I ingested my first tablet of LSD that evening when the rest of the La Honda crew, including Kesey, drove up to San Francisco and left me back home alone with Faye.

* * *

After the La Honda scene fell apart—a limit reached when the septic tank finally overflowed as more and more strangers and Hells Angels started to make regular visits—we moved down the coast to Soquel, a rustic little town adjacent to the then-sleepy seaside resort burg of Santa Cruz. I spent most of the next three-and-a-half decades there.

We rented an old farmhouse we called The Spread. It was there I learned that my affair with Faye had not gone unnoticed by Ken.

I was sick in bed one day with a urinary tract infection when suddenly Kesey and Mountain Girl breezed into the house and he said they wanted to use my bed. "I'm sick," I protested, "Find someplace else to screw."

"See?" Kesey told Mountain Girl. "I let him sleep with my wife and now when I'm just asking him to let us use his bed for an hour he tells me to go somewhere else!"

I had no idea how to respond. So I didn't.

THE BUST AT KEN KESEY'S PLACE

Exhausted by several days of Prankster foolishness we were calling "space travel," I was napping one pleasant spring evening in a back bedroom at Kesey's La Honda rustic house in the forested mountains above Palo Alto when I heard Michael Hagen's voice shouting something about a search warrant.

Search warrant? We'd been expecting something from the cops who'd been milling around La Honda, but I was in no mood to stick around to see what this particular search-warrant business was all about.

It sounded like Hagen was out front somewhere, so naturally I was up and heading in the other direction. I was halfway to the door out to the banks of La Honda Creek before I was even awake.

As I dashed into the darkness someone tossed me the mayonnaise jar with all the marijuana in it. Expecting a raid, we'd consolidated all the dope into a one-quart jar so it could be more easily disposed of in an emergency such as the one we were now apparently encountering. The jar was about two-thirds full. It was enough for two or three days.

I scrambled across a bed and started out the door, hoping to hustle the few yards down to the edge of the creek and, under cover of the total darkness you find at night deep in a redwood forest, toss the stash as far as I could into the stream. Hopefully, I was thinking as I stumbled toward the door, the mayo jar would smash on one of the boulders in the creek and the evidence would be washed away westward to the Pacific, a few miles down La Honda Road.

The trouble was, as I scooted out the door I ran straight into the barrel of an automatic pistol that was pointed directly at my forehead. I could feel the gun at the bridge of my nose. It was cold! It was hard! It was scary!

"Stop or I'll shoot," the gunman shouted, displaying no originality, I thought, as I turned back toward the way I had come.

119

Foolheartedly, I didn't believe he'd actually shoot me over something as benign as a little illegal weed, so I scampered back into the room. The cop, probably as confused and scared as I, stumbled into the blackness behind me. He grabbed my ankle as I started to crawl back across the bed, the mayonnaise jar still in my hand. Realizing that the room was pitch black, I understood in that instant that he'd never be able to recognize me in the light.

On the other hand, of course, he could have shot me. So I kicked him in the chest and tried to break loose. Another Prankster, Hagen I think, dashed into the bedroom headed toward the door into the bathroom—which had two entrances, the other off the kitchen. I lobbed the mayo jar to Hagen and followed him into the john.

What a sight. There was Kesey, who'd been dabbing yet another touch of Day-Glo paint to the constantly expanding mural-montage that covered the walls, the porcelain, and every other surface of the bathroom. Only now he was busy with the more pressing business of flushing the grass down the toilet. The Best Foods jar was empty! At the same moment, a fat Asian man who turned out to be the late federal drug agent Willie Wong, ran into the bathroom from the kitchen, smacked Kesey's balding head with a huge flashlight, then jumped onto Kesey's back.

Now, Kesey had been a championship wrestler during his college days at the University of Oregon. He was strong, agile and, just then, operating on adrenaline. He stood up from the swirling toilet bowl, Agent Wong clinging to him. With a terrific shrug, Kesey tossed the burly narc from his back onto Page Browning, AKA Des Prado, who was standing frozen at the sink where he had been shaving. Somehow, despite the chaos going on around him, Page was still applying the razor to his skinny face.

Wong, armed with the huge Ray-O-Vac flashlight, landed on Page like a sumo wrestler as he was tossed from Kesey's back. The pair of them, Wong and Page, tumbled into the bathtub. Page still held the Gillette razor in his hand.

Suddenly the bathroom window was shattered by a huge

automatic pistol thrust into the room in the grip of an anonymous, but clearly law enforcement, fist.

"You're under arrest!" the gunman shouted from outside the bathroom window. Agent Wong, who'd regained his footing, shouted that he was charging Page and Kesey with resisting arrest.

("What else was I going to do?" Kesey told us he later asked a judge, when he finally went to trial. "I was raised during World War II. What would you have done, Your Honor? A big Jap jumped on me. I didn't know what was happening. I tossed him off." The judge didn't buy it.

(Neither did the jurist buy Kesey's claim, as Ken looked at the twelve good, nicely dressed citizens of San Francisco sitting in the courtroom, that they had failed to impanel a jury of his peers.)

After Kesey and Page were pulled to their feet, subdued and handcuffed, we were led at gunpoint into the living room. There were fourteen of us: Kesey, Neal Cassady, Page Browning, Ken Babbs, Gretchen Fetchin the Slime Queen, Hermit, Mountain Girl, Jerry Anderson, whose bride-to-be, Signe Toly, sang with a band called The Matrix, soon to change its name to Jefferson Airplane, Michael Hagen, a woman I was spending time with named Rosalie, three others, and me. We were handcuffed and charged with violating California's Health and Safety Code restrictions against the possession of illegal drugs, specifically cannabis sativa. They confiscated a jar filled with capsules of LSD straight from ace acid-meister Owsley—Augustus Stanley Owsley—but it turned out that lysergic acid diethylamide was still legal in California and remained so until October 1966. (Kesey, favored "Alice." But jargon is democratic and within days, it seemed, everyone called it "acid" as though it had always been thusly nicknamed.)

Standing there in Kesey's rustic living room, our hands cuffed behind us, most of us strangers to raids, search warrants and cops in general. We were scared, of course, but somehow didn't believe that we could face time behind bars for being in a

121

house where marijuana had been "found," even though I was pretty sure that Kesey had dumped our entire stash down the toilet. We had known—or suspected, or, at least, feared—that the authorities were fixing to raid our little scene in La Honda. Our motto in the previous few days had been "Be Prepared!"

So when the squad of federal, state, and county narcs and deputies hurried across Kesey's bridge armed with search warrants and automatic pistols on the night of April 23, 1965, we were ready. At least, naive and simple pot-and acid-heads that we were, we *thought* we were ready. Faye Kesey had gone over the place with a fine-tooth comb before leaving with their three kids and the dogs: Schnapps, a mean little dachshund Faye asked me to take to the pound a year later when we were living in Santa Cruz (Kesey never really forgave me for taking Schnapps on her final journey) and Lion Dog, the wire-haired Airedale that had never been the same, really, since the time she ate a handful of LSD someone had carelessly left lying around. (Kesey never fully understood that I was only following Faye's orders when I took Lion Dog to the shelter.)

Faye vacuumed stray marijuana flakes from the rugs. She had rounded up all the alligator clips and hemostats and artistic Squirkenwerks devices, many designed by my friend Jon Sägen, that might be considered useful as, and, in fact, were used as, roach clips. Not that we kept roaches—the butts of marijuana cigarettes—around for long; we usually tossed them down like a vitamin pill when they got too short to burn nicely. Faye had even picked errant pot seeds from between the floor boards in the house. We swallowed or smoked or got rid of all the DMT, Obitrol, DET, Dexamil, Dolophine, bennies, sopors, hashish, and other stimulants, depressants, and psychotropics, legal or otherwise, that we found stashed around the place—except for the LSD in the refrigerator, and that was still legal.

As far as I knew, the only pot in the place was in the mayonnaise jar, and that came from my cabin up the road when I was sent out on a "tether" a couple of days earlier.

Let me explain. We were under what we called "spaceship

conditions." Just as Kesey's dictum "You're either on the bus or off the bus" has entered our lexicon, for this spaceship endeavor you were either on the spaceship or off it. The front gate on our side of the raggedy bridge across La Honda Creek was locked. No one was supposed to go in or out. That gate, welded out of old tools, car parts, bucksaws, and odd pieces of scrap metal by sculptor Ron Boise was the "airlock" between our spaceship and the rest of the universe. At least until the narcs invaded. We were, in our drug-sparked protoscientific way, trying to discover what life would be like isolated in space, cut off from the rest of humankind, fueled only by a little food and a little dope, knowing that alien life-forces were out there ready to pick us off. We shut off the phones, told friends to back off, and put up signs shooing visitors away from the premises.

Of course this could have smacked of cult behavior, although none of us ever considered that possibility. We were experimenting. In the words of our pal Hunter Thompson, we believed that "we'd be fools not to ride this strange torpedo to the end." We were, in Kesey's own words, exploring inner space without the slightest damned notion of whether we'd get back to home base without losing our minds.

I met Hunter Thompson and his first wife one day when they stopped by Kesey's hoping to meet the famous writer. I was the only one at home. Kesey and the others were off pranking somewhere, I suppose. Hunter and I hit it off when the three of us headed for one of the few bars in tiny "downtown" La Honda and he invited me to stop by his place next time I was up in San Francisco. I took him up on that offer and visited Hunter every now and then at his apartment near the San Francisco campus of the University of California on Parnassus Street.

A few weeks after that unsuccessful attempt to meet Kesey, Hunter called and asked me to come up with Kesey to a San Francisco television studio to join in a panel discussion with him, Tom Wolfe, and some other local literary types. We got there too late for the panel discussion. But after he'd finished the TV show, Hunter took us out toward Hunter's Point and introduced us to the president of the local chapter of the Hell's Angels—and I'll tell the story of the Angels and the Pranksters in a bit.

* * *

Speaking of the possibility of cult-like behavior, often, in the years since La Honda, I've thanked Cosmo, as I call what people think of as God, that Kesey was more or less a benign Prankster leader. Had The Chief, as Cassady called him, asked or ordered us to do something evil would we have done it? I doubt it, but you never know, do you?

* * *

We knew that April day in 1965 that we might get busted. We'd seen sheriff's deputies watching us, including one atop the steep bluff across La Honda Road from Kesey's house. We could see him keeping tabs on us through his binoculars. Mountain Girl kept turning on the microphone for the huge and exotic sound system we'd spread across our hillside. She delighted in blasting invitations to the deputy to come share a cup of coffee. That veteran lawman later testified during our preliminary hearing in Municipal Court down in Redwood City that, as a graduate of an anti-drug course at some police academy, he could swear that he observed us walking about in a "floating" manner "indicative of people high on marijuana." He also testified that he had seen us using what he called "heroin, maroin, and peynotty." The prosecutor, hoping for damning testimony from the grizzled cop, was obviously shaken. We'd not used heroin at Kesey's and had never heard of the dangerous drugs maroin and peynotty.

During the day before the nighttime raid some neighbors stopped across the creek to shout at us that there were squadrons of deputy sheriffs gathering not far up the road. The neighbors, who tolerated us even if they didn't invite us over, were genuinely concerned for our welfare. But we were still simple-minded potheads who couldn't quite believe that cops would really break into the home of a famous writer and his pals just because we acted weird, looked funny, and used marijuana—even if we did have enough legal Owsley acid in the refrigerator to disable a major city.

Not all that many people wanted to be aboard our spaceship if we were going to be busted, or if there were even the slightest chance that we were in for any brush with the law. Kesey had asked Faye to take the kids and to spend the week down in Palo Alto with friends. Those fourteen of us "acid-nauts" who'd stayed had already spent three or four days, most of it awake on the last of the house "white cross" Benzedrine stash, watching the bus movie, forty-plus hours of *Intrepid Traveller and His Merry Band of Pranksters Look for a Cool Place*, and smoking the pot parceled out by Babbs from the mayo jar.

It might have gotten weird in there anyway: fourteen of us locked in together, not sleeping, barely eating, taking lotsa speed, smoking much more than our fair share of grass, destroying other pharmaceutical evidence at a rapid clip. It was always pretty weird at Kesey's, so how would we be able to tell?

When we ran out of weed, I was dispatched (on that invisible "tether") up the road to the tiny shack I rented on a nearby muddy mountain road aptly named Redwood Terrace. There was no terrace but my cabin *was* surrounded by plenty of redwoods. I was on a tether, in the sense that as I drove I talked into a portable tape-recorder (technology was fairly primitive in 1965) during my ten-minute round-trip from Kesey's, up to my pot stash in my cabin and back. It was our version of walking in space, I guess.

The marijuana I brought from my place was the stuff in the mayo jar, and what little remained of it went into the septic tank when Kesey flushed the toilet just as Willie Wong rudely bashed him with the flashlight and hopped on his back. So I was sort of surprised, after we'd been officially arrested and were milling around the living room in handcuffs, waiting to be transported down to the county jail in Redwood City, when I heard Babbs ask his girlfriend, Gretchen Fetchin, "Would you care to eat some joints, Miss Fetchin?" She nodded and he passed her a couple from a personal stash in his pocket that he had, as was his wont, hidden from the rest of us. Babbs and Gretch proceeded to eat the remaining evidence.

The narcs confiscated the acid, along with a jar of roaches, they said they'd found. We knew this was a lie. I can assure you that they didn't really find any roaches. We ate our roaches or, occasionally, when several joints were going at once, jammed a bunch into the end of what Kesey dubbed a "nose-cone," a cardboard tube from a roll of toilet paper, and smoked the whole shebang at once, like smoking a supercharger of marijuana.

Under the watchful eyes of the deputies and narcotics agents who set up shop at the huge, round redwood-slab dining room table into which we'd all carved our initials and anything else that had come to mind, I tried to act cool. I wasn't cool, of course, and sort of squeaked when they asked me my name and occupation. Like most of my fellow prisoners, I described myself as an employee of Intrepid Trips, Inc., not mentioning that just a couple of weeks earlier, after many months of life in La Honda with Kesey and the Pranksters, I had quit my job as a reporter for the *San Mateo Times*. I knew the managing editor down there, a guy who'd disliked me, my politics, my lifestyle, and my La Honda friends, would be tickled pink when he learned that I'd been busted for drugs.

Later quoted in newspaper accounts of the raid in my role as "public relations director" for Kesey's Intrepid Trips, Inc.—including a story that reported that "Kesey seemed queasy" when booked into the county jail—I tried to make it sound like Intrepid Trips was like one of your run-of-the-mill big time film companies instead of a congregation of acid heads with cameras and forty miles of film, much of it out of focus.

I was cuffed to a hushed Neal Cassady and put into the backseat of a sheriff's squad car along with Kesey, who was also surprisingly quiet. In fact, we all seemed pretty reflective as we were rushed down to the county seat. We were facing time behind bars, especially Cassady and another Prankster who would be charged as "three-time losers."

At the jail, where forewarned photographers from the San Francisco newspapers waited to snap our pictures, we were booked for possession of marijuana. Kesey was also charged with resisting arrest, operating a disorderly house, an archaic way of saying he owned the place where the drugs were found, and for possession of narcotics paraphernalia. The cops had found a hypodermic syringe full of machine oil we used to lubricate hard-to-reach gears in our armory of movie cameras, tape recorders, and film projectors.

We were locked into a couple of cells. I was in the drunk tank, with about five other Pranksters, a few winos, and a big black guy who commandeered half of the space to himself after revealing that he'd just slit his wife's throat with a butcher knife. The Hermit, who was completely cuckoo on speed by this time, took over another quarter of the cell by acting (or being) crazy, climbing on the bars, making hideous screeching noises and generally scaring everyone except the wife-killer and his fellow not-so-Merry Pranksters.

We were bailed out by our lawyers, Brian Rohan and Paul Robertson (Zonker's brother-in-law) at around six in the morning. The highlight of our release was Hermit's mother confrontating Kesey. A nurse at the same veteran's hospital where Kesey worked when he got the idea for *One Flew Over the Cuckoo's Nest*, Hermit's mom threw a copy of that novel in its author's face. "Go back to your cuckoo pad," she screamed at him. "You should have stayed in the nest instead of flying over it, you big cuckoo."

Kesey deftly snatched the book out of the air, signed it, and handed it to one of our jailers, who gratefully accepted the autographed novel by the famous local writer.

By the time we were on our way back home to La Honda we were in pretty good spirits again. For one thing, we were out of jail. For another, our arrest was front-page news in the *Chronicle*, the *Examiner* and the *San Jose Mercury* (where I later spent nineteen years as a reporter, editor, and columnist until I retired in 2001). We were basking in the oddly attractive limelight that surrounds cultural outlaws. Several dailies ran my photo, handcuffed to Cassady, being escorted with Kesey into the jail in the company of a pair of nattily dressed sheriff's deputies.

We were already, though, considering the down side of the situation: We could end up in jail or prison. Neal Cassady and Jerry Anderson, who had prior convictions on drug charges, faced life sentences for being three-time losers, an early version of California's occasionally popular Three Strikes And You're Out deal. That, essentially, is why Kesey eventually pleaded guilty to a possession charge, to keep Neal, especially, out of prison.

But that wasn't until after Ken's second pot bust with Mountain Girl in San Francisco a few months later, and until after we'd all split to Mexico. Kesey, a fugitive from American justice, was nabbed by the FBI when returned to the U.S.

Kesey spent five months at the San Mateo County sheriff's "honor camp" in the redwoods not far up the road from his La Honda home. After almost a half year at the camp, Kesey—who'd agreed as part of his guilty plea, ironically, to stay away from La Honda *and* the rest of San Mateo County—was determined to avoid any more time in custody, be it behind bars or on a county jail farm. He told me that he'd never again cop another plea to anything, no matter what the consequences to anybody else. He did not like being incarcerated; he did not like not being free.

While an inmate at the honor camp, Kesey filled several notebooks with a mix of notes and diary entries intertwined with colorful Pentel pen drawings, caricatures, and illustrations. The whole package was similar, in a way, to the artwork on his old 1939 school bus that Kesey and the Pranksters turned into an ever-changing, rolling work of art.

It took another three decades before Kesey felt he had

something ready for his publisher, and that was only after the technology was available to capture the colorful pages on paper. The journals were published two years after Kesey's 2001 death as the relatively unknown, *Kesey's Jail Journal, Cut the M************ Loose*.

One of the more poignant parts of the journals is a note written to Faye during his time at the honor camp:

"Dear Faye: Hi. How's life on the streets? I lost my fine tailor shop job. Why? Same old reason. Making waves. Using too/much/COLOR/Just when I was getting good at it, too. However, I have been promoted. To a digger of ditches dig dig dig dig dig."

Actually, both Kesey and Page Browning pleaded guilty in the wake of the La Honda raid. Charges were dropped against the rest of us. But the narcs were not going to sanction any arrest-resisting, not even by a hapless Prankster like Page, Des Prado, whose only resistance consisted of falling into the bathtub when Willie Wong came flying into him.

We started to think about our lawyers' fees. Rohan and Robertson said they'd work for free, both knowing their reputations would soar among dopers and long-haired acid heads if they defended the country's most prominent apostle of psychedelic drugs. But we still needed some money and none of us, Kesey included, was bringing in any income.

Kesey thought one way to make money was to sell articles, stories, novels, or anything else with his name on it. He suggested that I call his agent Sterling Lord, and see if he could make any deals. "Lee, you can write it and put my name on it," Kesey told me. "Write anything you want. We can probably make more money if they think I wrote it." I tried, but Sterling Lord wasn't at all enthusiastic about making any quick deals for Kesey (I didn't mention to him that I was going to be writing the stuff under Ken's by-line) and, frankly, the publishing business in those days was pretty stuffy. They figured if Kesey was using drugs he must be a burnt-out head case.

Paul Krassner later told me that when he'd learned about Kesey's suggestion that I write stuff and use his name as my nom de plume, he thought of it as "very Zen. Ken had no ego," Paul reflected. "Kesey saw that the Pranksters could use his name as a tool" to raise money now that paid speaking engagements were petering out. Educational institutions, the main venues for speaking engagements by prominent authors, were more frightened to think that they might have a drug-user on stage in the auditorium than they were about the idea that there might be a Communist in the sociology department.

I didn't agree with Krassner that Kesey had no ego. I think thought this was merely a case of Kesey the Writer deciding he wasn't going to write any more. Seriously, Kesey decided after the La Honda bust to quit writing, completely and forever. One day a lawyer friend, Jim Wolpman, took Ken to meet a banker. Kesey wanted to borrow some money. As usual, he wore some bright shirt cut from an American flag and his light-colored jeans with Pentel-pen doodlings all over them. "I love your novels, Mr. Kesey," the banker said, asking, "What are you writing these days?" "I'm writing on my pants," the famous author replied.

Which, of course, reminds me of a story: One evening, taking a nap on Kesey's living-room floor while the seemingly endless Bus Movie was showing, I awoke with my head on the rug under a little end table. I gazed up and saw that someone, probably someone who'd eaten a few Benzedrine tabs, had completely covered the underside of the table with intricate doodles and fine drawings and bright designs with Pentel pens in a variety of bright colors. The artist had not signed his or her work, which was only visible if you were lying beneath the table, but had entitled it, per a note in one corner, "The Sistine Table."

By the way, I realize that it doesn't sound all that outrageous these days to know that Kesey wore an American flag shirt down to the bank. But you gotta remember, in those days the flag was still . . . well, I guess you could say it was still sacred. When Kesey and the Pranksters started to wear flag shirts or when Kesey, in his bus movie role as Swash Buckler tied Old Glory around his head like a pirate's bandanna, he was truly doing something extraordinary, something bold at a time when America's law enforcement agents conflated anything a "hippie" might do with a flag with opposition to law and order and the war in Vietnam. Using the flag was seen as something dishonorable and even dishonest. No one had yet designed flag-patterned rugby shirts, let alone burned American flags to protest anything.

I mean, when folks saw Kesey with the Stars and Stripes draped around his neck like a scarf they didn't know whether to salute or call the cops. Kesey had a knack for coming up with things that someone else would quickly popularize and cash in on. It never occurred to him or to any of us, for instance, to make money by selling flag shirts. We never even suspected that any other gang of acid heads would ever want to slap a Day-Glo paint job on their old bus. That would be nuts!

* * *

The La Honda bust was big news on the front pages of Bay Area newspapers. There followed a half-dozen or more court appearances as our arraignment and preliminary hearing got underway in the old courthouse down at the San Mateo County seat in Redwood City. Sometimes we'd spend the whole day in court, with lunch breaks at noon and marijuana breaks at mid-morning and mid-afternoon.

They weren't called pot breaks. They were officially called ten-minute recesses. And we didn't carry grass into court with us, where it might be found were they to search folks entering the courtroom. We didn't even leave our stashes where they might have been found during a search of our cars; we might have been goofy, but we weren't stupid. Instead of holding the weed in our pockets or our glove compartments, we chewed some gum when we made our first appearance before the judge, then stuck it under the courtroom benches. While the Juicy-Fruit wads were still gooey we affixed joints to the undersides of our seats so we were always able to reach down to get something to smoke when we exited the courtroom for lunch or a recess.

We figured they'd never search us when we *left* the courtroom.

STATE OF GRACE

After we'd been busted for drug possession, even though the drug was only marijuana, Kesey found himself an outlaw on the Bay Area literary scene. Invitations to speak or to appear on panels, which he and the rest of us saw as opportunities to pick up some much needed income, dwindled or disappeared. For instance, Ken's scheduled participation in a panel discussion at Lowell High School in San Francisco was cancelled at the last minute. A school district official called an hour or so before we left for the city us telling to stay home. He said district regulations forbade known drug abusers from using school facilities. Man, why did they invite him in the first place? Our drug use at Kesey's place was not a secret in San Francisco. And hadn't they heard of the concept of being considered innocent unless proven guilty? There had been no trial, no convictions, just articles in the newspapers about our arrests.

We drove up to Lowell High School anyway, after famed San Francisco attorney Melvin Belli phoned to suggest that Kesey defy the ban. Belli hinted that he would refuse to join the panel discussion as scheduled unless Kesey was also allowed to go on.

So when we go to the packed auditorium we discovered that half the crowd was pissed because Kesey had been banned from the stage and the other half seemed pleased that he'd been told to stay home.

When the panel discussion was announced, Kesey strode up to the stage at the front of the auditorium and hopped up to join his fellow panelists. The moderator ordered Kesey off the stage. Some of the panelists were shouting, "Let him stay;" others were shouted, "Get off the stage! Get off the stage!"

The person chairing the panel asked a school district guard to come forward from the rear of the auditorium and to drag Kesey away. I could see in Kesey's face and his demeanor and especially in his body language, which was that of the heavyweight wrestling champion that he'd been at the University of Oregon, that he had no intention of letting any guards or school administrators pull him off that stage.

But, as the cop was about to put his arm on the angry Kesey, he suddenly acquiesced, shrugging his shoulders and moseying over to some steps leading down from the stage. Kesey came back to where Faye and a couple of other Pranksters and I were standing and motioned for us to follow him out to the car.

"Hey, man," I wondered, "how come we're leaving?"

"Well," he explained sheepishly, "I was reaching in my back pocket to get out my wallet and put it in my front pocket so it wouldn't fall out if we got in a fight—and I found a joint in there with the wallet. I didn't want to get busted again, so here I am. Let's go visit Margo St. James."

So we headed toward North Beach to see Margo, San Francisco's best-known prostitute and later the founder of COYOTE—Call Off Your Old Tired Ethics, an advocacy group for sex-workers and against repressive sex laws that criminalize prostitution. Margo, a longtime friend of Prankster Michael Hagen, wasn't home so we headed back down the Peninsula, home to La Honda.

(One afternoon when Hagen and I were smoking dope with Margo at her apartment above a butcher shop on Grant Avenue, in the middle of the North Beach bohemian-and-Italian neighborhood, she told us to go in another room when the doorbell rang. Hagen and I and a woman who was one of Margo's fellow sex-workers, stayed in the living room smoking joints while our hostess entertained her guest. When she walked him through the room en route to a bedroom I saw that he was a tall and distinguished-looking elderly man. He nodded at the three of us sitting in the corner and puffing away on our marijuana. After he'd left, Margo told us he was a judge.)

Despite the decline in speaking invitations from some quarters—you really cannot understand how verboten marijuana was among many people, even in San Francisco, in 1965—Ken did get occasional invitations to speak. Now notorious as a rebel as well as an author of fine, respectable novels, he fit the bill for progressive preachers, the kind who were experimenting with folk music services.

Some Unitarians, following the suggestion of one minister who soon became a friend of the Pranksters, invited us down to a conference they were holding at the venerable meeting center at Asilomar, in Pacific Grove, at the tip of the Monterey Peninsula.

I went along with Kesey and some other Pranksters, including my girlfriend at the time, Ginger Jackson, a local Santa Cruz girl. We tried to blend in with the crowds of starry-eyed Unitarians wandering among the Monterey pines and some fairly tame deer but at first I found the Asilomar scene to be, well, a bit boring.

Our second evening there, Kesey was announced as the guest speaker after somehow promising that he would use the occasion to perform a miracle.

His off-the-cuff remark drew a few scoffs from Ginger and me and the other Pranksters. We were used to Kesey's rhetoric and were never surprised if he managed to do something outrageous—in this case, work a miracle—or if he failed to pull one off.

So we were not exactly surprised when, as Ken was talking about miracles to the assembled Unitarians sitting at the edge of the Pacific and watching the sun set behind him, he suddenly actualized, is the best way I can say it, a fucking miracle! Not a major one, not a miracle of any particular benefit to anyone. But, as he was saying something about all of us being able to work magic and miracles, he suddenly turned and pointed toward the spot on the far horizon where the sun was dropping behind the curtain of the Pacific Ocean.

"See?" he said, intending to show that just the mere fact that the sun rose in the morning and set at night was a miracle, take it or leave it.

Instead, the congregation of Unitarians sitting in a semi-circle around him gave a huge gasp. Kesey himself seemed a bit surprised.

Out there at the edge of the ocean, as the sun disappeared for the rest of the night, the famous green flash so watched for in Hawaii suddenly, for an instant, turned that spot in the distance a brilliant, neon green. Just for a moment, just for a second. Kesey looked at us, eyes wide. He seemed to be asking, *Did that really happen?*

* * *

Did word of this surprising "miracle" spread? I don't know. But it wasn't long before Ken was asked up to an Episcopalian seminary in Marin County to address the young men studying for the priesthood.

Faye, Ken Babbs, and I sat in the front row, just beneath the stage, in the seminary's combination little theater and lecture room. Kesey was on stage right above us, yakking about whatever crossed his mind. He had a carafe full of coffee at his side and a cup on a small table next to him. He asked the seminarians to interrupt with questions whenever they felt like doing so.

A student behind me toward the back rows asked, "Mr. Kesey, what about grace? What can you tell us about grace?"

Kesey began to talk about grace, but he was describing athletic grace, the grace of a basketball player, the sort of grace that is often thought of as being physical in nature—not the sort of grace on the minds of young seminarians.

I could hear a sad gasp of embarrassment buzzing all about me. These seminarians, hoping for some deep insight about spiritual grace from the burly pothead author, instead believed that Kesey had misunderstood them completely. They wanted to hear about the grace of God, not the grace of basketball star Wilt Chamberlain.

It seemed to many that Kesey had not only missed the point but that he was getting himself into a bind. One of those situations where you start talking about something and get further and further away from the original topic and suddenly find yourself way out on a conversational limb with a chainsaw and no apparent way to stop sawing yourself off, no way to get yourself back toward the trunk. Fortunately, though, we knew that Kesey was at his best when tap-dancing on a tightrope—or when sawing himself off when he was at the end of a limb.

But the seminarians, well-mannered as such young men were expected to be, listened politely even thought their guest speaker was veering off the subject. They watched as Kesey poured a cup of coffee and listened as he continued to discuss athletes and the graceful way they moved.

Then he looked down at Ken Babbs, who was sitting next to me.

"Hey, Babbs," he asked, "can I have the cream?"

Babbs took the tiny pitcher of cream that was sitting next to a sugar bowl on a small table between our front-row seats and the stage. He held the small cruet of cream by its handle and tossed it through the air. Kesey, still talking, still declaiming on the grace of an athlete, hardly looking at Babbs, caught the pitcher by its dainty handle. He poured a dollop of cream into his cup and dropped the tiny pitcher back down to Babbs, who also caught it by its handle and replaced the creamer effortlessly on the little table, right where it belonged, next to the sugar bowl.

And as he did this, Kesey was suggesting to the crowd, now rapt in silent awe of their guest, that the grace of an athlete and the grace of God are one and the same.

They suspected that he was right. And so did I.

THE GREAT DUCK STORM/FURTHER INDEED

Having enlisted as a Prankster after Kesey and his gang returned from their well-publicized round-trip bus adventure to New York City, I was tickled as we departed La Honda on my first extended trip aboard the famous painted school bus that had been purchased and decorated with money from Kesey's advance for *Sometimes A Great Notion*.

We headed west a few miles down La Honda Road to Highway 1, taking that winding coast road north along the ocean and across the Golden Gate Bridge. Neal Cassady was at the wheel, continuing his endless monologue through the night until we found ourselves at a state park near Mendocino. We all dropped tabs of acid imported from Czechoslovakia, then a repressive Stalinist ally of the Soviet Union. *What the hell*, I used to wonder, *are they doing with LSD in a country run by the secret police?*

Richard Alpert, soon to be known, after an enlightening trip to India, as Baba Ram Dass, was our source for a batch of that Czech acid. I think George Walker was the Prankster who stirred it and diluted it and mixed it and put a drop apiece into thousands of small, clear gelatin capsules, where it dried into a tiny spot, sensitive to black light, at one end of the cap. George thought each capsule contained about three-hundred milligrams, but he got so stoned handling the stuff as he prepared and put it into the gelatin caps that there was no way he could measure it accurately. I can tell you this: It was either damned great LSD or there were two or three times as much in each cap as George had estimated.

LSD was still legal in the United States, of course, until the autumn of 1966. It was so new to our own branch of the Great Society, though, that no one had come up with a suitable nickname for this wonder drug that promised to change the world for the better, one head at a time.

There were heads, users, who thought the term "acid" sounded too toxic. They— and they included Kesey—liked the name "Alice," not only a reference, of course, to *Alice in*

Wonderland but also a cute pun, as in Alice-D. But before you knew it, and with no real debate or discourse, the term "acid" caught on and stuck. Jargon is democratic and within days, it seemed, everyone was calling lysergic acid dethylamide "acid," not "Alice."

By the way, I've always assumed that the so-called "Prague Spring," which began in early 1968 and was led by Alexander Dubček, was a direct result of some of that government-produced LSD getting out of the lab and into the hands of Czech young people. Just like what happened here.

Our adventure in the Mendocino state park was a typical outing for the Pranksters. We got high. We saw the universe or God or Cosmo or whatever was lurking in there as we peered into the pores on the backs of our hands or at the veins of wildflower leafs and petals.

We listened to loud music after plugging the bus's sound system into an electrical socket in a men's restroom. The racket didn't go over well with other park-users and the cops came to order us to turn it down. But they didn't know whom to issue the order to.

"Who's in charge here?" a cop asked me. "Who's in charge?"

Well, Kesey had jumped off the bus and fled in some sort of acid freak into the woods. Even if he'd been there, though, we couldn't have said for sure that he was "in charge" of a busfull of Pranksters high on LSD. Nonetheless, when confronted by the cops asking who was in charge (meaning who was to blame), we all pointed at Ken Babbs, a tall, handsome man who happened, at the moment, to be covered with feathers—after someone, probably his girlfriend Gretch, poured some sticky substance over his body followed by a pillow-full of goose down. Babbs smiled as the cops approached.

"Are you in charge?" one asked.

Nodding, Babbs quacked.

"What did you say?"

"Quack. Quack," Babbs replied.

"Huh?"

Babbs continued to quack. He quacked quite eloquently at them, punctuating his quacks with nods, grimaces and hand gestures, seemingly enjoying his duck-like discussion with the men in park ranger uniforms.

Eventually, unwilling to play along—as with most peace officers when confronted with absurdity—the rangers gave up and went to the men's toilet building, where they unplugged the bus's sound system. Then they ordered us to get the hell out of the park.

The problem was that we were missing Kesey, who'd vanished into the woods on what looked to me much like a Natty Bumpo trip. Despite his ever-present warning that "You're either on the bus or off the bus," no one had ever actually considered the possibility of Kesey himself being off the bus. But there it was. Kesey was off the bus—so Babbs got us all aboard and told Cassady to head out of the park.

Faye Kesey was having a snit. "My husband's still here," she cried at the rangers. "We can't leave without him." She told Babbs that we couldn't leave Ken behind. But Babbs, sensing hysteria on the horizon, quacked orders to leave. He stayed in persona as a duck for an hour or so after we'd departed from the park.

I was worried. How would we justify leaving Kesey behind while we drove away on his own bus? But then, like those small miracles of Kesey's always happened, as we drove out of the park exit a couple of miles from the place where we'd been enjoying the acid and the music and the quacking, Kesey jumped out of the brushy forest like he was one of The Last of the Mohicans and hopped aboard the bus. So, with Neal Cassady at the wheel, we headed Further.

* * *

Our typical LSD doses of three-hundred micrograms tended to keep one high for about eight hours. So we were still under the influence as night fell and we headed east from Mendocino deeper into the Northern California forest. I was atop the bus with my two closest Prankster friends, Zonker and Hassler. Never anticipating the psychedelic revolution that was about to break wide open in the Bay Area, in the nation and even throughout the world, I asked Zonker a question that in retrospect seems so naïve I have trouble believing I didn't see the stoned handwriting on the wall. "Wouldn't it be a trip if we saw another bus heading the other direction and it was all painted up and full of freaks like this one?" Zonker, real name Steve Lambrecht, Hassler (Ron Bevirt), and I laughed at the absurdity. (Zonker's name evolved from his amazing ability and predilection to pass out whenever he could; Hassler, who's entire Prankster moniker was The Equipment Hassler, was named after taking charge, in frustration because no one else would do it, of the bus's sound equipment and anything else that needed attention during the original New York bus trip.)

My blatantly naïve question came after a station wagon filled with some guys with long hair like us chugged slowly past as the bus labored up a hill. The guys in the station wagon waved and, remembering Winston Churchill and thinking briefly about the Them-and-Us split between acid heads and squares, I flashed those nascent hippies the V-for-Victory sign. They looked back in confusion for a moment. Then one laughed and gave me the victory sign in return.

Zonker, a handsome San Jose State grad who was the inspiration for the Doonesbury character, said years later that that moment was an important one. "Lee, you invented the peace sign," Zonker said. And he was right. Gradually, that V for Victory became V for Peace as hippies and long-hairs and acid heads flashed that sign in recognition when meeting in the street or on the road in a street demonstration or just sitting around doing nothing.

The Great Duck Storm occurred as the bus chugged up another hill. Those of us riding on top of the bus had a down sleeping bag that we wrapped around us for warmth. The bus below was crowded and none of us felt like heading inside to get away from the nighttime chill. Somehow, the sleeping bag cover got a rip in it and pretty soon it began to open and clouds of white down came spilling out into the wind, which blew the feathers back onto a car behind us—and that driver had to turn on his windshield-wipers to whisk the blinding cover of white feathers away so he could see to stay on the road! Zonker said we had just created The Great Duck Storm.

Eventually, I went down inside the bus and nodded off to sleep, as did everyone else who'd been on the roof. I was sleeping between Page Browning and some woman who was his girlfriend at the moment. Somehow, and certainly surreptitiously so Page wouldn't know I was still awake, I touched the woman's hand and she responded by carefully and slowly putting it between her legs. But meanwhile, Page, not realizing that I was between him and his girlfriend, grabbed my hand and started making those kind of masculine yet poetic little finger strokes and gestures that let the other person, in my case always a woman, know we're interested in them. Jeez, I worried, Page is gonna figure out that he's holding my hand and then he's gonna figure out that I'm holding her hand and then… And then I made a snore-like sound and jerked both hands away from my bus neighbors, and then I went to sleep.

When I awoke the next morning, the bus had come to a stop, obviously on an uphill slope. It was a sunny day and I stepped outside and saw we were on a narrow dirt road on a mountain with the kind of pine trees that grow fairly far up mountainsides, not down near sea level. The Hermit, who was later banned from Kesey's place after he tried to molest several of the Pranksters' young sons, a proclivity naively unknown to us at that time, was making a fire "the Indian way," he told me. Hermit had lived and foraged in the La Honda-area redwood forests for months before we saw him walking along the creek trying to spear steelhead one day and we invited him in for a sandwich. Someone gave him a Dexadrine capsule and within an hour I saw a crazy look in his eyes and knew this guy was going to be a speed freak. Sure enough, the last time I saw him, Hermit was running down Haight Street a year after most of us had left La Honda. He held his outfit, his hypodermic and syringe, in the air and was shouting the praises of methedrine. I did not stop to say hello.

So this was an Indian fire? I wondered, seeing nothing on the ground but some sticks. "Put your hand above it," Hermit suggested. I did. Despite the lack of any visible flame or smoke there was heat rising. Amazing.

Kesey wandered out of the bus and wondered where we were. Neither Hermit nor I had any idea. We shouted into the bus, trying to find out who had been the last one driving. It turned out it was Dale Kesey, Ken's cousin. "Where are we?" we wondered. Dale had no idea. "Well then," asked cousin Ken, "why are we stopped here?" "Oh," Dale nonchalantly replied, "we ran out of gas."

Some panic began to set in as Pranksters arose, one-by-one, wondering why we seemed to be stranded on a remote mountain dirt road. Those who were worried got more concerned when an old man came walking up the road and, when we asked where the nearest gas station was, told us to go back down the dirt road fourteen miles to the state highway, then turn right and go about twelve miles to the Shell station. That wasn't good. We had between us no more than a couple of dollars after buying some bags of potato chips before we'd gone to sleep and had been getting by fuel-wise with George Walker's Chevron gas credit card. The nearest Chevron station? The old man didn't know. Some aboard the bus decided that we were screwed.

"Don't worry, everything always works out in the end," Kesey promised. Having seen what seemed to be a series of almost miraculous events, marvels, really, since I'd been hanging around him, I believed Kesey. I wasn't that concerned, nor were most of the Pranksters. But still, there was some skepticism, understandable, I guess, when you're fourteen miles up a dirt road and God knows how many miles from the nearest gas station that would take George's credit card.

Deciding not to worry, most of us started to look around. Down the road a hundred yards or so we found a water tank with a spigot so trucks going to and from the copper mine at the end of the road, several miles up the mountain, could fill their radiators and water tanks, if needed. Some of the Pranksters stripped down and got under the waterspout and had just started to feel refreshed when we noticed a coiled rattlesnake just inches from Mountain Girl's feet. It seemed to be enjoying the shower, but we skedaddled, having no wish to disturb the critter as it took in the splashing water and the morning sun.

An hour or so later, all the potato chips gone, we heard a truck horn blare. The sound came from a Chevron gasoline tanker truck making its monthly delivery to the copper mine up the road. The truck driver stopped, filled the bus's fuel tank, took an impression of George's Chevron card, said goodbye and good luck, and headed up the road toward the copper mine.

Kesey, with a smile, boarded the bus, put Ray Charles' tune "Hit the Road, Jack," on the sound system, turned to Neal and said, "Let's hit the road."

ON THE BUS OR OFF THE BUS

On our way home from Mendocino and other Northern California back roads we pulled to a stop one night on the edge of the town of Ukiah. We were stoned, tired, in no condition to drive another mile. It did not matter the slightest when we figured out that we were, in fact, parked right in the middle of the Ukiah dump.

Sunrise at the dump was as wonderful, actually, as sunrise is no matter where you might be. We stretched, made some rudimentary ablutions, then hit the road. We decided to stop in town for some breakfast hamburgers and coffee, which we gobbled down before Kesey said it was time to get back aboard the bus. Cassady started the motor, we found places to sit and enjoy our breakfasts and then drove down the main drag of Ukiah.

After we'd gone a few blocks, one of us noticed Jerry Anderson, a recent Prankster hanger-on who was married to Signe Toly, lead singer of Jefferson Airplane, running behind the bus. He was shouting at us to stop and let him get aboard.

Now Kesey's dictum, "You're either on the bus or off the bus," has entered the lexicon to the point that it's probably used as a warning to children by anxious parents and by troop leaders trying to organize their squadron so they can pull out of some defensive position.

Originally, Kesey meant it literally. One was, at all times, either on the bus or off. Specifically, wherever Kesey happened to be was "on the bus." If you were with him and got on the bus with him you were "on the bus." If you didn't get aboard you were, therefore, "off the bus" if the bus left without you. The bus waited for no Prankster. And when Kesey boarded and started the music playing ("Hit the Road Jack," our On the Road theme song) the bus left, no matter where we were parked, you got left behind if you weren't on the bus.

Jerry Anderson wasn't on the bus when we left the hamburger stand. Perhaps he'd been in the bathroom, I don't know. I do remember that he was pretty fucked up after an acid trip a couple of days earlier from which he had clearly not come down.

* * *

No one disputed the unspoken understanding that being "on the bus" meant being there, or anywhere. The on-or-off-the-bus deal extended to all corners of our group dynamics and it was all related to whether Kesey was there. After all, we clearly knew that it was Kesey's bus, purchased with the fruits of his writing. Where Kesey wanted to take the bus was where we went, always.

Aside from the concept of actually being on the bus, the real, 1939 International school bus, Pranksters were similarly on or off the bus no matter where we were. Yes, we were followers, although, fortunately, not in the sense of followers of a cult leader. Rather, we followed Kesey, or frequently followed him, because he led us to places we'd never been, places we'd never even suspected were there. Psychedelic places, for the most part, places in our heads that I know I might have been reluctant to seek, at least at the beginning of my season in psychedelia.

Some Pranksters never questioned Kesey. Others, myself included, might challenge him during a conversation or a group discussion, either of which could easily turn into a Kesey monologue—because he was peerless at commanding and holding attention, he was without equal as a teller of tales, or making and expressing strange connections and amazing images and outrageous but true similes. Ken had charisma. He may be the only person I've ever known who really had it.

From time to time I would do or say something that tried Kesey's patience, that would derail some story he was telling or some discovery that he wanted to reveal. Most of us did. The disdainful glances Kesey gave to someone whose interruption of his monologue failed to meet his high standards had the immediate effect of making any one of us feel that we were off the bus.

It seemed after a while that Kesey was more likely to take issue with big men who interrupted him than with slighter men, or with women. In fact, Ken spent much of his adult life coming to terms with the belief that women are men's equals. He was a cowboy at heart and thought of most women either as potential (and often the potential was realized) sex partners, or as little ladies who needed to be left alone to sew and cook and raise the children.

In those days I was tall, six-foot, four-inches, but not very heavy, probably one hundred and seventy pounds. But I was tall enough and big enough that on more than one occasion I felt he was sizing me up, as though our discussion or my interjections in his monologue might lead to some sort of testosterone-fueled macho wrestling match. But when I'd make some comment that either extended his own argument or that opened some new insight, Kesey was effusive in his making me feel that I was solidly on the bus.

Prankster Julius Karpen, who'd been my first editor on the overnight shift at the City news Bureau of Chicago when I was nineteen and who'd given me my first joint and my first Benzedrine tab, was shocked when he heard Ken make a negative remark about homosexuals:

"As always, Kesey was at the center of the group and the discussion. He made some remark I thought was anti-gay and I was shocked, then I responded. I told him that I thought his comment was wrong and that there was no reason to consider gay people as being worth any less than anyone else.

"He considered what I'd said and he responded that I was right. He apologized. And I was thinking, *Man, he's talking to me as an equal.* I was quite flattered. I was mind-blown."

In other words, Julius felt he'd suddenly found himself "on the bus."

* * *

The bus itself aged, as did we all. Kesey, who looked a bit like Paul Newman when I first met him, got balder and whiter-haired and let a thick fringe of curls grow around the sides of his head until he looked more like Bozo the Clown.

The bus was parked in a thicket on Kesey's farm in Pleasant Hill, Oregon, where Ken intended to let it slowly melt back into the earth—as sort of an example of his frequent statement, "Nothing lasts." It was similar to the Buddha's revelation that everything that is put together, created, built, will eventually fall apart.

Recently, Kesey's son Zane has, so I've heard, towed the rusting, rotting hulk of the bus out of the swampy thicket with an eye to restoring it—and probably somehow making some money with it.

In the late 1980s, Kesey bought a newer, slightly smaller old school bus and had it restored and decorated professionally. It was that bus that we took on a trip from his farm to the Smithsonian Institute in the nation's capital, where it would supposedly rest in a place of honor.

When the Smithsonian folks found out that it wasn't the original bus Ken was going to deliver to them they backed out; they sent him a letter telling him No, they didn't want the new bus. Kesey didn't even open the envelope. He tossed it to the wind as we drove from his farm toward Washington, D.C.

We got as far as Stockton, where Kesey had a speaking engagement at University of the Pacific. That was as far as Kesey had intended to go.

I was aboard, along with some other old Pranksters no longer used to sleeping on top of other sleeping Pranksters on the floor of an old bus. I was sending dispatches from the trip to my newspaper, the *San Jose Mercury News*.

My editor was extremely put out when he learned that Kesey had called off the trip to Washington. I was glad the journey was over, though. I was ready for a clean bed and to see my dogs.

As he was speaking to the University of Pacific students, one Prankster, George Walker, ran in and shouted, "Kesey, they've taken the bus. The kids have stolen the bus!"

Just as we'd intended, the younger Pranksters, including Ken's son Zane and some of his pals, had driven the bus away after drawing a chalk outline of it on its parking pad. Then they quickly slapped a coat of whitewash over the decorations and sped home to Kesey's farm.

The university students were baffled. The rest of us headed here or there. Kesey and I and a couple others hitched rides down to the Bay Area.

For once, *all* of us were off the bus!

ADIOS LA HONDA. ALOHA, SANTA CRUZ!

Anyone who's read much of the literature about Ken Kesey and the Merry Pranksters and the Bay Area Sixties' scene is familiar with the Hell's Angels party at our place in La Honda. Allen Ginsberg wrote a poem about it. Hunter Thompson wrote about it. Tom Wolfe featured it in *The Electric Kool-Aid Acid Test*.

It was a hell of a party. I think the genesis of the whoopdeedoo began one quiet afternoon in 1964 when I was by myself at Kesey's house when a nicely dressed young couple, looking like what later would be called Yuppies, drove across the bridge over La Honda Creek and honked at the gate—a piece of metal sculpture by Ron Boise, notorious at the time for his Kama Sutra statues.

Those erotic, finely crafted little sculptures had been confiscated as evidence in the 1964 San Francisco obscenity trial of the owner of the Vorpal Gallery for selling pornographic art. A jury found the gallery proprietor not guilty of the obscenity charges. During the trial, Boise testified that he had sculpted statues of individuals before deciding to create sculptures of two humans together. Why had he depicted the couples in sexual communion? He told the jury that there were only so many ways to show two people together: "They can fight each other, ignore each other, or embrace."

Later, a much-huger-than-life bronze Boise Kama Sutra statue of a man going down on an equally large woman sat in Kesey's yard until it was purchased by Fritz Maytag and moved to the roof of his Anchor Steam brewery in San Francisco. When hooked up to the plumbing at Kesey's, water gushed from the juncture of the man's mouth and the woman's crotch.

I'd hung out with Ron as he'd welded a rusty old bucksaw and parts of some wrecked cars and some other hunks and strips of metal into that gate. At the time, Boise and I were the only two around the Prankster scene who drank alcohol, a situation that changed a few years later after Kesey and Babbs and a few others went back up to stay on or near Kesey's farm in Oregon. They were downing a lot of booze, Kesey preferring schnapps, it seemed, whenever I visited.

I'd watched with wonder as Boise used his scarred and calloused mitts to grab the red-hot, even white-hot, pieces of iron and steel as he fashioned them into Kesey's gate, which was set on the inland side of the log bridge across the creek. I don't know what happened to the gate but I know that much of the bridge washed out during a flood season after Kesey and the rest of us had abandoned La Honda.

* * *

The young man and woman honking at me at the gate introduced themselves: Hunter Thompson and his wife Sandy, from San Francisco. Hunter, still unknown at the time, said he was a writer and wished to meet the author Ken Kesey. I told him everyone else was gone but would be home some time later in the day or evening. So, instead of wasting a trip down from San Francisco, the three of us spent the afternoon drinking tequila at a bar up the road in the tiny, rustic La Honda "downtown." Hunter and I hit it off and later, before he became famous, pulled up roots and ended up in Colorado—where, of course, his remains were fired out of a cannon manned by actor Johnny Depp—Hunter and I would hang out at his apartment on Parnassus Hill, across the street from the UC-San Francisco campus and medical center. He loved to talk about writing, the biker gang book he was researching, and about a novel he'd finished and wanted to get published. Hunter loved to drink. In those days, so did I.

One day, a week or two after we'd met, Hunter called me at Kesey's and asked if I would bring Ken up to the city to meet him—and to appear on a show (about literature in the Bay Area, I think) with him and Tom Wolfe and a couple of other writers. Ken, Faye, and I arrived at the public television station too late for Kesey to get on the show, but afterwards Hunter asked if we'd like to accompany him out to meet the president of the Frisco chapter of the Hells Angels. At the time he was working on what became his first book, *Hell's Angels: The Strange and Terrible Saga of the Outlaw Motorcycle Gangs.*

Many months later, when Hunter's book was published, the Angels, as they were known, characteristically beat the crap out of Hunter when he made what could have been a fatal mistake for someone who wanted to ride with the gang: He bought a British bike instead of a Harley-Davidson.

But things were still cool between Hunter and the Angels when we left the TV station and drove out toward Hunter's Point to meet the president of the Frisco chapter of the Hells Angels. He appeared to be a quiet, unassuming guy, a family man, it seemed, as well as a gang leader. During the afternoon we drank beer and Kesey said he and his outlaw motorcycle pals ought to come down to La Honda sometime. The guys seemed intrigued, particularly those who remembered seeing our photo in the *Chronicle* with the headlines about a drug bust at Kesey's home.

Kesey later said that had probably been the first time the Hells Angels had been invited to go anywhere! He came to believe that their classic *modus operandi* of roaring into a small town, getting drunk and high on barbiturates, getting into fights with locals, getting arrested, getting tossed into jail, and finally roaring out of town in a cloud of smoke and dust was an expression of masochism. They expected to get beaten up, Kesey theorized—and this was after a few years of a sort of friendship between Pranksters and Hells Angels—and they usually were.

Their traditional mode of behavior eased, though, when many members of the Hells Angels got into serious drug distribution. Oh, they were still prone to violence but now they had a real mission. They were businessmen.

Before long, Hunter, the Angels, and Kesey had set the date for a party at Kesey's house. As might be imagined, La Honda went nuts.

The local paranoia was touched off, I guess, by a big sign painted by a Merry Prankster so merry that the rest of us were in awe at his zaniness. Paul Foster, a bedraggled, stuttering genius and speed freak, lived on a platform in a huge tree in front of Kesey's house. He worked one day a week as a computer programmer down in what would later become Silicon Valley. His large sign, prominently displayed on Kesey's gate, where it was read by every La Hondan, who had always suspected us as dangerous madmen and –women, read:

PRANKSTERS WELCOME HELL'S ANGELS.

Paul subsequently placed a sign out front facing motorists arriving on La Honda Road, where they turned left across the bridge to Kesey's:

NO LEFT TURN UNSTONED.

* * *

Hours before the party was to begin San Mateo County sheriff's cars—the same vehicles that had transported us down to jail after our bust—started cruising slowly up and down La Honda Road. Our neighbors cruised past. We weren't sure if they were sightseeing or forming a vigilante posse with trigger fingers at the ready.

Suddenly we heard the unmistakable roar of Harley-Davidsons coming down the road. Then, with sheriff's squad cars leading them much like cops might escort a parade, the Hell's Angels, maybe three dozen of them, their old ladies jammed behind them on their giant modified bikes, roared across the bridge and came to a halt.

Behind them in a pickup truck was Sonny Barger, nominally president of the Oakland chapter but in fact the big cheese in the whole Hells Angels gang statewide and even worldwide. Sonny parked behind the bikes, shook my hand and a couple of other hands, then pulled a very long and very heavy steel chain from the bed of his pickup and strung it through the front wheels of each of the thirty-plus motorcycles. He snapped a huge padlock through two links and said he thought things would be a bit more civilized if none of his fellow gang-members could leave the premises until the next day, when the refreshments had worn off. (It was a good move. During the night several, perhaps a half-dozen, Angels kick-started their bikes and tried drunkenly to drive away, only to come up short when the chain ran out. Cursing and shouting, those Angels fell to the ground instead of roaring away into the darkness. Their Harleys stayed put, per the order and the chain installed by President Barger.)

After some hellos and handshakes, Sonny gave six-hundred bucks and the keys to his truck to a young Angel named Little Steve and told him to go back to town and buy some beer. I said I'd show Little Steve the way to the closest store with beer. We drove up to the small market and general store that was about half of the entire retail district of La Honda. When we walked in, the proprietor, who'd clearly been warned about the party up the road and who had obviously seen the procession of Harley-Davidsons roar past his little store, reached his hand down toward a shotgun propped against the wall behind the counter.

"We'll take six-hundred dollars worth of beer," Little Steve boomed.

The merchant looked stunned, then took his hand away from the shotgun and beamed at Little Steve.

"Why, yessir!" he said, leading us to the coolers where shelves were stocked with Coors, Bud, Schlitz, and the few other brands commonly available in 1965.

When we left the storeowner gave us a hearty salute and said, "Now you boys come back any time."

The cerveza was a big hit and before long the Angels started to mix up their usual cocktail of beer and reds, a combination of intoxicants designed to make one pissed off and groggy at the same time, sort of like booze squared. While reds were regarded as sleeping pills—they were the pills usually referred to in tabloid stories about pill-poppin' Hollywood stars—they were unlike Quaaludes and other so-called sopors that were just starting to hit the public's consciousness. Quaaludes, as my pal Ben Pesta pointed out, "are for when you want to fall down." Reds were what newspapers meant when you used to read about movie starlets dying after overdoses of pills, or about stars committing suicide. Reds were just the ticket for overdoses, suicides and, mixed with booze, nasty fights.

None of us Pranksters wanted to watch the Hells Angels act like Hells Angels, so it wasn't long before the pot and the psilocybin and the mescaline and the bennies and the LSD were making the rounds. We were hoping the Angels would keep their barbiturates in their pockets. And with all the possible combinations of drugs on hand it's likely each of us at the party was fucked up or high separately, in completely different ways.

Allen Ginsberg came by, as did some other friends and acquaintances up from Palo Alto and Stanford or down from San Francisco. And the deputy sheriffs had stopped cruising by and had parked on the edge of the road across the creek. The swirling red lights atop their squad cars sent goofy waves of color across Kesey's yard, where most of the party-goers hung out yakking or stoned or passing out or waiting to get into the backhouse, where a bunch of the Angels and, to my surprise, a couple of the Pranksters, took turns gang-banging a girl who'd arrived with Cassady. She didn't seem to mind, but the scene made me uncomfortable, to say the least. I watched for a while but left when a Prankster pal, caught up in what seemed to me, in his case, to be a sort of sexual mob hysteria, took up where a dozen Hells Angels had just left off. And I was embarrassed for Neal, who was out in the yard engaged in one of his endless pastimes: tossing a small but heavy sledge hammer in the air and catching it by its wooden handle, all the while pointedly ignoring the gang-bang nearby. I knew he was feeling bad. For the only time in the years I knew him, Neal was not talking.

But the sheriff's deputies across the creek were.

"Mr. Kesey! Mr. Kesey!" the deputy sheriffs barked through the loudspeakers on one of their squad cars. "Are you all right? Do you need help? Mr. Kesey? Do you need help? Do you want us to come over to help?"

Man, even if we had needed help none of us was going to invite the cops to the party. Get real! We were, for the most part, having fun and didn't need help. After a while, I incorporated all the stimuli—the flashing red lights and the occasional loud-spoken questions about needing help, along with the rock music blasting from the speakers we'd placed throughout the Redwoods surrounding Kesey's place and on the bus parked under Paul Foster's treehouse and even on top of the bluffs rising from the county road across the creek and above the parked squad cars—into one symbiotic scene. Hells Angels and Pranksters and friends seemed to be getting along swimmingly, as they say. I could see that at first some of the bikers were put off by Ginsberg's demeanor, which they perceived as "faggy," but before long all of us were getting along like long-separated long-haired fraternity members.

One guy came to the gate wanting to join the festivities, making sure, though, with every word and every gesture that no one would allow him through the gate. He kept insisting to anyone who approached that "I'm cool. It's okay, I'm cool. I'm hip."

(The biggest secret about being hip or cool, of course, is that you never say that you are. It's like wearing a souvenir T-shirt: you *never* wear it at the place it advertises. You'd never, for instance, wear an "I ♥ New York" T-shirt in New York. I don't know anyone who's ever worn, as far as I know, a Hard Rock Cafe T-shirt, but I'm pretty sure that it would be even more unhip, or square, to wear one of those items of haberdashery at the same Hard Rock joint where it was sold. I mean, Hard Rock Cafe Indianapolis shirts should probably never be worn anywhere, but certainly not ever in Indianapolis. A Hard Rock Caracas or Bucharest T-shirt would be so much hipper, unless worn in Caracas or Bucharest.)

Someone called me over to Kesey's gate so I could talk with the guy, who told someone he knew Lee Quarnstrom's brother in Berkeley. My brother Dean did indeed live in Berkeley in those days.

"I'm cool," he told me, when I walked up to him." I know your brother Dean," he said. Against my better judgment I opened the gate and told him not to bother anyone and especially not to bother me.

But he was unable to take that word to the wise and kept telling various drug-and-beer-crazed Hells Angels that he was cool, that he really was cool. Really! The last time I noticed the guy I was walking through the house and saw him hanging upside down from the ceiling. Some Hells Angel had tossed a rope up over a redwood log beam and tied it around his ankles, then hoisted him up, where he would swing like a pendulum if someone gave him a shove. A Hells Angel named Tiny, meaning, of course, that he was the largest of all of the gang members, gave him a push every time he walked past.

I don't know how long he stayed swinging from the rafter or who eventually cut him down. But my brother Dean said a month or two later he knew the guy slightly and that after the party at Kesey's place he had pretty much become another crazy person ranting on Telegraph Avenue.

WHAT DOES "PSYCHEDELIC" MEAN?

So far, I've used the term "psychedelic" enough times that I should explain what *I* mean when I use the word. I've written about Kesey's psychedelic bus. We've heard about psychedelic rock music, psychedelic art, psychedelic T-shirts, psychedelic insights. Let's see what the dictionaries say.

The *Oxford English Dictionary* says the word is "relating to or denoting drugs (especially LSD) that produce hallucinations and apparent expansion of consciousness" or "(of music, especially rock) characterized by musical experimentation and drug-related lyrics" or "having intense, vivid colors or a swirling abstract pattern."

That is a simple and inadequate definition of "psychedelic." But so are the others.

Urban Dictionary, perhaps the most relevant and up-to-date compendium of definitions, says it "means 'mind-manifesting.' It is used to describe the state of consciousness typically experienced while under drugs such as LSD, mushrooms, mescaline, cannabis—consisting of various stages of ego-release and an often-startling alteration of perceptions."

Better, much better, but not perfect.

Nor is the *Merriam-Webster Dictionary* definition adequate. It suggests the word relates to "drugs (as LSD) capable of producing abnormal psychic effects (as hallucinations) and sometimes psychotic states..." or "imitating, suggestive of, or reproducing effects (as distorted or bizarre images or sounds) resembling those produced by psychedelic drugs," such as "psychedelic color schemes."

So, the word "psychedelic" has come to mean highly unusual, drug-induced, often vividly colorful, and distorted or bizarre sounds or images.

That, indeed, is what we often mean when we say something is psychedelic. But what my friends and I mean when we say that something is psychedelic is that it's impossible, yet true—that it is something so unlikely to be really happening, yet really is happening, that it causes an instant of amazement so deep and significant as to approach, perhaps, a moment of *satori,* as Zen Buddhists call a flash of enlightenment.

In fact, a common verbal response to something psychedelic, at least in the 1960s, was, "What a flash!"

So, the Prankster bus was psychedelic in the sense that there had been nothing like it before it and therefore, it was so bizarre that it often registered upon first sight as something patently impossible. Who the fuck would paint a bus like that, with so many bright colors and strange patterns and designs and so many layers of visual, verbal, and artistic meaning that *it is not possible that it really exists?*

What if you saw a nun actually flying or a duck talking or a whole universe in a pore on the back of your hand? Now, those would be psychedelic!

Anything billed as psychedelic, such as a tie-dyed shirt or a band that sounds like the Grateful Dead or some daubs of paint on someone's face, is, on the face of it, not psychedelic at all. It is derivative. Yet by common use, if a shirt has a bright, tie-dyed pattern or a band makes music reminiscent of Quicksilver Messenger Service it is considered psychedelic, I guess, but only in the sense that it is *called* psychedelic. It is not psychedelic at all in any sense of causing a moment of amazement or *satori* or touching off a flash of insight.

I'm willing to let people refer to our bus as psychedelic solely because they know it was odd and colorful—but only if you're willing to allow me to use the word with a far deeper meaning—and in this sense the bus was, in fact, psychedelic. The Prankster bus at first glance, at least in those pioneering days in the mid-1960s, suggests something so profoundly startling that it stretches reality, distorts it so far into previously unknown corners or dimensions that it blows your mind.

CAN YOU PASS THE ACID TEST?

Although Kesey was present at the first few Bay Area Acid Tests—including the premiere, held at The Spread, the old farmhouse we'd rented in Soquel, on the outskirts of Santa Cruz—he was missing for many of the rest. In fact, when we took our LSD-fueled extravaganza on the road to Los Angeles and beyond, our goal was to party our way down to Mexico and eventually meet up with Ken—who'd taken a powder over the border to avoid time behind bars for his two drug arrests.

After he and Page Browning were convicted in the wake of the bust in La Honda, Kesey was arrested again, this time for smoking a joint with Mountain Girl on the San Francisco rooftop of a North Beach apartment building. He complained to the judge, after looking at the jurors who'd been selected to hear the case, "You honor, this is not a jury of my peers. These are not my peers." He meant it, of course, in the psychedelic sense. None of his jurors looked like someone who'd probed the outer limits of reality with LSD or any other technique.

Kesey ended up incarcerated after his return many months later from Mexico—where we did indeed meet up with him in Mazatlan and where I accompanied him and Mountain Girl to Mexico City in the hopes of seeking political asylum from the government of our neighbor to the south. (He didn't get it.)

Kesey went on the lam before we left the Santa Cruz area and joined the Grateful Dead in L.A. for a series of Acid Tests. By now Kesey was the subject of a federal fugitive warrant. Before we headed south we all became familiar with FBI agents who followed us from La Honda to Santa Cruz, seeking the elusive and apparently dangerous "Mr. Kesey."

The feds made frequent visits at The Spread, where we'd moved to get away from the mess we'd created in La Honda.

An accumulation of crap, essentially, had driven us south from La Honda, down the coast highway to Santa Cruz. There was literal crap that plugged the septic tank and made a visit to the bathroom a touch-and-go situation at the La Honda house. There were too many visits by too many Hells Angels and their pals. And there were far too many "tourists" from the Bay Area—kids, criminals, dope addicts, freaks, creeps, would-be weekend bohemians—hoping to say they'd rubbed shoulders with Kesey and the Merry Pranksters. And believe me, over the decades since, I have met or heard of plenty of folks who've somehow convinced their coterie of friends, perhaps even themselves, that they made their psychedelic bones by either hanging with the Pranksters or by being "on the bus." Sure, they may have climbed aboard the bus for a moment when it was parked here or there in San Francisco and environs. Or they may have stopped in uninvited at La Honda. And if they did, they were part of the reason we all pulled up stakes and moved down to Santa Cruz.

All of us wanted to escape the ceaseless gloom and mold beneath the La Honda redwoods and we had the sense that it was time to move on from San Mateo County.

We knew it was finally time to go one morning when the kitchen sink refused to drain. I'd wandered into the kitchen to make some coffee and Ginsberg and his longtime boyfriend Peter Orlovsky, and Peter's brother Julius, and Neal Cassady wandered in a minute or two later. Before I could stop him to report that the drain was completely clogged, Ginsberg walked over to it and hawked a gob of snot from his nose and throat into the half-filled sink. When I informed him that the sink wouldn't drain and the nasty-looking phlegm would probably stay floating in the gray dishwater, Ginsberg told me, "Don't worry, Lee, I have a mantra that'll clean it right out."

And he did.

Ginsberg began to chant some Indian raga or Tibetan mantra, bobbing his head, or davening, and chanting toward the plugged-up sink. Neal, who'd known Ginsberg almost forever, looked at me and shook his head in a bewildered and almost disillusioned sort of way. He said softly to the Orlovskys and me, "Man, Ginsy's got a mantra for *everything!*"

We knew we'd be comfortable down in Santa Cruz, about an hour south of La Honda. For one thing, our fellow Prankster Hassler and a friend, Peter Demma, owned the Hip Pocket Book Store, the first beachhead of hip in a town that has since become known as The People's Republic of Santa Cruz, a city with even more hipsters, artists, and lefties than Berkeley. The seaside city was a fading resort town in the mid-1960s when more than twenty-thousand University of California students came to the new local campus. Within a few years the influx of student voters had changed the complexion of the city council from Rotary Club bluebloods and businessmen to an array of social and environmental lefties.

In true left-wing style, electoral victories meant that factionalism quickly raised its smarmy head. Even the self-styled socialist-feminist councilman, a Marxist university professor, was blasted from the left as a tool of wealthy property owners. He happened to be, as far as I could tell, the only council member with a sense of humor.

Artists and writers and poets and musicians and bums congregated with local surfers in Santa Cruz the way thirsty camels head for oases in the desert. Hassler and Peter Demma's Hip Pocket bookshop was the downtown center of most of the action. In nearby Scotts Valley, The Barn, opened by North Beach beat restaurateur Eric "Big Daddy" Nord and later run by Neal Cassady's prison psychiatrist, was the local center of rock music and dancing. It was obvious from the get-go that Santa Cruz was a beachhead for what outsiders were calling Flower Power.

Santa Cruz is a great town. It is laid back, a surfer's dream, a place of aloha. I think of it as the easternmost place in the Hawaii Islands. I stayed there for most of the next thirty-five years.

* * *

Cassady sped into the Hip Pocket Book Store, where I made a few bucks every day stocking the shelves and running the cash register. He was with Allen Ginsberg and Ginsberg's longtime lover, companion, and fellow poet, Peter Orlovsky. Neal was on the lookout for a rumored party, a little jam with some Grateful Dead players, some Ginsberg chanting and some Czechoslovakian LSD. We invited a few regulars who hung out at the Hip Pocket, a couple of friendly surfers, and a few pals and girlfriends. The party turned out to be the first Acid Test.

* * *

One of our more popular sections at the Hip Pocket was the nudist magazine rack. We sold nudist magazines to men (we always checked IDs) who were older than our youthful regulars. With no porn and few prostitutes available in what was a blue-nosed town before the university population mushroomed and morals modernized, these guys would sneak in during the slow dinner hour, snatch up a Jaybirds Playing Volleyball magazine (in which people as naked as jaybirds, in the old cliché, played outside sports in the raw. The naked athletes were definitely NOT turn-ons), hand me or the other clerk a couple of bucks and whisper, "Put it in a bag, will you?"

Often, my fellow clerk, Tony Maggi, a talented painter and a craftsman at the local leather tannery when he wasn't working at the Hip Pocket, would, were he behind the cash register, open the tame, sepia-toned nudist magazine, hold it above his head and shout to me in the back of the store, "Hey, Lee, look at the tits on this one!" Then he'd put it in a bag and give it to the customer, who would pull his collar up around his face and hurry out to his car and speed away.

A fundamentalist minister up in Scotts Valley had begun to attack the bookstore on his weekly program on the local right-wing radio station. When he'd inform his listeners that "there is a sewer running through the main street of Santa Cruz and it is called the Hip Pocket Bookstore," we assumed he was mostly talking about the nudist magazines. But Jeez, they were so lame that you could have distributed them to horny high school boys as part of a family planning program centered on preventing such lads from ever having erections.

The radio preacher would occasionally send his teenage grandson into the store, hoping that we'd sell the underage kid a naked-ladies-playing-tennis magazine. But we not only checked IDs, we knew what the reverend's grandson looked like.

We were hassled, though, by Santa Cruz cops, who sent their truant officer—yes, there really was a truant officer—around to keep us truant-free. The fire inspectors said we couldn't put a motorcycle in the window as part of a display because it might suddenly burst into flames and destroy the building, including the hotel next door, an SRO joint where old men spent their final days until they were hauled out early in the morning, often while I was sweeping the sidewalk, and driven away to the county morgue.

* * *

When he hurried into the store and asked in his raspy croak, "Where's the party?" I sent Neal, with Ginsberg and Peter in tow, out to The Spread, a couple of miles away. I told him I'd be there later, that the Grateful Dead was coming, and that we'd set up Ron Boise's Thunder Machine—a piece of musical sculpture fashioned from the wreckage of Hassler's 1958 Chevy. (There'd been no old Chevy wreckage for Boise to work with until I'd driven the car off the road into Rodeo Gulch on a recent rainy night.) Boise fashioned the large chunks of Chevrolet into The Thunder Machine and local artist Joe Lysowski had painted it with bright acrylics. Someone, probably Boise, added strings to pluck for "music" and there were plenty of places to pound on for percussion. It was…psychedelic!

"Yes, yes, out to The Spread, yes, Ginsy, the Grateful Dead, see ya there, Lee," and Cassady was gone. A few minutes later a young woman, a Santa Cruz native with boho instincts and a taste for rock 'n' roll, joined me and we took her car out to that first Acid Test.

It was nothing spectacular, but it was important, I think. Real musicians, Jerry Garcia and his bandmates, were joined by Pranksters with no talent, really, on the Thunder Machine, Ginsberg chanting, everyone dancing and here and there, a touch of LSD. Festivities were mostly confined to the living room at The Spread and there were probably no more than fifty people present, mostly friends we'd invited, and only a few party-crashing guests who'd heard there was a bash in a farmhouse on the edge of town. In a sense it was just a continuation of the Saturday-night "happenings," as squares called them, that we'd been putting on in the woods in La Honda.

* * *

The best of those La Honda performances was on the night before Mother's Day 1965. Church of Satan founder Anton LaVey and his pal, well-known "underground" filmmaker Kenneth Anger, sat and watched, for a while, as we Pranksters pounded on some of Boise's musical metal sculptures and tooted on flutes and caused great echoes and loops and spooky sounds to fly around the intricate series of hi-fi speakers wired throughout the La Honda redwoods. At precisely midnight Page Browning was chosen, by the spin of a wheel as the chosen one to axe a chicken. We intended this to be satire, an ironic take on LaVey's diabolic church and some of the darker S&M features in some of Anger's films.

The hen had been resting in a cage on a stump at the bottom of a natural amphitheater on the wooded hills behind

Kesey's home. Page reached into the cage and grabbed the bird. As he lifted it out, ready to dispatch the bird so Gretchen Fetchin could cook up some middle-of-the-night chicken stew, we discovered that, as the clock struck midnight and Saturday became Mother's Day, the hen had just laid an egg!

Then Page chopped the chicken's head off. Gretchen Fetchin took the carcass down to the house, plucked *most* of the feathers off and put it in a kettle of boiling water. It turned out, though, that Gretch had never cooked a freshly killed chicken. She didn't know about the part where you clean and gut a bird before you toss it into a pot of boiling water.

A god-awful stench begun to seep through the house and into the midnight woods. Surprisingly to us, LaVey and Anger, perhaps because of the smell but more apparently because they thought they'd suddenly found themselves at a sacrificial cult ceremony, fled soon after Page killed the hen.

No one ate any of the stew. It was one of several culinary disasters during those Acid Test days and nights. There was the pineapple chili disaster at the Unitarian church in the San Fernando Valley and, a quarter-century later, there was the venison chili mistake at the Oregon Vortex.

* * *

That original Acid Test at The Spread was the first time I met Tom Wolfe, a stranger in a white suit who was jotting down notes for his upcoming book about Kesey. Unknown to most of us but present at The Spread with Kesey's apparent blessing, Wolfe sat quietly in a corner, watching and writing. Most of the rest of us, having taken acid, were either joining the music-makers or dancing or sitting in another corner engaged either in foreplay with our mates or dates or else noticing once again that by god, or by Cosmo, as some of us called that universal entity, we could see the whole fucking thing, *everything,* in that tiniest pore in the palm of our hands!

The evening high was briefly brought down in typical fashion by a Prankster associate we called Pancho Pillow. Zonker and I had bumped into the guy, who was, indeed, shaped like a pillow, one afternoon in Palo Alto. As soon as we'd taken him, at his request, up to Kesey's place in La Honda he began behaving, as he did for the rest of time that we knew him, as a designated bummer. Pancho was like a cloud that blotted out the sun. When the conversation, sparked by psychedelic drugs or not, got higher and higher—particularly when Kesey was letting his mind wander out into space and facilitating a rising feeling of expanding consciousness among the rest of us—Pancho Pillow would inevitably interject a few words that brought everybody crashing back down, back from the other side of the psychedelic veil or back to the surface from Wonderland. Kesey might be explaining, for instance, how all the things that ever happened were happening, really, at the same time and we're merely observing just this one momentary slice of the wheel of time and Pancho might ask, "Hey, are there any weenies in the fridge?"

The last time I saw Pancho Pillow was a few years later in downtown Santa Cruz. He stepped out of a car arguing with a woman who was in the front seat of the beat-up old sedan. She got out of the car and told Pancho to "get it." He reached in to the back seat and stood back up holding a huge pumpkin in his arms, just about as big a pumpkin as a man could possibly carry. The woman thanked him sarcastically. Pancho Pillow turned, stumbled over the curb and dropped the gigantic pumpkin, which smashed into a thousand pieces of shell and pulp and seeds and goo. "Hey, Pancho," I said as I nodded and stepped around the mess on the sidewalk, "what's happenin'?" I was gone before he could reply.

Subsequent Acid Tests, as we now called them—with the slogan, "Can You Pass The Acid Test?"—were held, among other places, at a decrepit Victorian house in San Jose, at an abandoned nightclub on the Palo Alto-Menlo Park border, up at Stinson Beach north of the Golden Gate—and as part of the three-day

Trips Festival put on in January 1966 by Stewart Brand and us and scores of other psychedelic pioneers. We were *all* quickly discovering that we were not alone and that there were *lots* of people discovering LSD and the other psychotropic drugs and that we could have a huge party and we could get stoned out of our minds if we so wished, with no trouble, no hassle, no violence, no need for cops or security guards.

The Trips Festival, San Francisco's first big homecoming party for the Bay Area's far-flung family of mind-expanded artists and freaks, unfolded at the Longshoremen's Hall near the San Francisco Bay. The affair was, appropriately, Kesey's final San Francisco appearance before fleeing to Mexico. He was facing two marijuana convictions and he did not want to go to jail.

Disguised in a Mylar space suit and helmet, Kesey hobnobbed with Pranksters and anonymously with other festival trippers but, knowing he was the subject of a federal fugitive warrant, he didn't reveal himself to strangers. He did, however, use a microphone wired into the festival's fabulous sound system and announce that he was running for governor of California. There were, of course, some FBI agents lurking in the crowd but try as they might, they could not pinpoint which costumed celebrant was announcing his bid for the Golden State's governorship.

Then Kesey wrote a suicide note and vanished. We didn't see him again until we took the bus down to Los Angeles for some more Acid Testing and crossed the border to hook up with our fugitive friend in Mazatlan.

In the most-brilliant fake suicide ever, Kesey appointed his look-alike cousin Dale to deliver his fake suicide note to the edge of a cliff in Northern California. Dale drove up the coast in a Chevrolet panel truck, one of the old and almost-unusable Prankster vehicles. Dale had his cousin Ken's bogus suicide epistle ready to let the world know that he had jumped off a cliff because he couldn't take it any more and didn't want to go to jail.

Now, Dale is a very nice man. Lovable, actually. But he is a bit of a *naif,* unable at times to see the big picture if there's a problem with the small one. So when the truck broke down a few hundred yards or so from the edge of the cliff, he asked an obliging local farmer with a tractor to help tow the Chevy out near the tip of the precipice. Then, as the farmer drove away wondering why someone would want to be towed up to the edge of the sea cliff, Dale followed cousin Ken's wishes and left the suicide note on the front seat and a pair of Ken's shoes and socks at the edge of the ocean bluff. Then he walked out to the highway and hitchhiked home.

Well, the FBI didn't know what to make of the apparent suicide of the famous writer who was the subject of a federal fugitive warrant as a convicted dope-user on the lam. They came to visit us at The Spread and asked if we'd tell them where Mr. Kesey was, where he *really* was. We think he killed himself up north somewhere, we'd tell them. They'd visit the Hip Pocket Book Store and, between customers looking for Beat poetry or unconventional psychology tomes or nudist volleyball pictorial magazines, ask us where they could find Kesey. "We think he jumped off a cliff," we'd reply. And they weren't sure, they just weren't sure if we were telling the truth or putting them on.

There was and still is our motto, "Never trust a Prankster!" and these feds didn't trust us, but they didn't know if maybe they should.

They shouldn't have.

One day we all grabbed a minimal amount of clothing, including some colorful Prankster shirts that Gretch and some other Prankster women had sewn, and we drove the bus out of Santa Cruz toward Mazatlan, with a long stop planned in Los Angeles.

This mention of sewing (and the earlier reference to cooking the chicken that stunk up the joint) seems as good a time as any to report that feminism was barely a mote of dust that had not yet irritated most men's vision in 1965. Men did "men things," in our case fixing broken equipment, doing any work that required digging or pounding or sawing, working on the film from the New York bus trip and, in my case, going down to San Mateo to collect unemployment checks every couple of weeks to help keep the La Honda scene going. Women cooked and sewed and cleaned and took care of the kids and, in other words, did all the real and difficult and important work. Women were like the ants in the fable, while we men were more like the fiddle-playing grasshopper who lay around having fun most of the time. Only when it rained or we got hungry or horny or got a rip in our jeans would we men ask the women take care of us, and they did, unlike the ants in the fable who at first locked the grasshopper out when winter came, teaching him some lesson that many of us never learned. Consciousness evolves slowly, it seems, whether you're an ant or a Merry Prankster.

I think we men, who told ourselves we were—and we really were—seeking some higher, maybe ultimately high consciousness, were totally unconscious about the roles that men and women were stuck in, including us. Some of the women, Mountain Girl, for instance, worked and played with the men, spending much of the time in La Honda with Ken in the so-called Backhouse where they were trying to cut the forty miles of film and somehow synch it to the audio tape that refused to synch and was not coordinated to the film for another forty-five years.

It wasn't until the Prankster scenes at La Honda and Santa Cruz broke up and Ken and Faye Kesey and their kids returned to Oregon and the rest of us dispersed around California or up to Eugene and Springfield to stick near Ken, that we started to see the reality that we men—Pranksters, acid heads, hippies, long-hairs, beatniks, bohemians, dopers—had been living the same sexual paradigm as our parents, as the squares. I imagine that many of my pals from those days still feel shame, or at least embarrassment, at our sorry early adulthood relationships with women—women we loved and women friends and women in general. I do, at least.

In retrospect, knowing, as I do now, we men may have had blinders on, but women knew what was going on. They had decided, I guess, that beatnik men, acid head men, bohemian men, were either too stuck in their 1950s upbringings to consider women their equals or so stuck in their "masculine" roles that it just wasn't worth trying to enlighten us. Until they did, until they let us know loudly and clearly that they weren't second-class persons and weren't going to put up with that treatment any longer.

Younger readers of Beat literature, the novels and poems and broadsides that were written in the post-Second World War, pre-psychedelic era, must shudder when they learn how male-centric the whole thing was. Men chased women and fucked women and used women and lived off the earnings of women, but rarely thought of women as peers. I guess women knew the score, but they seem to have kept men in the dark about sexual equality until the Sixties turned into the Seventies.

(I believe, by the way, that what most people think about when they recall or learn about the Sixties was not the entire decade. Rather, the iconic Sixties was the brief period between the assassinations of the two Kennedy brothers, John and Robert. Before JFK was murdered we were still, essentially, in the Eisenhower era; after Bobby Kennedy was murdered we found ourselves sinking into a dark, dystopian era that seems still to be flourishing.)

Oh, it certainly occurred to me, on the day that my Sixties began, that women had power. The fact that my first wife took the kids and split on November 22, 1963, the day JFK was killed, was coincidental. The fact that all I learned was that women could leave men as easily as men could leave women was inadequate. I failed to understand that we were equal as human beings. I was still buying into the old male-female dichotomy, the Dagwood and Blondie way of life. Not too many men were as hip as we thought we were in the 1960s.

My first inkling that things were not equal *and* that women might resent it was one day in the 1960s when I read a poem by a woman, perhaps by Diane De Prima or Denise Levertov, asking why she had to sleep in the wet spot every time she and her old man fucked. I knew the poet was right-on, literally correct. I knew, in fact, that I had always tried to roll back to the dry side of the bed. It occurred to me that women I'd slept with might have been less than pleased with my unconscious belief (if I even thought about it) that I, as a man, didn't have to spend the rest of the night on the damp spot on the sheet—if, in fact, a mattress I happened to share with a woman actually even had a sheet. I could dig what the poet meant, but I had not yet evolved to a point where it changed my attitude or anything else. That took at least a few years. But things do evolve, attitudes change, women began to be more assertive, and eventually I began to look for wet spots in life where I could take turns doing the dirty work. I know I wasn't the only man who could finally hear the shouts of women, just as most of us had heard the shouts from people of color, demanding that we not only see them as our equals but that we treat them as such—and that we not only treat them as equals but that we fucking well do the really difficult work of actually, really, *seeing* them and *hearing* them as our peers in every way that we could imagine, hearing their words not as nagging, not as bitching, but as a cry for justice.

These days we seem to be backsliding. Without turning this into a political tract, let me say that we seem to be going back to the pre-psychedelic days of an era before the 1960s. It seems we're moving backwards into the years before the psychedelic revolution or the civil rights movement without stopping to ask what the hell is going on.

Men, lots of men, I fear, are forgetting the lessons we learned during the days when men discovered that to free ourselves we must free our sisters.

Just like many of the other evolutionary societal gains made during my lifetime, particularly in the wake of the Sixties, I fear that the recognition that women and men share strength and power is devolving. Religious leaders of many ecclesiastical stripes find scriptural proof for their preachings that women should be subservient to men. Women still make less than men for doing the same work—and that's the simplest, easiest to understand, example of what we've been talking about for the past half-century. And no doubt many women still find themselves having to nod off to sleep at night on the damp spot on the bed.

ELECTRIC KOOL-AID

Cassady drove the bus south on Highway 33, a two-lane road that took us almost all the way to Los Angeles without encountering much in the way of freeways, highway patrolmen and, for that matter, any people at all. We received police escorts through a couple of rural burgs, notably Taft, an oil town where a pair of policemen stopped the bus, listened with total bafflement to Cassady explaining our mission and destination, stuck their heads in the bus, then declined to step aboard. The bewildered peace officers finally called for backup to make sure we caused no mayhem in their little city. Local Taft residents, who stared and waved friendly greetings at the oddly painted bus, apparently thought we were being escorted down the main drag because we were somehow important, not because the cops were worried that we might be Venusians on some nefarious earthly mission.

That encounter with the Taft police was typical of our brushes with law enforcement when we were aboard the bus. Keeping in mind that this was still before brightly colored buses and vans dotted California's highways and byways and before word about exotic, and no doubt dangerous, psychedelic drugs spread into the hinterland, it was no wonder that sworn officers of the law had no idea what we were up to. They just didn't want us to get up to it within *their* city limits.

In fact, a few weeks later at the Acid Test we held in Watts—a mere five months after the so-called Watts Riots of August 1965—there were at least a dozen baffled L.A. cops on the scene plus a few federal narcotics agents, who openly told anyone who asked that they were observing our behavior so they'd know what to expect when LSD was officially made illegal, which it was later that year. They checked my pupils with a little flashlight and took notes so they would know what to look for when the witching hour passed in the upcoming month of October and they could begin arresting acid heads instead of just observing us.

The Watts Acid Test might have been the best, as far as I was concerned. It was held in an old warehouse or automotive garage that we rented for the weekend. It may have been the only time that Pigpen, the bluesy soul brother of the Grateful Dead, got stoned on acid, and it was the time that we underestimated by a factor of six, I believe, when we mixed the ampules of Owsley LSD with the Kool-Aid.

We quickly realized, as Pranksters and the Grateful Dead roadies unloaded and set up speakers and amplifiers and strobe lights and black lights and all the other Acid Test paraphernalia, that we were going to attract a lot of Watts neighbors to our shindig. Many of the white hippies who'd been looking forward to partying with Pranksters and the Grateful Dead said later they chose not to come to the South L.A. neighborhood that had so recently been wracked by gunfire, blocks of homes and businesses ablaze, mob violence and police violence. Too bad for them.

As the afternoon turned into evening and as neighborhood men and women and children wandered in and out of the building seeing what we were up to, someone, maybe Wavy Gravy, or Hugh Romney, as he was still known at that time, made the wise decision to set up two plastic trash barrels to be filled with Kool-Aid: one for consenting adults, and the other one for children—the latter, of course, free of the drug behind the Acid Test moniker. We cautioned the older folks that there was something more than flavored Kool-Aid, something even more powerful than marijuana, in the bigger barrel, something that was gonna get them really high. Most of them enthusiastically gulped it down anyway. We steered the kids to the LSD-free tub of Kool-Aid. Everyone seemed to dig the Grateful Dead, even if they were all white boys making the music.

I thought of this recently when I saw Mountain Girl quoted in a *Vanity Fair* article looking back at the San Francisco rock scene during the so-called "Summer of Love." Always elegant and spot on with words, MG described Acid Tests as safe places for people to get high. And that's what we made certain of at the Watts Acid Test—that it was safe for our guests and safe for us.

When the Watts neighbors dug us in our goofy, brightly colored Prankster clothes and high-visibility red paint, colored clown makeup, sparkles, or whatever we happened to smear on our faces, some of the old men from the neighborhood went home and came back with their own crazy costumes, hepcat stuff they might have worn to Halloween parties when they were young and cool or when they danced in tap reviews or had sung in R&B quartets. These old cats were *stylin'!*

Babbs, who had assumed as much control of our bus gang as it's possible for anyone to have when everyone, including the leader himself, is berserk, or getting close to that state of mind, got together with some of us and tried to determine how much acid we should put in the Kool-Aid. The object was to get everyone who drank just one little Dixie Cup of the brew a little bit high. Eventually, it was determined that one of those little shot-glass sized paper cups full of the Kool-Aid solution would contain fifty mics of LSD. That meant that anyone who wanted the usual three hundred-microgram dose should have drunk six little cups of Kool-Aid.

Later, after most of us realized we were just about as high as we'd ever been—and then some—we recalculated and concluded that each cup had, in fact, contained a full, three hundred-mic dose. In other words, most of us had ingested some eighteen-hundred micrograms.

It was around this time that Babbs invented what he called "Babbs' Law," which is that "If you take a bad situation and irritate it, it will get worse." That's what happened with the overdosage of the Watts "electric" Kool-Aid.

No wonder that I was so stoned that I couldn't move for hours.

No wonder, as I watched the band getting ready to play as they snacked on some take-out fried drumsticks that a thoughtful neighbor picked up for the musicians at a nearby chicken shack, that each member of the Grateful Dead stopped in his tracks, frozen in time and space. Even Pigpen, who never, in my presence, at least, took acid or even shared an open bottle of anything lest he get dosed, stood motionless over his keyboard with a half-gnawed drumstick held an inch from his ready-to-gnash teeth. It seemed like that musical chicken-eating tableau went on for a long, long time. Of course, maybe I was so pleasantly fucked up that in my head I turned a one-second scene into an hour; or maybe the Dead really did stand like statues while minutes and minutes more ticked away.

But they did start to play and people started to dance or to wave their arms around under a strobe-light or to stare into some personal infinity they'd found in the palm of their hands. The Watts men and women liked these white hipsters playing rock and roll and everything, as they used to say, was groovy.

The cops joined the rest of us as we followed the mournful plaint of a woman whose voice jumped around the room, from speaker to speaker, on the intricate, echo-relay-feedback-delay system devised by Owsley, Babbs, and others. She was one of the Santa Cruz fans who followed us south so she could keep trying to pass the Acid Test. (I cannot recall all the names of the Santa Cruz gang; I do remember two of the guys were named Hey Man! and Lunchmeat.) The Santa Cruz woman somehow grabbed a microphone and started moaning, her cries distorted by the reverb and repetition and other hallucinatory features that may seem as commonplace now as strobe-lights and the black light, but were as unknown to folks in the mid-1960s as cell phones and videogames.

"Who cares?" she cried loudly into her microphone. "Who cares?" Again and again her poignant question circled the room, one speaker at a time, repeating over and over until she moaned it again, "Who cares?"

Babbs, applying Babbs' Law, rushed to a corner where the woman was sitting on the warehouse floor. He made sure the mic was near enough to pick up her every word. Most of us had no idea where she was and from where her sad if important question was being asked.

As often happened when Babbs' Law was applied, the woman shifted consciousness into some less-threatening state and the "Who cares?" cries slowed, quieted, then stopped circulating around the room. We turned our attention elsewhere.

The next morning, after most of us had come down from our unintentionally massive doses of LSD, we cleaned up and reloaded our gear on the bus. Page Browning, who'd painted half his face black and the other half silver for the previous night's Acid Test, was standing by the bus when yet another squad of police officers showed up to see just what the hell was going on. For some reason they arrested Page. I noticed a few years later on the old Jack Webb *Dragnet* TV show an episode about crimes committed by, and the apprehension of, a dangerous and drug-crazed madman called Blue Boy. This character was supposed to be Page, who at some point around then gave himself the nickname Des Prado. As I recall, the *Dragnet* show ended with Sgt. Joe Friday, the Jack Webb character, giving his patient and quiet partner a lecture about the outbreak of murderous lunacy by dangerous young people who "experimented." But who was experimenting? We didn't experiment. We got high!—with LSD and other illegal substances that led to mayhem and madness. In that, or some other episode, Sgt. Joe Friday revealed his feelings about psychedelic drugs to a hapless druggie:

"Marijuana is the flame, heroin is the fuse, LSD is the bomb. So don't you try to equate liquor to marijuana, Mister, not with me. You may be able to sell that jazz to another pothead, but not to somebody who holds some sick kid's head while he vomits and wretches on a curbstone at four in the morning. And when his legs get enough starch into them so he can stand up and empty his pockets, you can bet he'll have a stick or two of marijuana. And you can double your money he'll turn up a sugar cube or a cap or two. So don't you con me with your mind expansion slop. I deal with kids every day. I try to clean up the mess that people like you make out of 'em. I'm the expert here, you're not."

Joe Friday was tough as nails. He must have been elated when October 1966 came and LSD became illegal.

* * *

Our first stop in greater Los Angeles, the week before the Watts Acid Test, was at a Unitarian church in Northridge, in the San Fernando Valley. Kesey and the Pranksters had befriended the pastor, Paul Sawyer, who invited us to stop by when we were in the neighborhood. And there we were, in the neighborhood, weary from the bus ride south from Santa Cruz, and hungry—a situation that led to a culinary disaster and, hours later, the untimely arrival in the onion-domed church-in-the-round, of the generally oblivious Pancho Pillow.

Somehow, the Northridge Acid Test had received mention in a Los Angeles alternative newspaper. This drew a small crowd, but most of us were too tired and too famished to care. We just wanted something to eat. Wavy Gravy and my Chicago friend Del Close, former director and occasional star of the famed Second City improv troupe, were on hand. Roommates with Tiny Tim— yes, that one, the "Tiptoe Through The Tulips" falsetto singer and ukulele player—Wavy, Del and Tiny Tim were the stars of the show. Wavy and Del joined Neal Cassady in a virtuoso three-way rap on three mics from three different points of the compass in the circular church, each anticipating what the other was about to say and each remarking on it before it had even been uttered. *Word jazz!* Listening to those three wonderful wizard of words riffing off one another, each carrying on a simultaneous monologue and harmonious rap that was, to me, a verbal equivalent of a combo of musical giants such as those on the recording, *Jazz At Massey Hall*, that 1953 concert featured Dizzy Gillespie, Max Roach, Charles Mingus, Bud Powell, and Charlie Parker, who, because he was contractually unable to record with the others was listed as "Charlie Chan." And Tiny Tim, "Mr. Tim," strummed his ukulele and sang Depression-era songs not only in his famed falsetto but in a range of registers from the lowest bass up through a tender tenor to a falsetto that was an ironic takeoff on a falsetto. The thing was, Tiny Tim could really sing! When he wanted to, he could sound like one of the musical heartthrobs from the early days of recorded music. And he could play the ukulele right-handed and left-handed, which is not merely a mirror image of right-handed picking and strumming, it is actually upside down and backwards.

Like most of us at the Northridge church, I took acid and hoped for something to eat.

Somewhere in the Unitarian facility a few of the Pranksters, including Julius Karpen and Gretchen Fetchin, were said to be cooking up a batch of what they billed as "delicious pineapple chili." By the time it was ready, everybody was too stoned to eat. I hope somebody tasted some of it. I was far, far too involved deep somewhere in my own mind to feed my stomach.

"Trust your head," was the phrase that everyone on the scene told themselves and everybody else in those days. And I did. I trusted my head, which told me not to waste time chowing down on chili while my front doorway of perception was open and I was looking down a long hallway, seeing the reflection of the secret of the universe. Whatever that is!

Disaster struck the next morning when we woke up after a couple of hours of shut-eye. There were still great gobs of congealed pineapple chili left in the kettle in the church kitchen. It was cooked solid. It was inedible. It needed to be disposed of.

Oh, man, I didn't want to help get rid of a gigantic tub of pineapple chili! I reached that conclusion after one second considering whether to join the chili-disposal crew. But some helpful souls did attack the job of dumping of the stuff. Unfortunately, they chose to dump it down the toilet. Within seconds the chili had completely clogged the sewage-disposal line leading away from the tabernacle. Morning ablutions, bowel movements, etc., were quickly postponed after a few efforts brought the disgusting and disastrous hazardous waste problem to the surface, as it were.

The church's Sunday services were scheduled to begin, as usual, in just a few hours.

We went about the business of loading the bus. Most of us were like zombies, still asleep but walking around trying to be helpful, or, at least, trying to look like we were trying to be helpful. It was not an inspirational moment. Everybody's ass was dragging.

And suddenly the main door of the church flung open. In came a blast of fresh air and a too-bright beam of sunlight. There in the doorway, looking around the circular room, seeing passed-out Pranksters and stumbling Pranksters, and a few hearty Pranksters trying to unplug the plumbing, was the overstuffed figure of Pancho Pillow. Despite our best efforts to cover our tracks, Pancho had somehow tracked us down. He'd just blown into town and was looking to have some kind of fun. Pancho looked around with anticipation. He thought he'd arrived on the scene just in time to party. I could see he wanted to shout out his usual greeting, "What's happenin'?"

But I could see in his eyes the sad recognition that once again he had missed the main event.

Pancho looked from Prankster to Prankster and to the occasional new face among the bodies lying on the floor or trying to sit up or carrying a plunger into the bathroom or, in a few cases, carrying sleeping bags and speakers and various knickknacks out to the bus.

"What happened?" Pancho asked. And that said it all.

* * *

We took the bus to East Hollywood and parked on Lemon Grove Avenue in front of an old bungalow occupied by Hugh

Romney, Tiny Tim and, in the basement, my pal Del Close, from my days living in Old Town, on the North Side, and hanging out in Hyde park, on the South Side, of Chicago. They welcomed us and invited us in for much-needed use of toilets, showers, spare beds and mattresses—and friendship.

Some Pranksters left for other parts of L.A. to stay with friends, such as Zonker who headed to the Sunset Strip to see if he could bunk with Sensuous X, his lovely girlfriend from the New York bus trip. I slept on the bus, parked in front of the Lemon Grove bungalow.

Kesey was lost in Mexico by this time. His absence was felt by most of us. Everybody liked Babbs but I know I wasn't alone in thinking that his Marine training proved itself in his Prankster leadership style. He led more by edict than by moral authority. When he insisted that we all chip in money to a communal fund to keep the bus rolling we complied. When I craved a ratburger, as we called cheap hamburgers, I kept my complaints to myself because I'd turned over my few dollars to Babbs. But when I saw Babbs and Gretch a few blocks away, each with juicy cheeseburgers from a joint in the L.A. Farmers' Market, I was really pissed. At least I was upset for a few minutes. I wanted a cheeseburger all my own.

From then on, I think each of us squirreled away a few bucks every time we happened to come into any cash. My body needed cheeseburgers.

We didn't actually spend much time in the house. Hugh Romney, Del Close, and Tiny Tim were doing a nightclub show they called the Phantom Cabaret at a small, nearby joint catering to hippie customers. We mostly used the house for showers and as a place to receive phone calls.

I often looked for inspiration at a three-by-five card taped to the wall above the sink in the upstairs bathroom at the Lemon Grove house. Someone, probably Hugh Romney, quoting the old Mexican prophecy after the assassination of revolutionary leader Emiliano Zapata, had written:

"Ken Kesey is alive in the mountains with his white horse, waiting to return when his people need him!"

Every now and then I thought we needed Kesey. We needed him to come down from the mountains, or, in this case, up from Mazatlan, to spark some inspiration aboard the bus. I thought we needed him to get the Acid Tests going and to remind us why we were doing this. We did need him. I think we still need him.

* * *

I became a real fan of Tiny Tim. I was taken by his singing and I grew to admire his role in the world. Mr. Tim, as he liked to be called, lived in a room right off the kitchen. He preferred to eat without people watching him, so he didn't have far to go to eat in privacy. (I gathered from watching him load up his plate and carry it to his room that Mr. Tim ate only seeds, nuts, and dried fruit. I couldn't imagine why he didn't want us to see him eat it and, in my own head, I tried to imagine what sort of incredibly perverse and disgusting ways he could have of ingesting those sunflower seeds and filberts and desiccated prunes.)

Physically, Tiny Tim was perhaps the least-attractive man I'd ever seen—not counting men with gross deformities—like the guy who hung out in front of Cooper Union across the street from the bookstore where I worked on Third Avenue and St. Mark's Place in NYC, the fellow whose nose consisted entirely of two-inch-long tendrils hanging like pieces of Chef Boyardee canned spaghetti off the place above his upper lip.

Speaking of noses, Mr. Tim's was unusually large and beak-like. His hair was very long and quite stringy and seemingly unbrushed and uncombed, although you could tell that he spent more time than most of us did shampooing and fluffing his 'do. Mr. Tim wore some sort of makeup that could have been rice powder or just plain, all-purpose Betty Crocker flour patted lightly on his face, and the sports coat he usually wore could never have been in fashion. He did not cut an elegant figure.

Yet, I concluded, after I first heard him sing at the Phantom Cabaret, that Tiny Tim was an artist. His voice was sweet and angelic, or, depending on the song, a rich and deep baritone. He could sing duets, both parts of the duets, as in "Indian Love Call," singing both roles—Sgt. Bruce of the Royal Canadian Mounted Police and Rose Marie, the lass whose brother is on the scout. In his own way, Mr. Tim sounded as stalwart as Nelson Eddy, who played the Mountie in the movie, and as lovely as Jeanette MacDonald, as Marie. And, although I could barely believe my eyes, Tiny Tim really did play his ukulele rightside-up and upside-down, switching positions (and having to do an upside-down reconfiguration of his fingers for each chord) as he accompanied the Mountie and the plucky Marie on his tiny instrument.

The three housemates—Tiny Tim, Hugh Romney, and Del Close—had a heck of an act at the Phantom Cabaret, some of which they'd perform when they showed up at some of the L.A.-area Acid Tests. Hugh did his angry comic rant. Del did stand-up comedy and performed some sword-swallowing and fire-eating that he'd learned as a youngster working in carnivals. (He told me one day that after testing all available lighter fluids for his fire-eating act, he'd decided that Ronsonol was better than Zippo for spewing plumes of flame from your mouth because it tasted ever so slightly better than the Zippo lighter fuel.)

Tiny Tim sang old songs, most of them ballads by 1920s composers and songwriters, Irving Kaufman being his favorite. Mr. Tim seemed to prefer singing as a tenor, a bass, or a baritone. But he always sang falsetto on "Tiptoe Through the Tulips," which, of course, is what made him famous as well as the object of late-night television ridicule.

One day Mr. Tim, ukulele case in hand, left the house early. He said he was going to the NBC studios to tape that evening's Johnny Carson show, his first foray onto national television. He was back long before night fell and joined us in the upstairs TV room where we gathered to watch him on "The Tonight Show." We were all thrilled for Tiny Tim.

Preceding him on the show was the comedian Professor Irwin Corey, who billed himself as "The World's Greatest Authority." A real funnyman whose comedy showed a true social conscience, Corey in 1974 helped author Thomas Pynchon burnish his reputation as the greatest recluse this side of J.D. Salinger by going to the American Book Awards ceremony to pick up Pynchon's prize for *Gravity's Rainbow* and to give his own nonsensical speech to a crowd hoping to hear and see and meet the very elusive Pynchon.

That night in the upstairs television room, however, the estimable Prof. Corey did something that turned me off forever: Sitting on that famous sofa to the right (and our left) of host Johnny Carson, Corwin had a querulous look on his mug after Tiny Tim made his TV debut by singing "Tiptoe Through the Tulips" in his high, girlish falsetto. As Mr. Tim came over to take his seat between Corey and Carson, The World's Greatest Authority began a series of demeaning gestures and comments questioning Tiny Tim's sexuality. Now, there's nothing wrong with questioning his (or for that matter anyone's) sexuality and it might be natural for stupid people to make fun of a man with long hair who wears makeup and sings in a girlish voice and it was 1966, not today. But it was not becoming of a famous comedian, a man who identified himself with many praise-worthy left-wing causes, to objectify and poke fun at a man sitting next to him as though he were not there, and, essentially, to make homosexual jokes about a fellow performer. As far as I know, by the way, Tiny Tim was as straight as Irwin Corey or Johnny Carson.

Sitting next to Tiny Tim on that couch on the second floor of his Lemon Grove Avenue house, I turned to Mr. Tim and expressed my anger at Irwin Corey's rude behavior.

"Ooooh, Mr. Lee," Tiny Tim said chidingly, in the girly voice he used for everyday conversation, "please don't feel like that. Mr. Irwin Corey is a *very* nice man." It was then that I was certain that Tiny Tim was an angel.

SOUTH OF THE BORDER

Mountain Girl and I could not have stood out more from the passing crowds on Avenida Juarez in downtown Mexico City had we been naked. Each of us towered almost a foot or more above the average José we passed on the sidewalk. My hair was long and bleached very blond. MG, almost exactly nine months pregnant with Kesey's baby, had quit dyeing her hair a year earlier and had six inches of her naturally black and beautiful hair leading down to another six or eight inches of bleached yellow locks falling almost to her shoulders. Mountain Girl's ponderous pregnancy was enhanced by her outfit, featuring what must have been at that time the shortest skirt ever worn by a reputable gal in Mexico's Federal District.

Kesey, MG, and I had headed to Mexico City after the bus crew reunited with Ken in the resort city of Mazatlan. Like most Pranksters aboard the bus, I hadn't known until a few days earlier that we were even going to Mexico, let alone that we were supposed to get together with Kesey once we reached Mazatlan. That plan was a secret between Kesey and Babbs. (Remember, the FBI was hot on his trail.)

Ken had been on the lam in western Mexico while the rest of us were Acid Testing in Los Angeles and a few other Southern California locales. After leaving L.A. and spending some time in a beach parking lot in San Clemente, not far from the house that would become Richard Nixon's "Western White House," we headed east to Arizona, then south to the border. We crossed at Nogales and wended our way to Mazatlan.

It never occurred to me that when and if we reunited with Kesey that he'd be at least half out of his mind.

To say that Kesey was paranoid, fearful that he was under constant surveillance by the Mexican *federales* and our own FBI, is a gross understatement. He was haunted, checking each passing stranger as though he might be an undercover agent. Nor did he trust us. His eyes darted back and forth, checking out each of his old Prankster pals to make sure we weren't stooges or some sort of doppelgangers.

Kesey finally relaxed a bit the next day, when he and Mountain Girl and I traveled to the capital city, but he was still pretty wacky.

It was clear the moment he jumped out from behind a tree and leaped aboard the bus near a crowded beach in Mazatlan that Kesey was paranoid. He'd been lurking about the periphery of the beach parking lot since we pulled to a stop after circling the lot several times. Whether he and Babbs had agreed to this time and this place for a rendezvous, I do not know. I assume they had.

We noticed Kesey trying not to be noticed. He was acting blasé, if a paranoid fugitive from American justice can ever act blasé, acting as though his own brightly painted bus wasn't sitting a few yards away. First, he circled the parking area in an old car. Then he moseyed up close to the bus. Then he'd hidden—or lurked—behind a tree. Finally, he came aboard. At first, I assumed he was play-acting as he went through this pantomime of a man on the run in the Land of Mañana. Then I realized he really was about half-nuts. This wasn't an act. He suspected there was an FBI man behind every bush.

Once aboard the bus, Kesey kept glancing out the windows, staring suspiciously at motorists in passing cars, turning suddenly to watch some tourist crossing in front of the bus, occasionally holding his hat in front of his face so any feds lurking outside might not recognize him.

Why, I wondered to myself, would someone so obviously fearful of being recognized by a passing *federale* seek anonymity aboard his own infamous and highly noticeable psychedelic bus? Oh, yeah, he was as crazy as a bedbug.

After a quick meeting with us, Kesey left the bus and vanished back into Mazatlan. We agreed to meet him at a seedy hotel we'd found. He wanted to talk about seeking political asylum in Mexico and the rest of us wanted to talk about getting off the bus and swimming in the ocean.

While we waited for Kesey to join us dozen-or-so bedraggled Pranksters crammed into a small hotel room, we went about our business. Zonker fell asleep. I tried to nap. Hassler, who'd picked up some fungal disorder or something even worse in his general crotch area earlier in the Acid Test journey, complained to anyone who'd listen about pain and itching.

After several days of listening to Hassler's bitching about the condition of his groin, perineum, and testicles, we'd begun referring to his ailment as "Hassler's Asshole." As far as he knew, there were no pills to relieve his pain.

But, it seems a Los Angeles doctor had instructed Hassler to get some relief by having a daily prostate massage. We didn't know who'd done it up till now. He probably ignored the doc's advice. But now, lying on the hotel room floor and whining that it's impossible for anyone to reach, let alone massage, his own prostate, Hassler sought volunteers. You might even say he begged for someone to massage his prostate—which, of course, would entail sticking one's finger up Hassler's butt and digitally manipulating the gland in question. Volunteers? There was, of course, none. Some Pranksters seemed disgusted at the idea. Others were just not interested or too bored to get involved.

Finally, George Walker—the Prankster Iron Man who would do any job that the rest of us were too weak or too bored or too lazy or too preoccupied to do—said he would do the dirty deed.

Hassler gave George explicit instructions just how to grease his finger, just how to stick it up his rectum, just how to recognize the prostate and just how to massage it—and what to expect after a bit of stimulation of that deep-seated organ. George looked around for a rubber glove but there wasn't one. I suggested that he use a condom—and George looked even more-disgusted as he steeled himself to stick his sheathed and greased finger up Hassler's rectum.

But he did. And while some of us watched and others napped and others looked the other way, nothing happened, as far as Hassler was concerned.

"I'm supposed to ejaculate," Hassler said. "And this isn't doing it."

I suggested to George, "Tell him you love him!"

And, as George clenched his teeth and continued his workmanlike vigorous digital stimulation of Hassler's unresponsive prostate, the door suddenly burst open and into the room filled with some of his closest acolytes, companions whom he'd not relaxed with for so many months, strode Kesey. He stopped. He stared with disbelief at the tableau of Hassler, on his knees with his ass in the air, and George with his Vasolined, be-condomed finger up his fellow Prankster's butt, and the rest of us sitting around watching,

"So," said Kesey sadly. "It's come to this."

* * *

If Kesey hadn't been temporarily crazy at the time of our trip from Mazatlan up to Mexico City, the bizarre appearance of Mountain Girl and me might have taken the attention, off the fugitive *Norte Americano* writer. After all, back in California we'd fended off months of questioning about Kesey's location from FBI agents who'd show up every now and then, wondering where he'd flown when he flew the coop. We continued to swear that we didn't know. And, to tell the truth, most of us had no idea just when and where or even if we'd ever meet up with the man wanted now on a federal fugitive warrant for jumping bail and fleeing from two marijuana convictions in the Bay Area.

(Actually, the feds cut back on their Prankster interviews

after one visit to The Spread outside Santa Cruz. The two men in suits could hardly wait to leave after Babbs and Gretch, each in white coveralls covered with Day-Glo images, parts of American flags and rags and other motley, Pentel doodlings and assorted other decorations, had invited the agents inside. Like the most-affable of hosts, Babbs and Gretch explained in minute detail just why and how they'd added each doodad and illustration and patch to their jumpsuits and why they'd painted nutty pictures on the living-room floor and why they had side-by-side sewing machines where they were turning out colorful Prankster shirts—and would either of you care to try one on? One of the feds seemed particularly stressed after Babbs, noting a ring the man was wearing, gave the startled FBI agent the old fraternity handshake, which the guy couldn't help returning even though he tried to fight that knee-jerk manual reaction with gritted teeth.)

Always a showman, even when in hiding, Kesey could not bring himself to blend in with the Avenida Juarez crowds that seemed fixated on the bleached-blond *gringo* and the pregnant *gringa* in the miniskirt. Instead, Kesey insisted on drawing attention to himself by attempting to act the way he thought an American bird-watcher would act. A drama major in college, Kesey now talked constantly into a tape-recorder, muttering in an annoyingly prissy voice (the way he imagined an ornithologist might sound) about various finches and titmice and jays and thrushes he was supposedly seeing here and there in the crowded center of the second or third-largest city in the world. He wore a sport coat and tie and with his balding head and curly blond Bozo-the-Clown fringe sticking out from beneath the brim of a shabby fedora, he was actually attracting almost as much attention as Mountain Girl.

The really crazy part, though, was more than just his disguise and bird-watcher role-playing. His paranoia was so bad that he actually thought there *were* American agents among the brown-skinned Latino *hombres* and *mujeres* whom we passed.

* * *

Kesey had asked Mountain Girl and me to join him for this trip to Mexico City for vastly different reasons. He hadn't seen MG for a long time (he hadn't seen me for ages either, but then he didn't miss me the same way he missed the woman who was carrying his baby). The thing was, I had lived for a half-year in the capital in 1960 and more or less knew my way around town. We were going to meet with an attorney who might want to represent a famous American writer seeking asylum to get away from government harassment in *los Estados Unidos*. His argument was that the authorities were after him just because he'd used a harmless drug, marijuana. The lawyer he wanted to talk with had an office near the center of town, on a street near Avenida Juarez.

To make a long story short, the Mexican lawyer was not interested in a laughable attempt to seek protection south of the border from the American government's anti-drug laws. So the two tall *gringos* with the bright-blond hair, with the silly looking birdwatcher in tow, hit the sidewalks of Mexico City to wander aimlessly until we decided what to do next.

Our wandering—Kesey the Bird-Watching Man always ten feet behind, constantly lisping ornithological nonsense into his portable tape recorder—took us away from downtown. We wandered over to Avenida de los Insurgentes Sur, the main street out to the National University, where I'd taken some classes. I took some English language classes in Mexican history and some classes in *español* but I'd spent most of my time in Mexico City hanging out, meeting new *amigos,* wandering around the city and out in rural areas, and being in love for the first time.

As we walked, Kesey blabbered away into his tape-recorder—I could hear occasional references to wings, beaks, habitat—and Mountain Girl and I saw the sights. Beside us as we strolled aimlessly south toward the university, traffic on the broad *Avenida* barely moved. What had been a thoroughfare when I'd lived in town six years before had by 1966 become little more than a barely moving traffic jam.

I happened to peek into a car stuck in traffic as we walked past. I looked at a pretty woman and then did a double-take as I glanced at the driver. It was my dear friend Eric List, my friend from my 1960 sojourn in Mexico City, my *compadre* after whom I'd named my son! Here on one of the busiest streets in one of the world's largest cities was a man I hadn't seen for five years. Eric and his wife Ady, sitting in a car that was one of what? perhaps a half-million automobiles in Mexico City?

Coincidence is no surprise to anyone who believes that it's the nature of the universe. And it certainly was no surprise to a trio of acid-heads, the sorts of goofy people who come to believe anything and ascribe it to God or nature or some other wooie-wooie power that we Pranksters happened to refer to, at the time, as Cosmo.

"Hey, Eric," I shouted over the honking horns of cars halted in the traffic jam. Eric looked up with wide-eyed surprise that turned immediately into a huge grin. Ady opened the car door and stepped out to let the three of us cram ourselves into the back seat and we took off toward the "village" of Coyoacan, out toward the university, where they lived.

"I thought we'd bump into them," I whispered to Kesey. He looked at me with an odd uncertainty in his paranoid eyes. "No, no, man," I continued, "I'm kidding. It's just coincidence! It's just Cosmo!"

"Oh, yeah," he nodded.

* * *

By the time we headed out of Mexico City a day or two later to join the bus, our fellow Pranksters had moved down the coast to the seaport of Manzanillo. They'd rented a place to live (and park the bus) a few kilometers north of town just off the highway. The building had somehow once been involved with the sale of Purina animal foods and had a painted Purina checkerboard sign on its roof. It quickly became known as *La*

Purina Casa. Even the local taxi drivers knew what we meant when we asked to be driven there.

By now I was getting the bus version of cabin fever. I was itching to go home, wherever that might turn out to be. It was crowded at the Purina house. Mountain Girl was getting ready to have her baby and at least two Pranksters, Hassler and Julius Karpen, had been injured in an auto accident. I knew it was time to get off the bus and into something or some place else.

After MG's baby was born, by the way, someone learned that the child could have dual citizenship—Mexican and American—at least until she reached her eighteenth birthday. There was a catch: the baby had to be legitimate. The baby's father, Kesey, was already married to Faye, of course, so Mountain Girl was faced with a problem. She needed a husband so she could register the baby. She needn't have worried. George Walker, always the Iron Man ready to do what needed to be done, agreed to become the bridegroom and he and MG got married by signing some document at city hall. Then the entire wedding party, including the newlyweds, headed to another clerk's office to register the child.

"And what is her name?" the registrar of new babies asked.

"Solana," he was told.

"Solana? *No es possible!*"

"Solana!" insisted Prankster Julius Karpen in a voice that would brook no further questions.

"Okay," said the bureaucrat, "*ella es* Solana."

And so, the girl who in English would be called Sunshine and who would eventually gain some fame of her own as Sunshine Garcia when her mom later married Grateful Dead member Jerry Garcia, was entered into the Mexican population records as Solana—or, in English, Sunporch.

* * *

My life as a fulltime bus-riding Merry Prankster was over. With a few goodbyes and an *adios* or two, including farewells to Ken and Faye and others with whom I'd shared life aboard the bus, and after a conversation with Neal Cassady that was as close to an intimate talk he and I had ever had, I joined Zonker and Hassler aboard a first-class bus to the border. When we got to Tijuana we stopped in at a *farmacia* to buy some Dexamyl, the last legally purchased speed I was going to buy for a long, long time, and headed toward the border crossing into California. At the last moment, just before leaving Mexico, we each bought a beer and, now fearful of getting caught smuggling in the amphetamine that was legal where we bought it but forbidden a few hundred yards to the north, gulped the *cerveza* and swallowed all of our green-and-white capsules before we reached the border.

Wide-awake now, really wide-awake, we hitchhiked north, catching a ride in San Diego from a guy who introduced himself, "Hi, I'm Harry White and I'm as queer as a three-dollar bill." And he was. He started hitting on all three of us right off the bat.

Harry bought us dinner somewhere in South Orange County and then, expecting some payback, pulled off a darkened stretch of the midnight highway and told us what he wanted. And what he wanted was for Zonker to show him his cock while Hassler and I whipped him with our belts as he masturbated.

My belt was a soft, woven cloth strip I'd picked up in Manzanillo. Hassler's was something similar. You couldn't have hurt a kitten with those two belts but we were obliging young men and we did as we were asked. I could tell that Zonker was embarrassed but he zipped down his fly and let Harry see what he wanted to see.

There was a full moon above the field that night we crossed back across the border from Mexico, back to *quien*

197

sabe?—who know? There was a full moon when we knocked, late that night, at an L.A. apartment where we knew we could find some food, some shelter, and some loving, too.

A WINK, *EL NORTE*, AND THE SUMMER OF LOVE

Kesey and a dwindling posse of Pranksters stayed in Manzanillo for several weeks, playing, working on the film of the original bus trip to New York and, paramount in Kesey's mind, avoiding the authorities back in the USA. I visited for a few days with my new companion Space Daisy. We stayed in a hotel in town but spent most of our time at *La Purina Casa*—much of it talking with (but mostly listening) to Neal Cassady. It turned out that would be my next-to-last conversation with Cassady.

When I walked back into the *casa's* front room and edged up to Cassady so I could get a taste of his ever-weird-and-fascinating chatter, I realized that he was carrying on the same, the *exact* same, conversation (with, as ever, a fascinated coterie of listeners) that he was having when I'd last seen him several months earlier. I pointed this out to Neal, who looked at me with a grin and to my incredible surprise, a wink. This was for me a moment of such amazing closeness from someone who seemed so embedded in his own self-honed persona that he seemed inured to intimacy.

By winking, it seemed, Neal was letting me know that I had somehow stumbled into a secret part of his head, the part that differentiated between what seemed to be an unfiltered spill of ideas and images and language from his expansive and generous mind and a self-conscious awareness of what he was saying and to whom he was saying it. In this case, I understood, he had returned in his head to the very sentence he had been speaking when we'd said *adios* to one another months earlier as Hassler, Zonker, and I had split for California.

Space Daisy, or Judith, as she had been named at birth, and I returned by a very slow train to Guadalajara and flew home to the Bay Area. I was off the bus, as it were. But in San Francisco and in our house in the gloomy redwood Zayante canyon in the Santa Cruz Mountains, the psychedelic life continued. I saw Neal once again, in Zayante, when he and Ginsberg and Peter Orlovsky dropped by our house and hung around in the bathroom as I soaked in a tub of hot water. As always, though, he had sped on toward his next port of call by the time the water had cooled and I'd dried myself off.

Space Daisy had been Ron Boise's girlfriend. She and her three kids had been living with my sculptor friend when I'd returned from Manzanillo to Santa Cruz and found a place to sleep in a decrepit old Victorian mansion rented by Bill Laudner. Bill, who gained recognition within the rock-and-roll music business as equipment manager for Jefferson Airplane, was the ex-husband of a former girlfriend of mine, Ginger Jackson. (Bill was known for roller-skating through airports, rolling speakers and amplifiers and other essential equipment with wheels attached, to and from the jets that flew Jefferson Airplane to gigs around the country. A mutual friend saw Bill at San Francisco International Airport one day skating a load of speakers away from the luggage claim area as a helium-filled balloon floated his blond ponytail aloft.)

A lifelong surfer, Bill slept in the one inhabitable room in the decaying Victorian house. The other rooms were filled with fallen ceilings and mounds of broken furniture and other junk. When I, and then Hassler, moved in we had to share that one good room with Bill. We slapped two or three mattresses together in the only space available. So, when the surfer-girl I was seeing and a young woman Bill and Hassler were sharing stayed the night, we had a boy-girl-boy-girl-boy fivesome on the makeshift bed.

Ron Boise died in a local hospital of a faulty heart valve or congestive heart failure. I remember I was listening to my car radio outside the crumbling Victorian when Babbs' wife Anita, who was visiting someone inside, stepped out to shout that Space Daisy had called to report that Ron was dead. When I got this bad news I was listening to the Rolling Stones' "Paint It Black" for the very first time.

Boise had been a good pal and, as the only other drinker in the Kesey crowd when we'd lived in La Honda, had shared a few good and drunken nights at the nearest barroom in that mountain community, Boots & Saddles.

I noticed in later years, when I'd visit the Keseys at their farm outside Springfield, Oregon, that I was no longer the only drinker in the group. In fact, Kesey had developed a taste for schnapps, for some reason, and some of the other Pranksters drank even more than I did in those days.

On one of those Oregon trips, Kesey and I were the last two awake in the end of the barn that he'd fashioned into a home. Faye and the kids and a handful of other Pranksters and friends were asleep in their beds or in various nooks and nests in the agricultural portion of the barn. Kesey flipped on the television without checking to see what was on. We began to watch what I realized—but he did not—was the film version of his first novel, *One Flew Over the Cuckoo's Nest*.

"Oh, man," he said after a minute when he realized what movie was playing. It was the very movie that he'd vowed never to watch after a serious dispute with the producers who'd hired him, originally, to write the screenplay for *Cuckoo's Nest*. He jumped up and flipped the TV to some other channel.

"You ought to watch it, Ken," I told him. "It's pretty good." In fact, it was so good that it won a fistful of Oscars, including best picture and best screenwriting of material from another source.

"Yes," he admitted, "I've heard that. But by God I swore I would never watch it and I'm not going back on that now."

So we watched a few minutes of *The Tonight Show* and then took off for our beds.

It wasn't as though I rushed right over to comfort Space Daisy when I learned that Boise was dead. First of all, Ron told me before he went in the hospital that Space Daisy's husband, a well-known San Francisco rock radio disk jockey, had threatened to kill him "for stealing his wife." Secondly, I knew that that very same husband had been killed very recently when his car went off the road at a high rate of speed and crashed into a section of a concrete overpass pillar. Man, I thought, she must really be bummed.

Also, I was content with the young surfer woman I was hanging out with. She was smart and pretty and I enjoyed her company. The only downside of our relationship was her occasional need to get up, after checking the tide chart in the previous day's paper, at four in the morning to catch the waves out at "The Hook," a surfing break off a nearby seacliff known as Pleasure Point—the same neighborhood where I would later, within a couple of years, be delivering mail as a substitute letter-carrier.

Somehow, though, it wasn't long before I found myself in bed in someone's house with Space Daisy. I'd just bumped into her while visiting some other friends. She said she and her kids had moved up to Zayante. A few weeks later I moved up there, too, and in with her—and her three kids and a dog and a whole posse of cats. It wasn't exactly that she was a cat lady, but Space Daisy did have a heck of a lot of cats.

She had some money; I didn't, which eventually led to my brief career as a mailman. My last source of income had been some tiny weekly unemployment benefit after I'd quit the *San Mateo Times* almost two years earlier. But we lived like rich people for a while. We bought a pool table for our living room, meaning I didn't have to drive down to the bars in the small mountain community of Felton to shoot eight-ball, only to drive home half-drunk afterwards. We drank good brandy. We smoked good dope and we flew down to Guadalajara and took the train out to the coast to visit Kesey and the Pranksters at *La Purina Casa.*

One day I asked her if she wanted to get married. She said "Sure." I suggested we get hitched during a rock-and-roll dance at the Fillmore Auditorium, the scene of an early Acid Test and by this time the main venue for famous San Francisco bands such as Jefferson Airplane, the Grateful Dead, Big Brother and the

Holding Company with Janis Joplin, the Loading Zone, Quicksilver Messenger Service, and Country Joe and the Fish. She loved the idea.

Some friends, including Julius Karpen—not only a fellow Merry Prankster and Acid Tester but several years earlier my editor at the City News Bureau of Chicago—had formed a music-business partnership. His partner was another Chicago pal, Ron Polte. They called themselves West Pole. Julius managed Janis and Big Brother and Polte managed Quicksilver. A third West Pole associate, George Smith, managed an all-girl group, the Ace of Cups, which featured a lovely lady the Pranksters had named "Mary Microgram," and whose real name was Denise Kaufman, who now teaches yoga in Los Angeles.

Polte, by the way, had one of the best LSD-sparked ideas I ever heard. One day when he and Julius and I were sitting in Julius' living room, each of us high as kites on acid, and each of us staring at our hands, as people high on the drug are wont to do, seeing endless universes in each pore, Polte suddenly asked, "You know what I'd like to have?"

"No," we replied.

He told us, "I'd like to have five tiny fingers on the tip of each of my fingers." We sat there considering Polte's statement. It was, of course, the best idea any of us had ever heard.

I talked with Julius and Polte about getting married at a rock dance and then with the late Fillmore Auditorium "impresario," as they always called him, Bill Graham. Bill had jumped into the local music scene by helping organize the Trips Festival and stayed on to become more or less the boss of the Bay Area rock music scene. He not only said he'd be happy to have our wedding on-stage during an upcoming dance—this was when rock dances were actually dances, not concerts—but that he would throw us an after-dance wedding reception. Bill said he would lay in some food and wine and hire our friends, the Anonymous Artists of America, a band built around a Buchla Machine, a

music synthesizer built by a genius named Don Buchla. The Triple A included some close friends, among them Len and Toni Frazer, as well as Lars Kampman, the first man I knew to die of AIDS. The Anonymous Artists later played at the Acid Test

Graduation after Kesey and the Pranksters returned from Mexico. Space Daisy and I attended the graduation long enough for me to pick up my diploma, which announces that I have, indeed, passed the Acid Test. Then we drove home to Zayante.

The best thing about our wedding at the Fillmore was having such a crowd in attendance. Julius told me he has a photo of me shadowing my eyes from the bright lights as I gazed across about two thousand rock-and-rollers in the auditorium trying to pick out my bride-to-be as she approached. I think I took the microphone and asked the crowd to clear an aisle so she didn't have to push and shove her way to the stage.

We found a Unitarian minister to officiate and as we exchanged vows, although I don't recall that we actually vowed to do anything in particular, the Quicksilver Messenger Service played a song that one band member told me they'd written for the nuptials, "Acapulco Gold and Silver."

The Fillmore was the first venue for that San Francisco rock and roll sound, but it certainly wasn't the only one. Chet Helms and the Family Dog operated the wonderful Avalon Ballroom, scene of many famous rock dances and concerts that were immortalized in some of the classic psychedelic rock posters. And Bill Graham not only opened a new Fillmore Auditorium, he also opened Winterland, a former ice skating rink, as a rock auditorium in 1971.

Meanwhile, as San Francisco's rock scene was garnering national attention, Kesey joined the trickle of Pranksters returning to the States. In keeping with his dramatic nature, Ken came over the border as a broke cowboy singer. He borrowed a horse and a guitar, and disguised himself as "Singin' Jimmy Anglund," just a typical down-and-out drunken, singing cowpoke, broke after a rough weekend in a border town in the Land of Mañana.

Kesey was still a federal fugitive, yet came back to the Bay Area, where he was caught and taken into custody. I don't think it was hubris; I think Cosmo finally decided that Kesey had been on the run long enough. As he was being driven along the

Bayshore Freeway, by Hassler, as I recall, the passengers in the car next to them in the heavy traffic turned out to be—remember, Coincidence is the Nature of the Universe—federal agents, FBI men. They were the very dudes who'd endlessly asked us in Santa Cruz many months earlier if we knew where Ken Kesey was. Now it was evident to these crime busters that Kesey had *not* leaped to his death from a Northern California seacliff. There he was in the adjacent vehicle. They pulled the truck over and took Kesey into custody.

Ken eventually spent five months at the San Mateo County jail farm, located not all that far, really, from his La Honda home, the place we'd abandoned when we pulled up stakes and moved to Santa Cruz. He agreed to imprisonment after the two pot convictions were somehow merged and after authorities dropped charges against Neal Cassady and another Prankster, both of whom would have faced serious time behind bars as what was called in those days a "three-time loser." Sort of like "three strikes and you're out." Exactly like it, in fact.

Neal, for those who don't know, eventually died in Mexico, walking, alone, along a railroad track in a rural part of the country. The rumor at the time was that he was counting railroad ties and that his last words were something like "Ten thousand, seven hundred forty-two." But *¿quien sabe?*—who knows?

When Kesey was freed after serving his sentence, he returned to his Oregon hometown to live on the farm his brother had purchased for him. He told me later that he would never, ever again plead guilty to anything anywhere. He did not enjoy his confinement, although while on the jail farm he did write and illustrate *Kesey's Jail Journal*, subsequently released by his publisher, Viking.

Ken Kesey's time in California had ended. Sure, he visited from time to time and appeared on stage here and there and, in 1990, even took a new-and-improved replica, almost, of the original bus to the Golden State. I was able to join that trip with a primitive computer to send dispatches from the road back to my employer at the time, the *San Jose Mercury News*. But Ken was an Oregonian at heart. He had gone home to that farm near Springfield, and had buried his nineteen-year-old son Jed out in the pasture, the same pasture where in 2001 he, too, would be buried—next to his boy.

* * *

Kesey still appears frequently in my dreams. He was, of course, a majors figure in my life, in my development into whoever I am today. And tomorrow, Cosmo willing.

Since those heady days, I have always known I was lucky, that all of us in the Merry Band of Pranksters were lucky, that Kesey was a benign and mindful ... leader, I guess is the word. I doubt that many of us would have been attracted to him had he exhibited any of the evil insanity that in those unsettled times brought so many young men and women under the sway of mental and spiritual fascists like Charles Manson. Kesey didn't have any rules or dietary restrictions. There weren't any requirements that we follow his precepts to improve ourselves, any dictums that might in any way put himself above the rest of us. It wasn't a democracy, but the only way you could figure that out was if you were left behind when the bus pulled out.

After all, Ken did own the bus. That was why you had to pay attention. When Kesey wanted to leave, the bus left from wherever it was, regardless of where you were. His frequent admonition that "You're either on the bus or off the bus" has now grown from a friendly warning to fellow Pranksters to a common aphorism about commitment in modern America. Kesey meant the bus warning metaphorically as well as literally. I remember the time after The Great Duck Storm when we left Jerry Anderson in a town where we'd stopped for gas. Jerry was married to Jefferson Airplane's first chanteuse, Signe Toly, a woman with a sweet voice and a totally different way of singing than her successor, Grace Slick. Jerry had been hanging around the Pranksters since a bunch of us had met him at The Matrix, one of San Francisco's first rock-and-roll hangouts. The Matrix was owned, at least in part, by some members of Jefferson Airplane.

Jerry had hopped off the bus for some reason in Santa Rosa or some other town north of San Francisco. Whether he had meant to leave for good or whether he was just tardy getting back aboard, Kesey reiterated that we're either on the bus or off—and we departed. Kesey's "on or off the bus" standard also meant, of course, that if one's mental or spiritual or ethical standards indicated that it was time to leave the bus, one was indeed free to leave at any time or place. Personally, I think Jerry left the bus because he knew it was time to bid us *adieu, adios*.

Our only other rule, and this covered all of us, including Kesey, was "Never trust a Prankster." Don't!

Not only was Ken Kesey not interested in power over any "followers" or over a cult of devotees, it was clear to all of us, including Ken, that we were exploring this new psychedelic frontier as comrades in arms, as pioneers with the same ground-breaking curiosity as all of our Prankster colleagues. Most of this trail was as new to Kesey as it was to me. He did get a head start on psychedelic drugs during his sessions getting paid to test pharmaceuticals for, as it turned out, the CIA, as part of the agency's MK Ultra program. The spies were interested in finding drugs to disable or confuse enemies. Kesey said that as soon as he took LSD and started to get high he realized he should keep his mouth shut about its potential because, he feared, it would immediately be banned for public consumption.

Kesey was a man of great insight and wit. He had far more knowledge of literature than any of us except, perhaps, Neal Cassady, and he was not afraid of saying what came immediately to mind without worrying whether it might lead nowhere or leave him out on one of those intellectual/verbal limbs where we suddenly lose sight of what we were trying to say, of what words should come next, of where this last thought came from, of what any listener might think.

Above all, Ken Kesey was a storyteller. He could hold an audience spellbound, whether it was a few Pranksters or a crowd of students or academics or church congregants skeptical of the Famous Writer with Day-Glo paint on his pants and an otherworldly grin on his face.

Kesey had been a drama major in college in Oregon. He put that flair to great use when telling stories. But he was not a performer who turned his character on and off when he entered or left a stage. He was fascinating, literally. I could sit for hours listening to him spin tales and invent stories and relate myths. He never demanded to be the center of attention, yet he almost always was. He never tried to stifle anyone who had a comment to interject or who held different values or had different beliefs. He never spoke as a leader, as someone demanding rapt attention. In fact, he really didn't seem to care if we listened at all. We listened because we could not help ourselves. You could not shut your ears if Kesey had the floor.

Yet Kesey did not suffer fools lightly, a term I only came to understand as I became familiar with a sort of anger that could smolder behind his eyes. That smoldering would happen when the conversation had reached such a far-out level that the interjection of some pedestrian remark could bring the high-flying atmosphere to a crashing halt. Kesey didn't express that anger as such. Instead, he would grimace in a sort of self-righteous and disbelieving manner and look at the offender as if they'd stunk up the joint. He didn't argue. He always knew when he was telling a good story.

Because many such bring-down interruptions seemed to result from the egoistic wish of someone at the table or in the room to show they were as smart or insightful as Kesey, we invented the Power Game. This consisted of a twirling device (that I built; it is one of the few things I ever made). The device allowed a spinning arrow to point at any one of us sitting in a circle.

There were two versions of the Power Game. In one, the person selected by the luck of the spin would have the power for a fixed amount of time, say ten minutes, to make the rest of us do whatever he or she wanted. There was always, of course, the option of not doing what we were directed to do, but it quickly became obvious that the person selected would show little imagination and would make such puerile demands that we had no problem following him or her. I mean, who is going to get offended when ordered to, say, follow the leader outside and around the house in the rain and back into the living room?

The other, tougher version, gave the person selected by the spinner *all* the attention in the room, usually for the same ten or fifteen minutes. If you think it's hard to give someone else all of your attention for a few minutes, think about how incredibly difficult it is to have a dozen or more people completely focused on *you* for that same period of time. You become aware of every part of your own body, your own consciousness, every tic and itch and sniffle and blink. You might try to deflect the absolute *seriousness* of all that attention by making a funny face or by attempting to act nonchalant. But ten minutes of total attention seems like a very long time and I saw more than one person get so weird about it that they got up and left the room and the scene. Sometimes forever.

It took some guts to be a Merry Prankster.

In fact, as I think of us individually and as a group of comrades, the one feature that was common to all of us was fearlessness, even if at times it was an uninformed, even silly, ignorant, or stupid fearlessness. We often had no idea where we were heading, physically, mentally, or spiritually. We felt like "Colonel Spaulding, the African explorer," of Marx Brothers fame, crossing unknown rivers, entering uncharted mountains, exploring hidden, alien forests and jungles, knowing not what monsters might be hiding, what sort of incomprehensible insanity might lie at the end of the trail, on the other bank, under the rock we were about to lift.

Yet, despite the dangers—and believe me, there were indeed victims among our companions in psychedelic explorations—as pioneers we trudged ahead—boldly. It seemed the only sensible thing for an explorer to do.

Among our friends and our acquaintances there certainly were those whose minds wandered into endless psychic mazes with no way out. There were those who turned into hopeless addicts: of drugs, of cults, of visions that required their total immersion, with no return routes or signposts pointing the way back to families and friends, visions so alien that neither those visionaries nor the rest of us ever wanted to see one another again, let alone to share each others' new "insights."

Such was rarely if ever the case with Pranksters. There were a few who came and stayed for a while and left for other scenes and other levels of sanity. The Hermit, for instance, who'd been busted with the rest of us at Kesey's place in La Honda: he was last seen by me waving his hypodermic and syringe while running crazily down Haight Street during the so-called Summer of Love screaming at passers-by about the wonders of methamphetamine. The Hermit was nuts when we first met him and when I saw the far-away yet ecstatic look in his eyes the first time someone gave him a tab of Benzedrine, I was certain his story would not have a good ending. As far as I know, it did not.

But as I think about Faye and Ken Kesey, Babbs, Gretchin Fetchin (the Slime Queen), Hassler, Zonker, Roy Sebern (the quiet but insightfully mindful artist who originally painted the bus), Michael Hagen, George Walker, Mountain Girl, Des Prado, Jane Burton, Paul Krassner, Ed McClanahan, and so many other Pranksters and Prankster pals, I see clearly that they were each fearless, We *were* fearless! Hooray for Captain Spaulding.

* * *

You know, there was one psychedelic political trope that fascinated some acid heads and frightened so many cops and other authorities, and that was that we would put LSD in the water supply. Frankly, there were serious discussions about what would happen if somehow everyone—all the cops and all the kids and all the parents and all the priests and ... everybody— was dosed with

LSD. That topic passed for cocktail party conversation when acid heads got together to smoke pot and listen to music in the mid-1960s.

Was anyone ever serious about dosing the water supply? Jeez, I suppose so. Personally, I thought it wouldn't do any good, even if it could somehow be done and even if you could find enough LSD to turn a public reservoir into a pond of Electric Kool-Aid. I had already come to the conclusion that there is exactly the same percentage of assholes among LSD-users as there is in the population at large. No doubt there are the same percentages of greedy bastards and power freaks and probably saints, too. The idea of giving everybody acid seemed ridiculous. (The only time I ever heard anyone say "Let's put LSD in the water supply" was in 1990 when Wavy Gravy was running for the Berkeley City Council. He shouted it through the sound system of Kesey's replica bus as we tried to chug "further" up a hill that eventually led to the city reservoir. Wavy was kidding. I think.)

But I did know that psychedelics for everyone would open that previously locked door of perception that Aldous Huxley wrote about and that each of us is either born with or provided as a legacy by our parents, our priests, and our school teachers. I just didn't think it would lead to world peace, which is something we worried about a lot in those days. I also didn't think dosing the water supply would lead to equality among the races or even to a universal version of what the squares called "free love" and what we called fucking or screwing or making love.

At big "gatherings of the tribes," as psychedelic celebrations and whoopdeedoos were often called, it did seem true that We Are All One. Anyone who attended Woodstock or the Human Be-In that covered a goodly portion of Golden Gate Park with acid heads and hippies and poets and rock bands, could believe, if only for a moment, that there was a spiritual revolution afoot in the world, or, at least, in San Francisco. We really thought that we, with the help of LSD, were changing the world.

But the Summer of Love was on the horizon and what had been foretold as a time of love and peace and brother-and-sisterhood started to show some wear and tear and, finally, some really ugly reality. San Francisco, where a pop singer had told runaways and lonely boys and girls and outsiders and everybody else to come and to wear a flower in your hair, started to be jam-packed with hippies. That often meant runaways, bums, would-be troubadours with guitars but no talent, and a hundred other varieties of street people. There wasn't room for everyone. There was no room to sleep, no room to fall in love, no room to encourage a sweet expansion of these newcomers' minds, at least as far as I could tell.

Space Daisy and I were down in the redwood forest in Zayante.

We rarely went up to San Francisco any more. There wasn't even room to park.

One evening when we decided to see if we could break into the local nighttime culture, we stopped for drinks at Lou's Rendezvous, a bar in the community of Ben Lomond. It was a hangout for people who didn't know people with long hair. "Hey, are you a boy or a girl?" was still a question shouted from passing pickup trucks when I and a very few others with longish hair would go into town.

We weren't exactly welcomed with open arms, but everything was cool until Space Daisy, in a brief, brandy-fueled moment of exuberance, tossed her glass at the mirror behind the bar. *Oh, Jesus*, I said to myself, *now they're gonna beat the shit out of me.*

And sure enough, Lou himself jumped over the bar and threw a punch, then wrestled me to the ground. I lay there on the barroom floor, watching in a far-too detached manner for someone getting the crap knocked out of him, as Lou slugged me again and again. But I could feel nothing; none of the punches hurt. I looked into Lou's eyes and somehow knew that this man did not have long to live and that his angry punches were harmless reflections of his impending death. Eventually, he got up and stumbled back behind the bar, where he stood panting and huffing.

I got up, put some money down, tipped a mariachi trio playing in the corner, and left with my wife. I read in the paper a month or so later that, just as I knew he would, Lou had passed away.

It was at this time, by the way, that I had seven monkeys living in a large wire-screened enclosure attached to the house in the front yard. The way one acquires seven monkeys is by getting one monkey. Then everyone in the county who hears you have a monkey brings *their* monkey over and asks if you want it. They're easy to acquire but hard to get rid of.

The best part about having seven simians in the front yard was that the Jehovah's Witness guy who tried to peddle *Watchtower* magazines each month to the few residents along Zayante Road always, when he got to my house, opened the publication to an article about evolution. The articles themselves were slightly different each month but the general tone, as expressed by the headlines in *Watchtower*, was along the lines of "We Are Not Descended From Monkeys!"

I always gave the young fellow a dime so he'd go away after leaving the magazine. It was well worth ten cents to keep from hearing his preaching. And it was interesting each month to watch the young Jehovah's Witness come to a dead halt in front of the monkey cage, after he'd taken my dime and given me the magazine. He would stare at the monkeys, at the three macaques, the two woolly monkeys, the capuchin, and the tiny squirrel monkey. And I knew what was going on in his head. If you stare into a monkey's eyes it is obvious that there is something in there looking right back at you, something bright and intelligent and even thoughtful. Something, in fact, almost human.

I spent time every day in the enclosure with my furry friends. The alpha monkey was a large macaque named Charlie. But when I was in the cage I was the alpha monkey and Charlie, as my henchman, or henchmonkey, would sit on my shoulder and snarl at his minions, saying, in monkey talk, "Look, I'm with the big guy. Get out of our way!"

In San Francisco, the Summer of Love approached. Community groups hoping to do something spectacularly peaceful and psychedelic—groups like the Diggers and some of the musicians, concert promoters, and neighborhood organizations—tried to pull off a real season of love and peaceful co-existence. But there was a lot of bickering and in-fighting and ego trips and a lot of the Summer of Love plans went by the wayside as the city was overwhelmed by crowds of hungry and homeless hippies, competing neighborhood coalitions, and some very big music business egos. I was happy to stay with Space Daisy and her kids and my seven monkeys in the deep woods of Zayante.

One day our friend Jimmy Byers stopped by. He had a haunted look in his eyes. Jimmy had just come home from a bummer trip up to the city.

"I was driving along Haight Street," he told me. "I was going to see this girl, and suddenly this guy steps out in front of my car, right between two parked cars and he's right in front of my car. So I slam on the brakes. And then these two guys in suits step out right behind him and they're cops and man, they shoot him dead right there on the street, right in front of me.

"So my heart is racing a hundred miles an hour and I get over to this lady's apartment and I get inside and I tell her what just happened and she says, 'Let's go out. Let's get away from the neighborhood,' and we open her front door and right there in front of her apartment door, man, right on the front steps of the building, there's this guy and he's dead. He's got a knife sticking out of him."

By the Summer of Love there was heroin everywhere. There were speed freaks stealing anything that would fit in their pockets or on their shoulders so they could sell it and buy more speed. That is the nature of amphetamines. There were guys, old guys, young guys, preying on the hippie chicks who were flocking to town. There were guys who told the girls they were music promoters who might get them a gig with a band if they could sing, and of course each one of them could sing. There were black guys who promised the white girls that they could be hip, and if they'd hang with them they *would* be hip. Some guys turned them out, some gave them heroin, some fucked them and left them, some were sweet and gave them love. But it was a crapshoot.

The last time I took LSD—although not, by a long shot, the last time I took a psychedelic, a milder, easier, psychedelic like magic mushrooms—Space Daisy and I swallowed some at our house. The kids were asleep, the dog and cats were content, we expected no visitors, and we had the whole night ahead of us. It turned out to be the only time I had a bad trip.

Bad trips originate in our own heads and no one is to blame, unless we want to blame our minds. Oh, yeah, if you take some LSD and go to a crowded Costco and mingle with hordes of nightmare shoppers, you might say that Costco is to blame. But you chose to go there, so blame yourselves. That night with Space Daisy I was definitely not enjoying myself when my wife assumed what she thought was a regal pose on the couch and told me that she was experiencing a former life, and that former life was that of Cleopatra.

Believe me when I tell you that Judith, Space Daisy, was not the first psychedelic companion to tell me she was a reincarnation of Cleopatra. Why, I have wondered and I'm sure many acid heads and former acid heads have wondered, do women tend to discover that they were Cleopatra in their past lives? How many damn Cleopatras were there? How come no one is ever Wanda the Slave Girl? Or Martha Washington? Or a Bedouin seamstress or Winnie Ruth Judd or Annie Oakley?

At the same time as I was getting annoyed at my wife's hackneyed reversion to the personage of the late Egyptian queen, everything else was getting scary to me. This went on for minutes, probably, but it started to feel like hours, days, centuries.

And then my head spoke to me. At least, that's the way I put it in my acid-head jargon, a patois that included the common psychedelic admonishment to "Trust your head."

I did trust my head. And my head, my mind, the part of me connected to Cosmo, said to me, "Lee, don't take any more

LSD." And of course, I haven't. I think we should all trust our own heads.

* * *

I still trust my head. I can still see huge patterns of inexplicably weird and unknown lights in the night sky. I can still see an almost-endless succession of images when I move my hand across the space in front of my eyes, much like we can see so many after-images of the "Nude Descending a Staircase" in the famous painting by Marcel Duchamp.

But those tricks of the sense organs are not the legacy of my hundred-and-fifty-or-so acid trips. That's not what I gained from Ken Kesey or from being a Merry Prankster, not what humankind at large, or the worldwide community of all creatures, gained from The Sixties.

There were, of course, tangible changes in the sociological sense: advances in civil rights, increasing and eventually overwhelming opposition that led to the end of the Vietnam war, more participation in decisions affecting their own futures by some previously hidden or ignored segments of our worldwide community. But as anyone who reads newspapers or watches the nightly news or keeps abreast of things online knows, such actual political and social changes are never permanent. Kesey said "Nothing lasts." Buddha said the same thing.

Some people I knew went to the South to join the struggle for black voting rights. A few I knew went to Canada or Sweden

to protest and to avoid the war. Many people I knew marched in front of federal buildings to express their feelings about peace and justice and the lack thereof in our America and in our world.

Once, we took Kesey's bus up to an anti-war demonstration in Berkeley. It was a well-noted scene in the history of the 1960s. It was a time when Allen Ginsberg and the Hells Angels, university students and street people, feminists and almost everyone in our half of the community wanted to let the other half know what we felt and what we wanted.

But the presence of the Pranksters at that scene was a demonstration of something different. In *The Electric Kool-Aid Acid Test*, author Tom Wolfe tells the story of Kesey observing an anti-war leader at that demonstration. After a few minutes of listening to the bald-headed man fire up the crowd with the usual anti-war rhetoric, Kesey turned to someone and noted that the speaker reminded him of somebody else:

Benito Mussolini.

I don't believe that Kesey felt that he or we had a mission there at that demonstration. We had decided to paint the bus a more-or-less solid color, maroon, to decorate it with a few militaristic-seeming symbols and to wear some Army or Navy patches on our clothes.

These were not political statements. We were pranking. In fact, naturally, all of us Merry Pranksters agreed with the anti-war sentiments of that speaker and of all the speakers. But we were there not to support any political point of view. Rather, we decorated the bus and ourselves to try to make some sort of a higher statement, a psychedelic statement, a statement that we believed—and I still believe—that the way to promote peace and to support justice is not so much to overwhelm any opposition but to evolve to a place where the people with whom we agree and those with whom we don't are *all* higher than we are now, all as close to enlightenment as we can be, each of us secure in the knowledge that we really are all one—in every sense but especially in the cosmic sense. In other words, the goal, as they used to say, was to "shift paradigms."

If there is anything approaching a lasting change or cultural mutation that has arisen from the 1960s—and I mean not only from the psychedelic drugs but from the music and the poetry and the widespread sense of communion with all of our brothers and sisters—it must be the evolution of consciousness, an opening, if you will, of those doors of perception, an intangible but very real upward tick of our inevitable but agonizingly slow progress toward attainment of God-ness. Maybe I can call it "Cosmosis."

The Sixties was a big tick upward, a kick in the pants to give us a bigger step than usual toward enlightenment, toward heaven, toward whatever one's vision might be of a land of milk and honey—and peace and love and equality and passion and all the other qualities that mean perfection.

It took humankind a long time to get to the 1960s and it will no doubt take even longer to approach perfection. But I suspect that many of us still alive who are veterans of those heady days of psychedelia believe that a better day is a-coming and that we'll need a few more kicks in the butt, or maybe just a few more kicks, before we get there.

DOPE, AN ASIDE

My wife, Chris, and I went to the same high school in Winettka, a Chicago suburb. But we didn't meet until our fortieth class reunion, in 1998. She says she'd known who I was, when we were senior classmates at New Trier High School, because I was editor-in-chief of the school paper. Unfortunately, or perhaps fortunately given that I finally did meet her and am a contented husband and man, I can't reciprocate by saying that I was aware of Christine Hultman in 1954 to 1958, our high school years.

One thing I was aware of, but barely, was marijuana. It must be difficult for young people these days to hear that most of us were unaware of pot back then or to know that educators themselves were even more completely in the dark about illegal drugs than they are today, and that's pretty deeply in the dark.

So, when we heard senior year that the police had arrested a student and possibly a teacher for possession of marijuana we on the staff of the *New Trier News* figured we had a great story on our hands. When word of our investigation reached the Dean of Students I was called to his office and told in no uncertain terms that we were not going to pursue the drug story any further. Obviously afraid of damage to the school's stellar reputation, the Dean—who had also been my geometry teacher two years earlier, a soporific with a bald head and two legs—threatened to pull the plug on the paper if we didn't agree.

Somehow, the marijuana case was swept under the carpet and, as far as we could discover, no charges were filed. No one was kicked out of school or fired from the teaching staff. And no one was any wiser or hipper about dope than we'd previously been.

Today, high school students know as much about drugs, or some drugs, as I did when I was a Merry Prankster. They smoke pot, they snort coke or speed, they take Ecstasy when they go to raves or rock shows and they use, or are used, by guys with a supply of roofies or other downers.

During one of my two stints as a reporter at the City News Bureau of Chicago (I got my first real journalism job there when I was nineteen; after nine months I quit and went to Mexico but returned for nine more months starting in late 1960) I lived with some fellow City News reporters in Old Town, on the Windy City's North Side. We drank a lot but mostly we smoked a lot of marijuana and listened to a lot of folk music. Until the paranoia got just too overwhelming, our dealer was a Chicago cop. His product, we believed, was dope he or other policemen had confiscated after arresting dealers who had brought the stuff up from Mexico.

Which reminds me, I had a friend a few years later who was a smuggler. He brought marijuana in bulk from the Mexican state of Michoacan across the border and sold it in California. Like many beat or hippie dope dealers, Barry, as I'll call him, was in it for the pot more than the money. Oh, he made some good money every once in a while, but he had access to the highest-quality Mexican marijuana available at the time—and he smoked up a lot of his profits. Since then, the quality of marijuana is so much better as growers have figured out how to grow strains of cannabis sativa that have much denser amounts of THC than the Mexican farmers knew about back in the 1960s.

One day Barry drove a decrepit and barely running old car packed with the illegal weed across the border into Texas. You'd be surprised how much grass can be sealed into welded sections of fenders and fuel tanks, doors, and other parts of an expendable automobile. His plan was to drive to a garage where the car would be dismantled and the dope could be driven quickly to San Francisco.

However, Barry got busted at the Rio Grande. Often, those arrests occurred because the go-betweens who dealt with growers and smugglers would notify the Mexican border guards, who'd confiscate the packaged kilos of *mota* and return it to those go-betweens. After paying those guards a bribe, the same guy would sell the same load of dope to some other American sucker hoping to make a big score.

Barry was well aware of the scheme and had taken steps to avoid arrest by the guards on the south side of the river. The American customs agents, of course, were suspicious and took the car apart and arrested my friend on the spot.

Now the story took a funny turn. The agents asked Barry where he was taking the load of smuggled pot in the rickety old car. He told them that he'd been paid a couple of hundred bucks to drive the car across the border and then west to Los Angeles, where he was to leave it in a few days in a parking lot at the beach, then walk away.

For some reason they believed him. They asked if he'd cooperate in a sting to arrest the (non-existent) people who were going to pick up the car once he'd left it at the beach. Man, of course he would! So, while some poor customs agent had to drive the crappy old stick-shift car—which was missing third gear and could only be driven in first or second—the government flew Barry to L.A., put him up in a motel until the appointed day, then told him to drive the car to the beach, leave it, and walk away. And Barry did.

When he got to the beach, Barry told me, it was a chilly winter morning. There were hardly any beachgoers and hardly any cars. Nonetheless, he said, the parking lot was dotted with obvious undercover drug agents—operating hot dog carts, picking up litter with those broom-handle sticks with nails in the end, fixing wires atop telephone poles, watching the surf from unmarked undercover cars, waiting. And, as instructed, Barry parked the car from Mexico, walked over to the Pacific Coast Highway and hitchhiked north.

He didn't get any rides. Instead, a zealous sheriff's deputy who knew hitchhiking was against the law in those days, pulled over and ordered my friend to get into the squad car. Barry tried to explain that he was part of an undercover drug sting—even though, of course, it was, at rock bottom, something he'd fabricated to avoid serious drug-smuggling charges in Texas.

The deputy was not impressed. "Let's just see about that!" he said sarcastically as he made a U-turn and drove back into the parking lot, the red light atop his car spinning.

And, naturally, the hot dog vendors and the phone company workmen and the guys picking up litter converged on the deputy's car and screamed at him to get the fuck out of there, that he was ruining a big-time drug bust. It took a while, Barry later related, but finally the officer turned off his red emergency light and drove out of the parking lot. He even gave Barry a ride north to Malibu.

Meanwhile, no one showed up to pick up the old car and the marijuana. The narcs were pretty sure that the deputy sheriff had ruined their scheme. They never contacted Barry again. He was off scot-free, except that he'd lost his carload of good Mexican weed.

* * *

I once wrote in my *San Jose Mercury News* local column that I believed that all drugs should be legalized with the exception of PCP, cocaine, and methamphetamine. Coke and speed dealers should be shot, I wrote, and PCP dealers should be turned over to the mothers of PCP users for appropriate punishment.

I still agree with most of that. I believe that those three drugs are bad, or have the potential to be bad, evil, corrupt, and I have trouble saying that now I think they should be legal, too.

The one time I smoked PCP the atmosphere seemed to gel into the consistency of snot. I could understand why PCP users tend to freak out and cause mayhem if not murder when "high" on this shit. (I'm not sure anyone smokes this animal tranquilizer any more; I hope not.)

Like so many people, I've had lots of fun snorting coke and using methedrine, as we used to call the injectable form of methamphetamine. I didn't use cocaine in my psychedelic days. It wasn't as available then as it became in the mid-'70s, when users like lawyers and businesspeople and flashy guys in bars started giving it affectionate and funny names like Peruvian marching powder or the diet of the stars.

Like Neal Cassady, although without his staying power, I swallowed hundreds, thousands, of amphetamine pills: Benzadrine, Dexadrine, Dexamyl, those speed-soaked wads of cotton in the old, now long-forgotten Benzadrine inhalers, Obitrol. Man, there were so many legitimate brands of diet pills and stimulants floating around that the pharmaceutical companies must have told their shareholders that the whole world was trying to stay awake and shed pounds. And for a while, in my case, anyway, it was so easy to find ampules of injectable methedrine in the mid- to late-1960s that every now and then I could stay high for days before crashing wherever I happened to find myself.

However, and this is important, I believe, I don't have an addictive personality. As I did at later times in my life with cigarette-smoking and serious drinking, I decided to more-or-less call it quits. Some of my friends didn't because they couldn't. Some stopped eating, which meant lack of nourishment. Plus the long speed runs meant no sleep. That combination turned those friends into meth zombies. And, as most of my beatnik and acid-head and long-haired friends did, I kicked speed freaks out of my home. Speed was so important to them that it overwhelmed their normal senses of decency, and even beatniks have senses of decency. A visit from someone shooting speed meant just one thing. That person was there to borrow money or to steal something of value they could sell for money to buy methedrine.

I do know people who turned supposedly controllable cocaine use into terrible habits. One friend spent a fortune freebasing, or smoking an extract of coke similar to crack. Others turned to crack, which is no doubt cheaper but still takes everything a user has.

So to me, the karma and effects of those three drugs—coke, meth, and PCP—are *so* awful that I would still toy with the idea that dealers should be shot—except that I'm a Buddhist and shooting dealers would be against the rules.

The word "dope," you know, is an ironic term, sort of a celebratory pejorative, used by pot smokers, mainly, the way "queer" has come back into use by gay men and women and "nigger" is used by some black men and women talking to each other. It was originally termed "dope" to describe what society thought a drug-user was. It's clearly a bit of pot humor to name the drug, which got someone high enough to understand the irony of it, dope. Funny!

The spectrum of psychedelic drugs that includes LSD, psilocybin, peyote, mescaline, MDMA, ayahuasca, "magic" or amanita muscaria mushrooms, and DET, as well as various tweaked analogs and an unknown number of flora and even fauna (such as toad slime) all open those "Doors of Perception" made famous by the late Aldous Huxley. For me, and many other people I know, the most-intense high comes from a substance so common it's almost something you'd find around the house, as they used to say on a radio quiz program. Actually, you'd find it around your dentist's office: nitrous oxide, *aka* laughing gas, used to sedate patients who are having ungodly and painful work done in their mouths. Actually, nitrous doesn't sedate you at all. It just puts your mind in another place. And, if you breathe enough of it (which you can't do in the dentist's chair because there's too much oxygen mixed in) you'll get as high as it's possible to get. Suddenly it *will* all make sense and by "it" I mean *everything*.

That high, unfortunately, only lasts for an instant, just the fraction of an instant. And then you'll spend the rest of your gas-breathing session trying to get back to that place where you're higher than you've *ever* been. Kesey compared it to ringing a bell. You ring the bell, you see everything—God, the universe, the meaning of life—then you try to ring it again and you just can't quite get there.

You used to be able to pick up a tank or two of nitrous oxide from businesses that stocked various gases for industrial use. I don't think that's so easy any more. Back when it was, however, Zonker used to keep a tank in the back seat of his car and have the hose up near his face so he could suck some gas whenever he had a yen for it. He even held onto that rubber hose, and the metal tank to which it was attached, when he crashed his convertible in Los Gatos back in, oh, 1968 or so, and was thrown out of the car on impact. The tank landed next to him and the ambulance attendants had to disconnect his hand from the rubber breathing tube.

The second-highest drug I've used is DMT. I've smoked it and had it injected into the muscles of my butt (by a sweet woman and Prankster associate we all called Sweet Generous). There were two problems with DMT. The high lasted only twenty to thirty minutes. Also, several people who joined me in smoking DMT noticed lizards or dragons or mean-looking little troll-like critters running toward them from across the room during their twenty-minute highs. Really! Two fellow-DMT smokers saw ugly little dwarves, holding knives in a threatening manner, coming at them. Others saw the lizard-like creatures. In every case, the obviously bad hallucinatory creatures came even closer with the next hit of a DMT-laced joint, close enough to stand at the feet of and to glare up at the smokers, the trolls with their daggers at the ready. None of those people wanted a third hit.

I never saw stuff like that on any psychedelic substance. I saw exaggerations of perspective, I saw the whole universe in a freckle, I saw that my fingers had fingers that had fingers, and boy, were they tiny. Several times I lay on the ground stoned, looking up into the night sky, watching the outlines of space ships of incredibly huge dimensions soaring across the heavens, undulating like gigantic but perfectly transparent jellyfish, so I could see the distant stars through them.

I saw everything, at least, everything I wanted to see—and more, so much more.

Yes, I think drugs should be legalized. For one thing, anybody who wants any drug at all can find it anyway with little or no sweat. Anywhere. Even in your little hometown. And secondly, of course, addicts would be able to satisfy their needs without having to steal your color TV or your mom's jewelry to pay for it. And that color television for which you paid several hundred bucks will get the hype, as we used to call junkies who used hypodermics to inject their stuff, no more than a few hour's worth of heroin or whatever he or she uses to get straight, to feel normal. (And maybe someone will invent a way to put some vitamins into methamphetamine and bottles of cheap wine and cheap vodka. And maybe, as the author of a book I read while living on the beach in Acapulco in 1960 suggested, the booze companies and drug dealers could prolong their customers' lives that way so they could continue to reap profits instead of having a regular die-off of under-nourished, unhealthy winos and addicts.)

Of course, if illegal drugs were made legal there would be no reason for those notorious Mexican drug cartels that control smuggling into the U.S. So far, almost fifty-thousand Mexicans, many gang members but many innocent bystanders, have been killed over the past six years, they say. They died for one reason. The incredible profits to be made when a dollar's worth of drugs sells for ten or twenty or one hundred times that much in the United States because it is only available illegally.

Mainly, though, I believe that drug-users—who are going to use whatever it is they want whether it's legal or not—should have the luxury of dancing to the music or watching the movements in the night sky or seeing God in the leaf of a fern without also having to worry that a narc might come busting in.

Sure, I think it should be illegal to dose another person without that person's permission. And it should be a major crime to give a woman or girl or anybody a soporific drug in order to commit rape. Maybe it should be illegal to drive under the influence of some drugs—although I've noticed that driving while high on acid was like driving a car in one of those old movies where William Powell, say, and Myrna Loy would be in the front seat and we could look past them out the rear window and see that everybody was driving at a "normal" speed and that William and Myrna were, too.

But I don't think driving occurs to most people high on psychedelic drugs. The few times I did drive after taking LSD, no matter how much I stepped on the accelerator, no matter what the speedometer read, I felt I was driving at a "normal" speed. The rest of the universe inside the car and out was crazy, chaotic, psychedelic, whack-a-doo. Looking out through the windshield, my speed felt just dandy. It felt normal. I didn't feel at all that the car was in any way out of control.

A friend told me he felt the same way when he was driving and knew that the ride was a little bumpy. He stopped and looked at the road to see if it was pitted with chuckholes. It wasn't.

But all four tires were flat.

IV.

ON THE ROAD, OFF THE ROAD

EXISTENCIALISTA

The single, best stroke of dumb luck in my young life was my decision to take my two favorite records with me when I left Chicago for Mexico City in January 1960. I still would have had an enjoyable half-year in Mexico without them, no doubt, but once word circulated around some expatriate and artistic circles that I had the pair of LPs, I was invited to parties, fiestas, small gatherings, informal dinner parties, and even to a cocktail party of pot-smoking diplomats where the short and pushy ambassador from Uruguay insisted that I looked like "a blond Adonis" and that I should immediately accompany him back to the embassy.

I declined.

In retrospect, those two records remain among the best jazz recordings of all time: Cannonball Adderley's *Somethin' Else*, featuring Miles Davis in one of his greatest performances, and Sonny Stitt's *Only the Blues*.

Some of the artists, beatniks, and bohos I met in Mexico City had heard one or both of the records but most of them hadn't and they really, really wanted to. Be-bop was hot, or cool, and I had the best of it. When I'd get invited over to someone's house for lunch or dinner or a party the invitation inevitably included the question, "By the way, Lee, could you bring those Miles and Sonny Stitt sides?" Of course I could.

I'd bump into some of the same American and European ex-pats at all of those get-togethers. No matter where it was or what kind of party it might be, I could always count on seeing self-confessed British remittance man, Colin, always prompt, always in the same shabby tweed jacket and tie, always in need of a shower; three Danes, two men and a woman, known, of course, as "the Great Danes," who lived and loved one another in the same apartment and, in fact, in the same bed; a black fugitive from a California murder charge who had a local jazz radio show and who'd played a tiger-skin-wearing African native in some Tarzan films that had been shot in the '40s and '50s in tropical jungles on Mexico's Pacific coast; photographer Bob Gordon, who rented a room in a downtown Mexico City whorehouse and whom I'd meet again many years later, when I was at *Hustler* magazine and he was a porn video director; and many more, most of whom I can't recall any more than they would remember me more than a half-century after twenty-year-old skinny, "blond Adonis" Lee brought his jazz LPs to Mexico City.

* * *

It was at a 1959 Christmas party that my roommate Ron Soble and I threw in our North Side Chicago coach house that I decided to quit City News Bureau and head south to Mexico. Besides Ron and me, there were a handful of our City News compatriots at the party and one, Bill Britt, was leaving for Mexico City after the holidays. I told him I'd meet him there and, like we do sometimes when we're considering a major life change, I committed myself to a Mexican adventure by telling everyone at the party, including other City News reporters, about my sudden new plan to quit and head south of the border. I probably referred to my desire to share Jack Kerouac's enthusiasm in *On The Road* when he wrote that he and Neal Cassady "had finally found the magic land at the end of the road and we never dreamed the extent of the magic." After nine months at City News I wanted some of that magic.

Following a cheap flight and a taxi ride I found myself, with no Spanish other than the ability to ask for a glass of water, looking for a room to rent in a neighborhood not far from two of Mexico City's main drags, Avenida de los Insurgentes and the Paseo de la Reforma. When I saw a sign that I correctly interpreted as Room for Rent near the intersection of Yucatan and Chiapas avenues, I felt that the magic had kicked in. In bios accompanying published copies of his ground-breaking poem *Howl*, Allen Ginsberg had pointed to "Satori in Harlem, Yucatan and Chiapas 1954"—and here was my first Mexico City digs—at

Yucatan and Chiapas, for fifty pesos, four dollars, a week. I moved right in. No Satori but everything was good otherwise.

I saw my Chicago friend Bill a couple of times and through him eventually rented a room from an American couple getting by, as so many gringos in Mexico City did in those days, on veteran's benefits and the G.I. Bill. They lived out toward the National University in a neighborhood called Colonia Florida. The husband, a Chicano, was an artist, an "action painter," and a grad student at the university. His wife, whom I'll call Sara, eight years older than I, was a beautiful woman, a Texan and the mother of their five-year-old autistic son, Marco.

They rented the room above their garage to a New Yorker named Al, from Far Rockaway, near Coney Island. Al was a student at the National University. For a while I enrolled in some classes taught in English on the magnificent campus, studying Spanish and some Mexican history. The highlight of that educational experience was the occasional attempt by student radicals to dynamite the huge statue of former Mexican President Miguel Aleman, who was to the young university students a symbol of corruption and betrayal of the revolutions of Emiliano Zapata, Pascual Orozco, and Francisco Villa and of the late president, Lazaro Cardenas. Every few days our classes would be disrupted by yet another unsuccessful attempt to blast the Aleman statue, located handily near the English-language classrooms, to smithereens. While the student dynamiters could never even chip a dent into the huge statue, I knew my old Olympic National Park trail crew buddy Tony Jacobsen would've been able to knock it on its concrete ass.

* * *

Those months in Mexico City, and in Valle de Bravo, a village a couple of hours west of the capital city, were among the happiest of my life. I was on my own, forced by circumstance to learn a new and beautiful language and to understand customs and beliefs completely unlike those I'd left behind in *El Norte*. I was familiarizing myself with an historic and cosmopolitan city, a metropolis where I never felt any fear and where the people I met and even those I passed on the street seemed friendly, kind, and generous. I learned from a passing woman who pointed at me and smiled, then turned to her friend, that a *norteamericano* with longish blond hair, a scraggly beard, no socks, and sort of shabby clothes was not, in Spanish, called a beatnik. "*Mira*," she said to her companion, "*mira la existencialista!*" "See the existentialist!"

The atmosphere in the huge city was so clear in 1960 that I could see a thousand times more stars from the seven-thousand, two-hundred-foot-high Valley of Mexico than I'd ever seen—and, shocking as it must seem to tourists and even to residents today, given that Ciudad de Mexico is now said to have some of the worst smog anywhere, Carlos Fuentes had just published a fine novel about the city, titled, in English, *Where The Air Is Clear*.

And I was head over heels in love, and in what certainly was also, at the very least, the most-severe case of lust I'd experienced so far in life. My landlady, at twenty-eight, was old enough to be, for my twenty-year-old self, the "older woman" that some men fantasize about. She was beautiful in every way and I could hardly believe it when I felt her returning my surreptitious glances when her husband was around. I felt comfortable talking with him about murals and mobiles and models but I could hardly wait, each weekday, for him to head off to class.

When he was at school I often hung around the house reading or listening to music, hoping that Sara would walk through the room and ask me to run an errand or to help with something that needed fixing or just to sit and talk over cups of Nescafe. I was so fascinated by her that I quit attending class at the university. And, when she crawled into my sleeping bag one morning, we began what was my first real love affair.

I learned to dissemble, to prevaricate, to feign interest in household table-talk at dinnertime or when all four of us living there would sit around evenings smoking and drinking or when we'd visit friends together or take day trips to explore

Chapultepec Castle and other sights. I was obsessed with looking at her and touching her and with waiting for her husband to leave the room so I might touch her breast or so she might reach for a quick feel of my cock through my jeans. I waited through the night for him to go to school the next morning so she and I could fall quickly into bed, beneath my sleeping bag on my narrow mattress in the "servant's quarters," a little room off the kitchen, or on the sofa in the living room or under the dining-room table or anyplace else where we might have privacy for even a minute. Once, when I needed to take a bus to the border to renew my tourist's visa, I managed to meet her in a tiny Texas town where she was visiting her sister. I even scraped together enough money to rent a cheap motel room for a night, a whole night spent making love with her.

I'd never felt anything so deeply, so passionately. My previous relationships, if I could even remember any, seemed puerile and as foreign to my new love as the meaningless headlines on front pages of English-language newspapers I'd occasionally see on the news rack at Sanborn's downtown. Other flings suddenly seemed insignificant in every way, as irrelevant to me as neckties or life insurance in this Latin nation of *indios* and *mestizos* who spoke an exotic language and who still recognized the old gods who still live in the incredibly beautiful Valley of Mexico.

I had never even dreamed of the extent of the magnificent magic—the magic of Mexico, the magic of love.

* * *

Friends Tom and Jerry, two gay men who found acceptance and peace in the quiet village of Valle de Bravo, had a Ford Foundation grant to educate Indian children who could neither read nor write Spanish. They had turned an old *casa* that had been a thread factory in the nineteenth century into the *Casa de Alfabetizacion,* a House of Literacy. They taught Spanish to boys and girls who spoke only a dialect of *nahuatl*, the language of the Aztecs who had once included what was now Valle de Bravo in their massive empire. Because the children didn't speak Spanish they couldn't attend school in the village. Therefore, they were more or less condemned to a life of poverty even below that of the poor but Spanish-speaking residents of the town and surrounding hills.

One day some sociology students from the National University came to Valle de Bravo en route to San Simon de la Laguna, a tiny Indian village in some nearby mountains. The five or six university students wanted to do some sort of study of life in the remote town and to help with any projects, such as developing in water and plumbing, if necessary, and to find similar good works they might do. They'd arranged with Tom and Jerry to take one of the youngsters from their program, a boy raised in San Simon de la Laguna, as a guide and they asked if I wanted to join them.

We drove their Jeeps up some rough trails and boulder-strewn canyons before we arrived in San Simon. There we found a church, an abandoned schoolhouse (with a photo on the wall of Mexican hero Benito Juarez) and a few huts beside a lake that seemed to double as a rice paddy. There were no people. The seemingly abandoned little village came to mind later that year in Chicago, when I saw a similar scene in the film, *The Magnificent Seven*, a town with no visible residents.

The boy who guided us cross-country to this village that was his home shouted in *nahuatl*. Suddenly, almost as in a trick performed by an illusionist, and much like it happened in *The Magnificent Seven*, the dusty little town was filled with people. They appeared as if by some pre-Columbian magic, some off in the distance, some standing right next to us. They seemed literally to have materialized from nowhere.

Our young guide, who had learned some Spanish down in Valle de Bravo, introduced us to the village headman and to his own parents. My *español* wasn't sufficient to understand the whole conversation, but I knew enough to understand that we were free to wander about and ask questions and share some tortillas if we wished. To me the highlight of an afternoon in San Simon was the small seventeenth-century church, empty by that time of pews and most furnishings usually found in Catholic places of worship. It was clear, however, that the church was still in use, although whether for Christian worship I couldn't be certain. There were brightly colored paper streamers and strips of cloth hanging from the rafters. Offerings of food and flowers and water were placed in front of the few religious statues on display, but the colorful banners and the offerings seemed less reminiscent of my boyhood Catholicism and more like decorations from a children's birthday party—or, as I've learned in subsequent years, like the altars and burial places of indigenous people throughout the world.

I've come to understand that those streamers and plates of fruit and bowls of water were similar to offerings and icons one might find on a hippie bus or pad, or at an ancient Hawaiian *heiau* or altar, or on a Native American grave such as the one I visited on a reservation near Mount Hood. I visited that Oregon reservation with a girlfriend whose mother was a tribal elder and whose grandfather was buried in the small cemetery where we stopped to leave some trinket on his burial mound.

Several months later I bumped into one of those university students in Mexico City. He and his comrades had tried to return to San Simon de la Laguna recently but had been turned back by rock-throwing villagers. It seemed that some terrible disease—he thought it might have been smallpox—had struck San Simon after our visit and the village residents blamed the students, rightly or wrongly, for bringing the plague to their community.

* * *

Even though I was twenty years old and as ready to fuck at the drop of a … hat as I'd ever be, there were times when Sara, the woman I loved, or even I, had other things to do. I did get around to art and historical museums and to walls and staircases and alcoves brightened by Mexico's great muralists Rivera, Orozco, and Siqueiros, and to ancient sites just then being uncovered by archeologists. Several times, usually alone, I wandered through Chapultepec Castle, originally home to an emperor and his empress, Maximilian and Carlota, later a military academy where six brave students, *Los Niños Heros,* threw themselves over the parapets to their deaths as the invading American troops stormed the buildings in the Mexican-American War of 1847. Nighttime was great for wandering among centuries'-old buildings in the central part of the city or hanging out with my new friend Eric List, a university student and son of German List, a revered poet of the revolution..

One day my housemate Al and I took his car down to Acapulco, where we rented a *palapa* on the beach. We swam and loafed on the sand during the day, eating fresh fish grilled by the same guy who kept filling our goblets with gin and grapefruit juice, food and drink being covered by our twenty pesos, or a dollar-sixty, daily rent. By night we usually headed up to Rio Rita, a scruffy red-light district, for dancing and more. We'd learned there were three whorehouse districts in Acapulco: one was nice, one was the tawdry Rio Rita, and one was even sleazier. I became familiar with Rio Rita because, oddly, we were renting our hut and spending our days and nights on what we later learned was the resort city's gay beach. It happened to be the off-season for gay tourists. We learned all of this when we woke up after spending our first night sleeping under our thatched roof: there were topless women actually "frolicking" in the surf. We learned they didn't mind having men watch their morning saltwater ablutions because men on the beach were generally homosexuals. When Al and I convinced them that we were not *los otros,* the others, as gay men were sometimes known, they adopted an "Oh, well," attitude and not only kept up their frolicking but returned for more of it the next morning. They also invited us up to Rio Rita, where we spent the next few evenings frolicking ourselves.

In this whorehouse part of town we danced and made new friends and could have, had we so wished, visited the short-time hotels located between the seamy bar-dance halls along the rutted mud street that was the Broadway, the Main Street, of Rio Rita. I was impressed at the efficiency of one of those dance hall-pickup bars when I noticed that right in the middle of the dance floor was a urinal so that potential customers who needed to pee but didn't want to leave their chosen partners just to go to the men's room didn't have to stop dancing and flirting and negotiating for more than the minimal amount of time necessary for relieving one's self.

* * *

One afternoon my landlord left school early, meaning that he came home early, and meaning that he found his wife and me in bed. Sara and I both feared for our lives, at least for an instant. But he didn't blow up, he didn't act macho, he merely said, "I am very disappointed in both of you."

I decided it was time to head north, back to the states.

I'LL TAKE MANHATTAN

I hitchhiked from Chicago to New York just after Christmas, 1960, to see a young woman I'd met several months earlier on a quick, Benzadrine-fueled round-trip drive up from, and back to, Mexico City. She and I had done nothing more than make goo-goo eyes at one another on that brief visit to New York and I thought it would be great fun to hitchhike from Chicago to see her.

I'd spent the pre-Christmas shopping season staying with my folks and working in a department store selling men's shoes. We also sold girls' and women's ice skates and, being the Chicago suburbs, where winters get *really* cold and where they freeze the village parks so locals can skate whenever they want, we sold a lot of ice skates to a lot of girls.

We also sold a lot of men's slippers for the upcoming Christmas holiday. These days most slippers are sold in four sizes, S, M, L, and XL; in 1960 many were sold by shoe size. And lots of wives and mothers and daughters came to the men's shoe department to buy for their husbands, boyfriends, sons, brothers, or fathers. When they'd say their husband wore, let's say, a size nine shoe and asked what size slipper he'd take, I always sold them a size twelve or a size six or some other slipper that would be an obvious misfit once hubby had torn off the Christmas wrapping. I sold hundreds of slippers, all, or most of them either too big or too small. That's why, when the head of the men's haberdashery department told me they wanted to keep me on after the Yuletide holiday and would pay me a larger salary to manage the men's shoe department I declined, telling them Christmas Eve would definitely be my final day on the job. I was not going to deal with scores of angry men demanding refunds. In fact, I was going to get out of town.

Since we sold all the ice skates available in the store, I had many young women and girls as customers, always with their mothers, usually wearing skirts or dresses. I would measure the girls' feet and go behind that curtain (there is *always* a curtain at the entrance to a shoe department's stock room) to find the appropriate pair of white ice skates. Invariably, as soon as I was behind the curtain, I'd hear a slapping sound, the sound of a mother's hand smacking a daughter's knee. Then I'd hear the mother's angry whisper:

"Keep your knees together!"

So *that's* how that bit of tribal information is passed from mother to daughter down through the generations.

Well, it turned out, of course, that hitchhiking through the freezing blizzards of northern Indiana, Ohio, and Pennsylvania was not fun. There were plenty of traffic—families going to and from Grandma's place for Christmas and weary truck drivers I'd ask for rides at gas stations and restaurants along the frozen turnpikes. Tired, hungry, and anxious to meet the woman I thought might just be my next honey, I eventually thumbed my way to New Jersey late at night and, sick of hitchhiking in the snow and sleet, took a commuter train the rest of the way into New York City, arriving, ultimately, at Penn Station.

My lady friend drove in from the apartment she shared with her parents out on Eastern Parkway in Brooklyn. They lived in a neighborhood of their fellow Calypso-speaking immigrants from the Caribbean islands. While she spoke lovely, private-school English, her parents spoke in a Barbados accent that was so thick I could only catch about every fourth word.

She dropped me off with her friend, a painter named Sal, who had a studio in the garment district somewhere around 28th Street and Seventh Avenue, I soon found my own place in an East 11th Street combination beatnik hive, group home, and flophouse. I rented a crummy room, a fifth-floor walkup, with no functioning toilet anywhere above the second floor and no hot water anywhere in the building. I pissed into the sink, tossed trash out the window into an interior building well that served as a garbage dump and compost heap, and ate so little I needed actual toilets only every other day. It cost fifteen dollars a week.

To make a longer story as short as it should be, we had sex, my dark-skinned Caribbean island maiden and I. She didn't much care for it. I guess I enjoyed the sex, not having had all that much variety of sexual partners by that time—or at least, not enough to be blasé. It *was* a bit of a downer when, after we'd finished, she asked, in her fine British accent, "You mean that's all there is to it?"

One night a week or so after moving to East 11th Street and disappointing my friend from Barbados I turned on the light in the middle of the night when I felt that something was wrong, really wrong. I was right: There was something wrong. Every horizontal surface in the room, including the bed and including my face, was covered with cockroaches. The plentitude of bugs was amazing. Disgusting, but amazing nevertheless.

I moved out instantly, at about 3 a.m. All of my belongings fit in my pockets.

I quickly found a better place to live in what was then Spanish Harlem, on West 96th Street between Amsterdam Avenue and Broadway. I paid thirty-five dollars a month for the room in an apartment where the tenant of record rented out rooms, even the dining room, to guys like me, without much money. He himself lived in the living room, where he spent much of the day masturbating before going down to Times Square to compete in matches in a chess club filled with shabby old men who, it turned out, were Russian masters and even, in one case, a grandmaster.

My fellow renters were a Belgian welfare worker who hated poor people and an Indian businessman who lived in the dining room and fasted all day every Thursday but began preparing his 12:01 a.m. Friday feast at about 11:00 every Thursday night, filling the apartment with the smells of curry. Generally, when I headed to the kitchen each morning to boil water for coffee, Badrash was standing in his dining room digs, eyes closed and hands clasped prayerfully, paying homage to a multi-armed statue of Shiva on his chest of drawers.

I kept a black cat named Lumumba but had to give him away when, several months later, I left to return to Mexico City.

I worked at a Village bookshop, the Paperbook Gallery, on Third Avenue just where it begins at St. Mark's Place, across from Cooper Union and where the Bowery turned into Third. Marty Geisler, the store owner, also had a small press going where he published screeds by Ted Joans, who had parlayed his position as one of the few black beat poets into a constant jamboree of getting laid, and Seymour Krim, a serious dude whose *Visions of a Near-Sighted Cannoneer* was one of our imprints. Both writers hung around the store, as did a variety of other local poets and novelists.

My favorite places to go after (or before) work included an artists' hangout, where drunken painters would express their feelings about one another's artistic output with a lot of swearing and occasional fisticuffs, and two bars where it felt good rubbing shoulders with other writers (who probably felt good, as well, rubbing shoulders with other writers) the Cedar Tavern and the Whitehorse Tavern.

Life at the Paperbook Gallery was easy, but the pay was low. I continued to count my finances in terms of the wieners sold at the kosher butcher shop on Amsterdam Avenue, around the corner from my rented room. The franks were seven cents apiece. So my fifteen-cent subway fare to work and the fifteen-cent return trip amounted, the way I was figuring it, to four-and-two-sevenths hotdogs just for transportation each workday. I ate the wieners raw and saved the rest of my income for beer.

My high school friend Wendy Griffin lived in Greenwich Village a few blocks from the bookshop, on Sullivan Street. When her pal Penny Brown showed up for a weekend visit from college in Pennsylvania, I fell head-over-heels in love-again. I had loved a woman in Mexico. But I had never felt like I was walking on clouds, never been so transfixed by a woman, and she by me, it seemed, that we couldn't go for more than a minute or two without having to touch and kiss and feel and rub against one another.

Wendy wrote poetry that her boyfriend, an actor known as Steve Phillips but who was really named Phil Stevenson, would read at touristy beatnik bars in basements along Bleecker and McDougall streets. Steve also made money by dealing in "keys," that is, sub-rental agreements for rent-controlled apartments that were so valuable, even then, in 1961, that potential tenants would cough up five-hundred dollars just to get the key and move in.

The weekend Penny and I met we not only fell in love, we participated in what turned out to be one of the first major sociopolitical events of what we have come to think of as The Sixties—the Washington Square folk music demonstrations.

The sItalian old-timers who'd lived in and around Greenwich Village for decades, and who had barely reached some accommodation with the bohemians who frequented their neighborhood, were down on folk music because the guitar-strummers and troubadours who gathered in Washington Square attracted beatniks and, even worse, *Negroes!*

In late winter of 1961, folk music was *the* thing in Greenwich Village. Reedy-voiced devotees of Cisco Houston and Woody Guthrie were everywhere. I was lucky, and I even knew it at the time, to hear Cisco Houston and then-unknown Bobby Dylan at Gerdes Folk City, not all that far from Washington Square. And I was lucky enough to fall for the crystal-clear voice of Joan Baez, who was just gaining celebrity in the neighborhood.

The so-called folk music (Beatnik) riots of 1961 began when city politicians called in the cops, who told the Washington Square musicians to move on. Folk-music fans swarmed in support, filling the park every weekend. And one weekend the proverbial "all hell broke loose" when a squad of mounted policemen trotted in, swinging nightsticks and smacking heads. Hundreds of young folkies and supporters and skylarking beatniks, marched. And sure, I loved folk music, but I was completely smitten by Penny Brown so I was only peripherally concerned about the plight of the pluckers, and strummers, and singers. Guitars, banjos, and unusual antique instruments played rousing tunes about the bastards who own coal mines and factories and, we extrapolated, city parks. We *were* the downtrodden coal-miners, the underpaid, overworked lumberjacks, the serfs driven into lives of banditry by heartless landowners. We were *The People!*

Of course, they were the cops and they were on horseback and they had the billy-clubs.

Ugly incidents abounded. Wendy, who was arrested for interfering with a police officer as she was trying to avoid getting stomped on by his horse, had her picture on the front page of one of the tabloids. It was either the *Post* or the *Mirror* or the *Daily News*. The photo showed her getting slugged by a uniformed cop. Penny and I bailed her out down at the Tombs. Many other musicians and supporters were taken to hospitals for treatment of their injuries or booked into jail for the night.

Many of us who didn't get busted found relief from the nightstick-brandishing cops when the pastor of an Episcopalian church on the south side of the park opened his doors and gave us sanctuary. After we were inside, the cleric insisted to the cops that we were in a safe haven under British and American common law. This baffled the police long enough for them to get bored and leave.

About a year later, in the very first edition of what turned out to be an unsuccessful attempt by Dow Jones to publish a weekly newspaper called the *National Observer*, there was a two-page photo spread about young people in America. There was a lovely portrait of Penny Brown and me, apparently taken by a photographer who was covering the 1961 folk music protests. It had this caption beneath it: "'What would youth be without love?' –Lord Byron."

Penny became the first woman to break my heart, but not until later in the spring after we thumbed our way cross-country and down to Mexico City.

That trip was remarkable mostly for an unbearable day and awful night spent in the hellishly hot cab of a diesel tractor-trailer truck parked in the foul-smelling stockyard area of St. Louis. It was also remarkable for the post-midnight argument I had with the driver of that truck. That debate happened hundreds of miles from St. Louis, deep in the middle of rainy Oklahoma. The trucker had determined that since we were beatniks we'd have no problem accommodating his desire to screw Penny right then and there.

This guy was a lot bigger than I. In 1961 I was a tall, skinny twenty-one-year-old without much skill in fighting other than bar brawls, where you can hit anyone at any time and scram when you want to. Of course, I was frightened but ready to defend Penny's honor, even if it meant that I was going to be pummeled and we were going to be tossed out in the rain at two in the morning in the middle of Oklahoma.

I finally convinced the trucker that he was a reasonable man, which, of course, he was not, and that it was unreasonable to kick us out just because Penny didn't want to fuck him.

He agreed that he was a reasonable person. But he didn't say another word as he drove us to the border between Texas and Mexico. There, he opened the back door of his rig, grabbed our two suitcases and tossed them on the ground. We said thanks, but he got back in the cab of the truck and drove away.

We took a bus from the border to Mexico City, where we met up with my former housemate, Al. Actually, Penny hooked up with him more than I did. A lot more. Which is how she became the first, but certainly not the last, woman to break my heart.

WHEN I WAS A MAILMAN

My brother Dean worked as a part-time mailman for several years before I donned the official uniform of the United States Post Office. This was my first post-Acid Test job.

Dean wasn't an actual government employee. Rather, he was the Assistant Asshole on the rural route where we each lived, about a half-mile apart, in Zayante, a dark and, in those days, sparsely populated redwood canyon in the Santa Cruz Mountains. The regular rural route delivery guy had a contract to pick up the mail down at the Post Office in the town of Felton, then deliver it in his old car up and down several mountainous roads in Zayante. His route also included nearby Lompico, another dark redwood canyon where the few residents, mostly bikers, drug dealers, and fugitives (not that the three were mutually exclusive) had as their community leader a fellow known as Touchy the Clown.

The regular mailman had painful hemorrhoids, a condition aggravated by the way he stretched his body across the front seat of his 1948 Chevrolet as he delivered the mail. He kept his left foot on the gas or on the brake or, when he shifted, on the clutch, and his left hand on the steering wheel or the stick shift while he leaned out the right-front window to deliver the letters and bills to the rural mailboxes scattered along the twisting rural roads. I could see how this might aggravate his hemmies.

Every few weeks he would honk his horn in front of my house, then shout to me, when I showed up at the front door, that he wanted Dean to sub for him for the next few days.

"Tell your brother my asshole is acting up," he would yell, noting that his excruciating rectal pain could only be alleviated by a few days away from the front seat of his old Chevy.

So I'd call Dean and tell him he was needed as assistant asshole on the Zayante-Lompico route for the next few days.

My brief postal career began when my wife Space Daisy and I ran out of money. It seems we'd spent what we had on a profligate life as newlywed boozers, dopers, and partiers.

Deciding that I had to go to work, I first looked for a newspaper-reporting job but there was none available within driving distance. So I headed down to the Santa Cruz Post Office and applied for employment as what was officially known as a "letter carrier."

In those days, prospective postal employees took a one-hundred-question government civil service test. I passed and joined a staff of mailmen and clerks who, for the most part, had passed their tests because veterans got a five-point bump on the civil service exam and wounded vets (in those years mostly from Korea, although some servicemen were starting to return from Vietnam) got another five points on their test results. The remaining mailmen, including myself, got by with no veterans' boosts but by the sheer skill it took to correctly answer multiple choice questions about as hard as those asked on TV by quizmaster Groucho Marx on *You Bet Your Life!* Questions like, "Who is buried in Grant's Tomb?"

(When I applied for an Associate Press job in Seattle in 1963 I took a battery of similar, but much more difficult, and timed, tests. When I finished the first page I realized quickly that the answers to the multiple-choice questions on page two were the same as on the previous page. The answer to the first question on each page was, for instance, B—and on the second question, D. I checked page three and it was the same situation. Ditto for the fourth and final page. I made sure I had all the answers right on the first page, then simply marked the same multiple-choice answers on pages two, three, and four without reading any questions and then turned the papers in to the editor. He told me later that not only had I scored higher than any AP applicant in history, I'd been the only potential employee ever to actually finish the test!)

Without reporting much about my life as a mailman, let me just say that the work was incredibly easy and so boring that each and every day for the entire nine months I believed I was getting more and more stupid by the hour. After watching most of my fellow mailmen bumble about the PO, I was convinced it was a miracle that a letter, *any* letter, actually made its way from one place to another. Several times as I dumped bags of incoming mail onto a huge tray where we would then sort it by delivery routes (there were about fifty in Santa Cruz in 1968) I would find envelopes dated a month or two earlier stuck in a crease in the canvas bags. Incoming mail would be sorted by the most lackadaisical group of government employees you could imagine. And if a letter was accidentally sent to the wrong desk to be "cased" by addresses for delivery, hell, it was just tossed back on some other desk for possible re-casing the next day. *Who cares?* was the order of the day.

After a day of "training," which consisted of an old-timer showing me how he could drive his mail truck backwards through a trailer park if he were in a hurry to get home and hide his truck in his garage so he could watch a Giants baseball game on TV, I was given my first route. I was a sub, filling in, as I did for my entire nine-month postal career, for regular mailmen who were either sick, on vacation, taking a day off, or temporarily assigned elsewhere.

On my first day of work, I got to the Post Office at seven a.m. and clocked in. I cased my mail, taking time to be extra careful so things would be in the correct order for delivery. Then I signed out my truck, loaded it with mail, and left the PO at about ten in the morning. My route that day took me out to the Pleasure Point area, a somewhat seedy neighborhood where surfers and artists and hippies lived in old summer cabins. In the late 1960s they were the cheapest rentals available in the Santa Cruz area.

I delivered my mail, stopping every now and then to chew the fat with friends and acquaintances among the long-haired Pleasure Point residents. Finally, at about noon, I headed back to the Post Office.

En route I saw another mail truck and waved. That other mailman flagged me down and shouted across the street at me, "Hey, where you going?"

"Back to the shop."

"No you're not," he ordered. "You don't get back there until 3:30!"

"But…"

"No buts! 3:30! Get it?"

"Oh." And I got it. Man, if a first-day mailman can finish his route and get back to the PO three hours early, it could throw the entire American postal system spinning out of control. Take your time, I learned. Be deliberate. Stop for a leisurely lunch. Fortunately, the route included a parking area with a vista over the beach and surf of Monterey Bay, a view I saw frequently during the next several months as I ate my sandwiches and drank my Cokes and read somebody else's magazines during long and comfortable lunch breaks.

One of the routes they frequently assigned to me included a lot of trailer parks, only they were called mobile home parks and the trailers were known as coaches. At the time, before the invention of direct deposit, all Social Security checks were delivered on the same day, the third day of the month. On that day many of the older folks living in those mobile homes along my route would be standing by their mailboxes as I'd maneuver my right-hand-drive, red, white, and blue van up and down the cul de sacs of the trailer parks. Little old ladies I'd see but once a month, on the third, would each have an excuse to be standing there by the mailbox, ready to reach for their government checks to make sure no hooligans or dark-skinned gang-bangers (there was none in town at the time) beat them to their mailboxes to rip off their monthly stipends. Usually, to justify standing out by their mailboxes in their housecoats, they'd have a piece of out-going mail to hand me, perhaps a utility payment, maybe a postcard to a child or grandchild whom I knew for a fact, as their regular mailman, never returned the favor and mailed postcards to them.

There were two old women, in two different mobile home parks, whose domestic situations were quite disturbing. Neither had an actual roommate in their trailers but each shared their mobile home with lifelike dolls that looked from a distance like real little girls. *And they changed their life-sized dolls' clothes daily.*

I cannot tell you how spooky it is to turn into a corner in a trailer park and see a little girl standing in the picture window of a shabby but nicely maintained coach, a little girl whose waving arm never moves and whose eyes you realize, as you get close enough, never blink, never move, never focus or squint or indicate any greeting or fear or delight or ... or anything human at all. And she's wearing a neatly ironed pinafore or a little beach outfit with a sunhat, or a parka or raincoat, depending on the weather. And she just stands there, her arm frozen in that spooky wave.

One sad side to delivering mail to old folks living in trailer parks was that they died at a faster clip than the younger families in middle-class ranch-house neighborhoods. Today's Social Security check recipient was tomorrow's subject of an obituary. Many clients along my route were the surfers and hippies renting run-down beach shacks that once served as summer vacation homes for wealthy farmers from California's Central Valley. In that vast and productive farmland, in the days before air-conditioning, it got so hot in July and August that dad would stay home to supervise the family's agricultural operations while mom and the kids would spend those months in the cooler coastal climes of the Monterey Bay area. In that region, morning fog is the summer norm, keeping temperatures relatively comfortable all day long.

The longer I worked as a mailman the clearer it became that the main reason for the existence of the U.S. Post Office was *not* to efficiently deliver letters, bills, magazines, advertising flyers, and picture postcards. No, the Post Office's main function, it seemed, was to employ a few hundred thousand men and women, providing jobs to veterans, slackers, and a few hippies who might otherwise be unemployed, jobless, and on the dole.

All that changed, I suppose, when the venerable U.S. Post Office, said to be the brainchild of Benjamin Franklin, was replaced by a new, no-nonsense, semi-private, non-profit corporation, the U.S. Postal Service. This new Postal Service, it was said, would run more efficiently. And it would be free of the politics that had long seen local leaders of whatever party was in power in Washington snap up appointments as local postmasters.

The most-notable difference, though, at least to this former mailman, and to my fellow letter-carriers, was that as the new Postal Service began to shake things up, the drab blue serge uniforms with the red stripes down the pants legs were replaced by drab blue serge uniforms with blue stripes down the pants legs. Otherwise, the new uniforms were exactly the same as the old. They looked liked bus drivers' uniforms, just like the old ones did.

Who in Congress or the Postal Service management, I wondered, had an investment in the blue serge uniform business?

V.

PORNOGRAPHER

THE REALIST

Paul Krassner had been one of my literary heroes long before we became friends. I'd begun reading his satirical political publication, *The Realist*, when I was living in New York City in 1961. Paul was a pioneer of a sort of journalism that had never occurred to me. He was also, as they say, "the Father of the Alternative Press." (Paul always demands a paternity test.)

I was living in the fifth-story walkup room in Spanish Harlem and working at the Paperbook Gallery, a bookshop on the fringe of the East Village. I was making fifty-five dollars a week.

Paperbook Gallery owner Marty Geisler was a First Amendment stalwart and loved to sell books that had been officially banned, in New York or elsewhere, along with various lefty publications and beat literature, and damned near every paperback book then available. When Henry Miller's *Tropic of Cancer* was published by Grove Press, located a few blocks away in the Village, Marty put a display of that banned book in the front window, hoping to attract some blue-nosed law enforcement officers who'd be offended enough to arrest whoever sold him the book. Marty assured us that he and Grove Press would bail us out if the cops came and arrested any of us clerks. Disappointingly, no cops came and no one in Greenwich Village bought the book because everyone had already picked up a copy in Paris.

Similarly, when Marty suggested we defy an atomic bomb safety day curfew, when all New Yorkers were supposed to seek shelter in subway stations or other underground places—where, we figured, it would take one or two seconds longer for the explosion or the radioactivity to kill us—we walked out to the middle of Third Avenue and walked around defiantly, showing that we didn't believe the government's lies about the nuclear bomb. Only one cop blew his whistle at us, but sadly, for Marty, at least, none of us was arrested.

Among the periodicals we carried at the Paperback Gallery was *The Realist*. While Paul Krassner never made himself known if he ever did come into the shop that wasn't the case for other neighborhood writers of note, most of whom had books or pamphlets on the shelves of the store. The late East Village beat icon Tuli Kupferberg was a regular at the Paperback Gallery, dropping off copies of a mimeographed poetry magazine, *Birth*. Tuli is said to be the guy in Allen Ginsberg's *Howl* who jumped off a bridge and wandered away with nobody knowing about his leap. Asked about it, Tuli told an interviewer, yes, he'd jumped off the Manhattan Bridge "but nothing happened. I landed in the water and I wasn't dead. So I swam ashore, and went home, and took a bath, and went to bed. Nobody even noticed."

Alexander Trocchi, often described as a Scottish Beat Generation author and known to most of us as a stone junkie, also frequented the store. He mostly dropped by so he could steal copies of the amazing chronicle of his life as a drug addict, *Cain's Book*. My first day at the store's cash register Marty Geisler came over and pointed out a thin fellow hovering around the fiction section. "That's Alex Trocchi," he told me. "Watch and see what he does, but don't bother him."

Trocchi brought a half-dozen or so of his novels up to the racks in the front of the store, the racks where Marty displayed best-sellers, or at least, the books that sold best in Greenwich Village. Marty and I conspicuously looked the other way while Trocchi lifted a bunch of books by *The Jack Paar Show* joke writer Jack Douglas and carried them back to stack on a shelf in the fiction section. Douglas' book, very funny, was called *My Brother was an Only Child*. Trocchi then put the copies of *Cain's Book* in the rack with the other best-sellers except for the one copy he stuck under his shirt and inside the top of his pants. Then he left.

Marty told me to let Trocchi steal as many copies of his own book as he wished. He used them, Marty explained, as evidence in court cases that he was a writer and that he wrote about drug use and therefore should not be considered a criminal drug-abuser because he was getting high for research. It was a good but somehow not quite persuasive argument. Trocchi must have been arrested frequently on heroin charges because he was in the shop at least once a week to boost a book to introduce into evidence.

I continued to read *The Realist* whenever I could find a copy. And finally, on the other coast, I got to meet and eventually become friends with Paul Krassner. In fact, it wasn't too long before I was writing occasional columns for him, features we called "Fables Without Morals," much like these memoirs.

In 1969, after my years with Kesey, I found a job as a reporter for the *Register-Pajaronian*, a small but highly respected and Pulitzer Prize-winning daily paper in Watsonville, a farming community in the south end of Santa Cruz County.

Paul, meanwhile, had moved to the edge of a cliff above Monterey Bay and close to Watsonville, where he shared a house with Hassler and his wife, Paula. I was happy to have Paul and Hassler as neighbors and started to spend much of my time over at the edge of that seacliff with Paul and Hassler. For a while there also was a lovely hippie girl who was an off-duty hooker staying at the house, relaxing by the edge of the Monterey Bay. (She was one of the primary sources of the long-whispered rumors about her one-time client, she revealed, the late comedian Danny Thomas and his supposed penchant for fresh feces deposited by pretty prostitutes onto clear glass plates for his pleasure.)

One night my wife Lupe, a sweet Filipina-Latina young woman who'd been our baby-sitter when I'd previously been married to Space Daisy, went with me to some local boxing matches. Then we drove out to Paul's place. He was sitting on a couch in front of the fireplace next to John Lennon and Yoko Ono, all three with huge stoned grins on their faces. Yoko was bummed when she heard me say we'd been at "the fights" but soon began to giggle when she realized she'd just asked Paul to please "throw another brownie on the fire." Pot brownies! No wonder they were grinning.

As neighbors, more or less, in California's Pajaro Valley, Paul and I spent a lot of time together in those days.

In fact, Paul credits me with being some kind of port in a particularly rough psychic storm he had to navigate during his stay near Watsonville. One day Paul called and asked me in a very odd tone of voice if I would come over to lend him a hand with something. When I got there I could tell that Paul was in the midst of some sort of paranoid freak-out, not necessarily anything out of the ordinary in the world of psychedelic drugs, but somewhat unusual in my circle of friends. Paul was talking in a hushed voice when he told me that a woman who lived down the road had some visitors from outer space *who could read entire manuscripts just by passing their hands over the whole thing.* I suggested he get in my car and come over to my place for a rest.

As we drove along the rutted dirt road away from his house, we came upon a land-surveyor who seemed to be peering at Paul's place. He was just the sort of guy you don't want to run in to when you are paranoid. He was looking through his transit—which looks to anyone, even if you're not completely nuts with paranoia—like a telescope. And it was pointed down the property line toward Paul's cliff-side house.

We passed within a couple of feet of the surveyor, who was wearing a hard hat and a high-visibility-orange vest, as he squinted through his scope. Paul, now terrified, suspecting that I was somehow in league with the man using a scope to observe his house, turned to me and said, the fright in his voice now replaced with certainty, "Lee, I've trusted you up 'til now!"

Paul did get ... better? Is that the word? Well, he got his incredibly quick wit and his sharp sense of irony back and he stopped believing, I think, that he'd encountered some beings from another planet who could read books and manuscripts by passing their hands above them. He no longer believes, as far as I know, that I am part of a cabal with agents either from outer space or from the FBI or CIA or DEA. Paul seems normal to me, but even I have to take that with a grain of salt.

One day Paul told me Larry Flynt had hired him, at an unheard-of (for a radical bohemian alternative press editor) annual salary, to become the new publisher of *Hustler*, which then, in late

1977, was an American cultural phenomenon. *Hustler* was the country's most-pornographic "men's" magazine and Larry Flynt was ringmaster to a three-ring circus of smut.

Paul asked if I wanted to join him at Larry's smut shop, working for the newly revived *The Realist*! Of course I did. I gave notice at the Watsonville paper and headed for Los Angeles.

Larry chose Paul to replace him as publisher for two reasons:

1) Paul had edited Lenny Bruce's autobiography and the late comedian and biting social critic was one of Larry's cultural heroes for his "fuck you"—literally—attitude. In fact, Larry had named his Ohio stripper clubs and then his magazine after a Lenny Bruce dictum, "Everybody's a Hustler."

2) Larry had gone nuts. Now he calls it a manic episode. Whatever it was, the staff was shocked, to say the least, when Larry announced that he had become a born-again Christian and that he was moving the company from Columbus to Los Angeles and appointing Paul Krassner as publisher.

In late 1977, flying high at the top of his particular line of work, Larry told his editors and writers, and the world at large, that he had been converted by his close friend Ruth Carter Stapleton, sister of then-President Jimmy Carter. He announced that he would "no longer treat women like pieces of meat," that he would add a religious tone to his magazine, that he was moving LFP, Inc. to luxurious quarters on the 38th floor of a skyscraper in Century City in West Los Angeles, that he didn't need to run photos of sexy women on Hustler's cover in order to sell it.

I should note that a year or so later, as a much different Larry Flynt and I sat in the photo editing room looking at slides of a potential centerfold model, he turned to me and, with the wisdom of a smut millionaire, imparted to me one of the main truths about the publishing business. It was for me an Aha! moment:

"Lee, always put a pretty girl on the cover of your magazine."

Larry pronounced "put" in his Kentucky coal country drawl as "putt," as in golf. "Always putt a pretty girl…"

Ruth Carter Stapleton was among several famous or almost-famous people I met when Larry would show them around our offices. She was pushing Larry in his gold-plated wheelchair when they knocked and came into my office. The well-known evangelist was smiling, pleasant, acting as though the stacks of porn and the nude photos tacked to the walls were no more offensive to her than, say, charts and graphs on the wall of an insurance company home office.

I can't say the same about disgraced former-Tennessee Governor Ray Blanton when he was shown through our offices. The man who'd been forced out of office after disclosure that some of his aides had accepted cash for gubernatorial pardons of convicted criminals or for commuting prison sentences, was quite seriously interested, in an obviously prurient way, in the photos of upcoming "girl sets" tacked or taped to office walls. The randy governor, who died in 1996, also served time in prison for accepting a bribe for issuing a liquor license.

Another notorious character I wanted to get into *Hustler* was my old friend Hunter Thompson. He told me that he didn't want to write for the magazine; he had enough writing assignments to last him for years. In fact, he was working on the series he'd proposed when he'd phoned me at home, drunk and barely coherent, late one night from Churchill Downs, where he was covering the Kentucky Derby, probably for *Rolling Stone*. He'd told me the derby, with all of its drunken parties and drunken big shots and drunken floozies and drunken touts and degenerate gamblers and hard-up jockeys made for one of the greatest bummers he'd ever encountered. And he'd encountered more than a few.

"Lee," he mumbled into the phone, "I'm sitting here in the middle of one of the great bummers and it's occurred to me that there's a book to be done and I'm going to do it, *The Great Bummers of America*. Think of it: the Derby, the Indianapolis 500, the Daytona 500, the Super Bowl, the World Series, the heavyweight championship of the world."

While Hunter didn't want to write for *Hustler*, he did want us to interview him. However, as it turned out, he wanted to be paid ten-thousand dollars for the interview! I told him that Larry Flynt had recently asked me to interview Tim Leary. I told Hunter that I took Tim to lunch and that Tim had been flattered that *Hustler* wanted to interview him. I told Hunter that Tim Leary then asked to be paid five-thousand dollars for the interview and I told him that when I'd informed Larry Flynt of this demand, my boss had responded with a simple, "Fuck him." So I doubted Larry would be up for his proposed ten-thousand-dollar fee.

"What if he flew us out to Fiji and we did the interview on a veranda of a straw hut looking out over the South Pacific watching the sun set?" Hunter asked.

"Out of the question," I replied although it sounded great to me.

So, we never did interview Hunter Thompson or Tim Leary but I did help Larry and another editor, perhaps Bruce David, interview Dick Gregory. Dick was around frequently because he'd been Larry's "health and spiritual advisor" prior to the assassination attempt on *Hustler*'s publisher, and Larry credited the incessant "cleansing" enemas prescribed by the former comedian for preventing a fatal infection after the would-be assassin's bullet tore through Larry's guts. (We illustrated Larry's wound with a graphic photo of him lying in bed with a triangular section cut from the skin on his belly, where the bullet had penetrated his abdomen. We referred to the picture as "the pizza-slice photo." It did look like pepperoni and cheese).

I concluded that Dick Gregory, whom I'd once thought to be among the funniest stand-up comics, was not only not funny any more, he was nuts. I came to that deduction after he described the earth as having a hollow center. In that hollow core at the middle of our planet, so his theory went, lived little people who controlled our lives. He was nowhere near as much fun as Ruth Carter Stapleton, and she was an evangelist, for Christ's sake!

Neither was professional atheist Madalyn Murray O'Hair a barrel of laughs. Madalyn had struck both Paul Krassner and Larry Flynt as someone worth paying attention to over the years because of her stands against the non-stop creeping tendency to blend church and state in the U.S. of A. We had her in for an interview and I have never spent as dull or as unpleasant an hour as that spent listening to O'Hair rant about damned near everything. She was so unpleasant that I'd bet that a lot of atheists would have submitted to baptism just to get rid of her. She vanished into thin air many years ago and, as they say, foul play is suspected.

Larry, not a religious man at all in his younger days, had been aboard an airplane with Ruth Carter Stapleton when he was converted to Christianity. Jesus made a personal appearance to convert Larry Flynt. High above America aboard his private jet, Larry sat with the President's sister talking about Jesus. Suddenly, Larry told me quite seriously, he saw Jesus.

"There He was Lee, right there, right in front of me, talking to me. He was sitting right there where you are!"

That religious condition, by the way, lasted for only a few months. Larry's craziness, at least that particular Jesus craziness, eventually petered out at about the same time he was shot and almost killed in Georgia. Larry had no trouble reconverting to the worshiping at what *Hustler* Articles Editor Jerry Kindela referred to as "the temple of butt."

Things returned to normal. That is, *Hustler*'s covers began again to feature barely attired women, as Larry lay in a hospital recuperating from his attempted assassination and after his wife, Althea, had taken charge. Althea believed beyond all else that if something worked, there was no need to change it—and the pre-Krassner girly covers had indeed worked, making *Hustler* one of America's newsstand best-selling magazines.

Althea, a worried wife and almost a grieving widow, came back from the hospital where Larry was being treated and realized that she had to take over day-to-day operations of the Flynt magazine publishing and distribution businesses.

One of her first moves was to fire Paul Krassner and to put an end to the revival of *The Realist* as a Larry Flynt Publishing, Inc., enterprise. I was out of work, but not for long. I got a job at *Hustler*.

FLIGHTS OF FANCY: LARRY FLYNT AND LAS VEGAS

The nurse poked her hypodermic into Larry's arm as we waited for takeoff from the AiResearch private airport adjacent to Los Angeles International. We were heading to Las Vegas and Larry needed this final shot of Dilaudid and cocaine to stem the pain until we reached our hotel. He winced a bit when the nurse stuck him, then he hummed a sigh of pleasure as the drugs hit his central nervous system. The nurse, a woman who looked like she'd smoked a lot of cigarettes and seen a lot of drug addicts, placed a tiny, round Band-aid over the injection point, then began packing up her outfit. Larry peeled a couple of hundred dollar bills from a roll in his pocket and gave them to her.

"Did you know Elvis used to own this here airplane?" Larry asked me as the nurse walked up the aisle to the exit door. Sitting across the aisle from my boss I recognized that he was just boasting, not asking for a response. He continued, clearly relaxing, yet seeming also to become more alert as the opiate and the coke went about their work.

"Lee," which he pronounced "*Lay-ee*" in his backwoods Kentucky twang, "this here is the Rolls-Royce of drugs." It killed the excruciating pain that had dogged him for about a year now, since a right-wing goon with a .44-Magnum rifle, had tried to kill him outside a courthouse in Georgia.

The shooter had been enraged by a photo spread in *Hustler* featuring a black man having simulated sex with a white woman. The sex was simulated because, in the late 1970s, that avoided a lot of legal hassling by local prosecutors around the country. To avoid legal problems in Japan, where *Hustler* was also a hot item among horny men but where depiction of genitals is illegal—as anyone knows who's watched Japanese porn and seen the pixilated groins of guys and gals—Flynt Publications hired a crew of women to put blue stickers, less than an inch in diameter, over all photographic depictions of pubic hair or genitalia of either sex.

"Heh, heh," Larry cackled one day as he explained his simple solution to distributing sex magazines in Japan, "all they have to do is peel off them little blue stickers and they can see all that pussy as good as you can here." His cackle always reminded me of laughs of the "evil Dr. Sivana" in the old Captain Marvel-Shazam comic books."

Larry's would-be assassin had missed a fatal shot but the terrible pain and the loss of control of all bodily functions below his navel must have seemed at times worse than death to America's most-notorious pornographer. He now depended on the "Rolls-Royce" cocktail of a narcotic and a stimulant to keep him from nodding off while the painkiller did its work.

After the nurse left the Lockheed JetStar, Larry signaled to one of the Uzi-toting bodyguards who accompanied him night and day since the failed assassination attempt. He ordered the thug to tell Althea's sister Marsha, the LFP office hatchet-woman, to "get out there and fire that nurse. Damn, it hurt when she stuck me."

* * *

Larry speaks with the peculiar accent of residents in the hollows, or hollers, of Magoffin County, Kentucky, where, he claimed, people were so poor they were jealous of the poverty-stricken folks over in better-known Hazard County. The biggest source of income for his old neighbors back home, he insisted, was jury duty. He'd hired a motley crew of relatives for various jobs in his publishing business but mainly, I think, he was helping them make a living when they weren't needed on Magoffin County juries.

Larry loved the ramshackle cabin he'd grown up in. When he was rich—his fortune based on graphic displays of female genitalia—and had the fortitude to face down local law enforcement officers and blue-nosed prosecutors who constantly hauled him into court—he built an exact duplicate of his rustic boyhood home in the basement of his Columbus, Ohio mansion. It was authentic right down to the chicken manure on the floor and the corncobs in the "outhouse."

Larry's mansion in Columbus, where *Hustler* got its start as a full-fledged magazine, was in the exclusive Bexley neighborhood. I think he wanted to live there not so much because it tickled him to be able to afford to live among the city's well-to-do, although it did; it was more that he wanted to rub the outraged noses of his fellow Bexley residents in the fact that their new neighbor had made his fortune as a smut-peddler.

But, like so many Americans on the make, Larry and Althea eventually decided to move their operations, and their home, to Los Angeles. That's when I was hired to work for LFP.

The Flynts purchased a Bel Air mansion that previously belonged to actor Tony Curtis. Larry frequently chuckled and cackled, when he thought about his rich and famous neighbors who now had to contend with such an unsavory character living next door or down the street. He was amused that Johnny Carson lived over the back fence and would have to put up, he said, with the howling and barking of the vicious guard dogs he acquired as back-up to his posse of vicious bodyguards.

Larry felt the same way, I think, about newsstands, where *Hustler*, a big money-maker for local magazine dealers, who loved its enormous profit margin, was placed butt-cheek-to-jowl on racks next to the *Ladies Home Journal* and *Sports Afield* and other "legit" periodicals. He loved to shock people and I'm sure he enjoyed picturing the outrage of people having to reach past *Hustler* in order to buy a newsstand copy of *Time* or *Newsweek*.

* * *

As Larry lay close to death, and, honestly, we never knew from day to day whether he'd make it, Althea moved quickly on several fronts to make sure the company didn't go down the toilet.

People who owed Larry Flynt Publications money were deciding not to pay up, now that it looked like Larry might die; and creditors like the printer were demanding cash on the barrelhead.

Althea's first moves were to cut some of the more-highly paid staff, including Paul Krassner, to sell her chinchilla-lined maroon Rolls-Royce (she'd won it in a successful bet with Larry that she could concoct Sloppy Joes superior to those of his previous three wives) so she could pay the printer to put out the next issue, and to start putting those "pretty women" back on the cover. She told me she had been no fan of Paul's decision, as temporary publisher, to have covers *without* photos of nearly nude women, including one cover, for a spring edition, depicting an Easter bunny nailed to a cross.

Althea made damn sure that Larry's new-found Christianity was not going to slaughter the cash cow that made them both rich and made her the highest-paid woman executive in the country. We didn't abandon the religious theme; we merely began to make fun of it. Larry, when he came back to his senses and always eager to make a joke at his own expense, loved it.

After some grim months during which Althea hired me, feeling sorry, I guess, because I'd lost my job when she'd folded *The Realist*, *Hustler* started to get back on its feet—although Larry never did. Confined to his gold-plated wheelchair, he started to recover from his wounds but not from the nerve damage that caused the infernal pain and left his body useless below the belt.

Once during his recovery, he stood in Althea's corner office, with some help from his wife and me. He tried to take a step. He lurched forward into another standing position. It wasn't really walking, but he believed it was, that he'd just taken a step.

"*Lay-ee*," he barked in that hillbilly twang, "call Clive (one of the staff photographers) and tell him I want a picture for the magazine of me walking on water!"

Althea gave me that look that meant, "Forget it, Larry's 'confused.'"

Aware of her prowess with a Sloppy Joe, I was not surprised one day when Althea called me into her corner office on the 38th floor and told me about her plans to pen the *Althea Flynt Cookbook*. She told me, and I had hellish visions of sexual perversions beyond anything anyone had ever thought of, as she drawled on, that it was going to be about "a hundred things you can do with hamburger."

Fortunately, I never had to find out what the ninety-nine uses of hamburger were beyond fixing up some tasty Sloppy Joes. Nor, as I had begun to worry, did I have to ghostwrite a cookbook that would have certainly included more intimate uses of ground beef.

* * *

Most of the editors who came out West with the Flynts from Columbus, the Ohio capital where Larry started the magazine after publishing a newsletter for his *Hustler* go-go clubs, didn't think much of Althea. I liked her, usually, and knew she was much brighter than most of those editors believed. Street smart, that is; she had a lot of street savvy.

Those editors also hadn't thought much of Columbus, which they referred to as "The City of Seven Flat Places." I was not enamored of Ohio's capital city myself after I had to spend a week there one winter waiting to testify in lawsuit.

I admired Althea's talent for getting things done, even if she was not the creative genius her husband was. What she wanted to do was to repeat Larry's success—which was always based on his unfailing ability to do something completely different, gross, and outrageous in each new issue of *Hustler*—and which of course, was what Paul Krassner had continued to do as publisher.

Althea wanted to replicate the last issue that her husband had overseen before Krassner had been hired and before Larry had been shot. It worked. Circulation, which had lagged when none of those pretty girls were on the covers, began to rise. In fact, one month *Hustler* hit what was then its all-time circulation peak, sales of about two million copies, as I recall. I felt good about that. I had written the cover-lines touting some old black-and-white topless snapshots of a prominent celebrity. We'd bought them from a guy who specialized in nude photos of stars before they were stars. (There are *a lot* of those snapshots floating around and this guy knew how to find them.) The topless shots were from some B-grade movie this star had appeared in early in her career. The cover-line read: **"Angie Dickinson Nude Inside."** It was a bit of an exaggeration but was not untrue. Generally, though, the staple of *Hustler* cover-lines was the word "shocking," as in "Shocking expose" or "Shocking pictures" or "Shocking confession" of someone or something prominent.

Althea was a demanding boss. When she'd tell the photo chief and me that she wanted some particular model to pose "like this," she'd lie down on the carpet, spread her legs and show us *exactly* what she meant. If she said, "This girl here should have a little black ribbon around her neck," she'd remember that detail a month later when the chromes, or color photographic slides, would come back from wherever they were developed. Woe to the photo editor if the model wasn't sporting a little black ribbon around her neck.

Actually, Althea had an amazing sense of what model and what particular photographs of her constituted the perfect *Hustler* girl. I assumed that her bisexuality contributed to her ability to pick out models who shared the desired combination of the girl next door and the wanton slut down the street.

One flaw Althea could not abide in photo shoots was dirty feet on the models. When she got a new set of chromes from the developer, the first thing Althea looked at was soles of the woman's feet. If they were dirty at all they were tossed (from *Hustler*, but used in some offshoots we published) and the photographer and probably the makeup artist were reprimanded or fired. After all, it was the photographer's responsibility, along with the studio crew, to make sure the models met Althea's standards.

Remembering her frequent offhand demands was one of two reasons I always carried a notebook when I talked with Althea. The other was that Althea was incredibly impressed that anyone would take notes when she was talking. It made her feel like a real executive, not like a former go-go dancer who used to let men familiarize themselves with her private parts for a buck or two at one of Larry's Hustler Clubs back in Ohio when she was a seventeen-year-old kid. It helped her forget, I think, about the night when she'd hidden under the bed with her sister when her drunken father came home and killed almost everyone else in the family, including Althea's mother and himself, with a shotgun.

I admired Althea for the time she stepped out of her limo and confronted some feminists demonstrating against *Hustler* in front of our office building. (Larry had asked how long the longest stretch Lincoln Continental limousine in Los Angeles was. When he found out, he ordered one two inches longer.)

Althea, who relished her domestic role in procuring women who'd have sex with her after they screwed Larry, waved a copy of *Hustler* at the demonstrators.

"If you'd spend more time looking at this," she told them authoritatively, "and less time between each others' legs, you'd be a hell of a lot better off."

Althea Flynt had an odd sense of propriety. She once circulated a memo demanding a change in editorial policy after having had lunch with a woman friend, the wife of best-selling novelist Harold Robbins. The Flynts and the Robbins had become good pals after Larry and Althea moved to L.A. and into the posh Bel Air neighborhood. After returning from lunch, Althea sent a memo to me and other editors saying she no longer wanted us to refer to female genitalia in the pages of *Hustler* as "cunts." From now on, Althea ordered, we would stick to "pussy," which apparently offended Mrs. Robbins to a lesser degree. As with many other directives from Althea—and, indeed, with directives from editors and publishers of every sort of publication, including daily newspapers—we worker bees knew things would change, that the latest directive would soon be forgotten and that we'd be back to the old way of doing business before too long.

Another time, Althea demanded that we actually interview the models whose nude photos ran in the magazine. "That way," she chirped when she told me her idea, "we'll be able to capture the actual personalities of these women when we expose their shaved groins and their cunts, er, ah, excuse me, pussies, to the world. What a wonderful idea!"

Well, it was a terrible idea. I knew that like all other directives from the Flynts this one, too, would eventually be forgotten. For a month or two I had to assign one of the editors, Michael Stott, I think, to meet the models at the studio and ask questions so he could write the so-called "girl copy." Michael was in the country illegally because he lied when they asked at Immigration whether he'd ever been a mercenary soldier and he denied that he'd ever been a gun for hire. Actually, Michael, who died not long after I left *Hustler*, had fought on various sides during rebellions in Congo and other African nations. But I knew he was the right man for the job because he loved porn, had a truly dirty mind, wanted to make porn movies and always wanted to get out of the office.

Sadly, it turned out as I knew it would. No matter how smart or sophisticated the models were, and no matter how hard Michael tried to pry some revealing personal information from them, all he was ever able to get them to say was that, like every woman who'd ever written her own sexual fantasies to *Hustler*, each enjoyed moonlight strolls on the beach, wanted to ride a horseback nude and would enjoy a threesome with, generally, her boyfriend and some vapid rock guitarist I'd never heard of.

Althea understood immediately that this new dose of reality in the girl copy was less than a turn-on to our male readers. (We called them readers rather than jack-offs because it sounded more professional.) We were soon back to writing our own girl copy, stuff like "Wanda loves having her tongue wrapped around a stranger's cock while he licks her clitoris until she screams with passion."

Althea died in 1987. She had AIDS and apparently nodded off and drowned in her bathtub. She'd been an on-and-off again junkie since she joined Larry in injecting his painkillers after the Georgia shooting. But, as many of us realized when we first heard she had contracted the disease, about which very little was yet known when she passed away, Althea could have contracted AIDS in almost any of the ways we've ever heard about.

* * *

Imitating the accents of Larry and Althea and coming up with absurd porn metaphors like "Mooring his throbbing, rigid speedboat in her welcoming port-of-call" were two of the most-popular pastimes in the editorial offices of Larry Flynt Publications. Things were rarely dull. And this may surprise you, but I found that the editors I worked with at Larry Flynt Publications were the smartest people I've ever worked with. Quick, witty, well-read, and sharp as tacks. For instance, the guy in the office next to me was Jerry Stahl, whose memoirs, *Permanent Midnight*, were about a comedy writer watching his life spiral out of control as his heroin addiction takes over. Jerry was played by Ben Stiller in the film version of his life story.

Also, oddly or not, we were mostly ex-Catholics. I made some good friends at *Hustler* and my apartment-mate Clare, an industrious, talented and beautiful lesbian I'd met when we were both working on the resurrected *The Realist*, was warm, friendly, and sexy. She never lacked for girlfriends and I heard her several times defending me when some of her gal pals questioned the wisdom of getting close to a man, let alone living in the same apartment with one.

Hustler editors were fast and free with homespun jargon and similes, writing to impress one another, not necessarily the

275

"readers." Despite Larry's optimistic belief that at least some of the men who bought *Hustler* actually read the articles between the pictures, the editorial staff was pretty sure that most actual readers of our smut similes, puns and allusions were our peers: other porn editors, not the stereotyped hard-hatted, cigar-chomping construction worker we touted as the salt-of-the-*Hustler*-earth. (In fact, demographic studies indicated our readership was exactly the same as those of both *Playboy* and *Penthouse*; men, as I recall, aged twenty to fifty with middle-class incomes and usually with wives, two cars, and two kids.)

The reality of the smut business was, for me, nothing like the sleazy underworld depicted in films such as *Boogie Nights*. "Wholesome" was not a word I'd use to describe any of us, but it was a word we sometimes used in the girl copy accompanying photos of those wholesome sweeties next door who just happen to spend their time out by the pool spreading legs and butts just like we all imagine they do.

Yes, there were indeed tough guys with flashy diamond pinkie rings involved in parts of the porn business. Distribution of magazines and videos, for instance, was commonly believed to be dominated by gangsters or guys with connections to that all-encompassing world of "organized crime."

I did have to call "organized crime figure" Reuben Sturman once to talk about potential problems we might face distributing an upcoming *Hustler* with a proposed "hard-core" porn photo set. Hard-core porn, in 1980, included photographs depicting actual insertion, meaning photos clearly slowing a penis entering a vagina. Simulated insertion was *not* hard-core; the real thing was. Erect penises were hard-core; flaccid male organs were not. In some parts of the country, the parts you'd expect, the areas where the Tea Party rose to prominence and where prohibiting gay marriage seems more important than national financial stability, hard-core versus soft-core made all the difference. Soft dick near open vagina? Okay. Erect dick entering open vagina? Arrests, fines, and other legal troubles—and not only for Larry Flynt. When local newsstand owners and regional distributors got arrested, Larry was always ready to jump in with his team of lawyers and First Amendment experts.

Reuben Sturman was a legend in the smut business and was a pioneer in the distribution of porn, legal and otherwise, particularly in Ohio. Centered in Cleveland, Sturman became for a while the country's largest distributor of publications featuring sexual content. Hassled endlessly by local bluenoses and self-righteous cops, he served time behind bars for a variety of offenses ranging from obscenity charges to extortion and trying to bribe a juror. He was the go-to guy if you needed to know whether a proposed feature was going to cause legal problems for local purveyors of our magazine.

"Fuck 'em," was his advice to me.

For the most part, the people I met and the people I worked with could have passed for bank clerks or, at least, used-car salesmen. The Larry Flynt Publications, Inc., offices looked for all the world like the regional headquarters of an insurance company—except for the pages of upcoming issues thumbtacked to hallway walls so we could stop and see how next month's *Hustler* was laid out and which naked woman was the centerfold. The LFP fellow workers with whom I got drunk after work every night didn't use any more cocaine than anyone else in the entertainment business—and I do think that we all believed that we were in that world, the world of showbiz. After all, Los Angeles is a company town for the entertainment industry.

Larry's optimism about the popularity with readers of *Hustler*'s prose kept the staff of bright and witty editors in business, running exposé articles about the greedy corporate bastards who run America, the psychiatric fascists who stifle the creativity of people like Larry by doping them with anti-psychotic drugs and especially about the prosecutors, politicians, judges and anti-smut crusaders who attacked Larry Flynt with nary a second thought about the First Amendment.

Larry, of course, had not heard of that particular section of the Bill of Rights until during a pornography trial in Ohio, when he learned that some famous and respected writers had run an ad in the *New York Times* stating that, while they found Larry's output repulsive, they had to defend his right to publish it because of the freedom of speech guaranteed by the First Amendment.

After that, *Hustler* editors wrote endlessly about freedom of speech and only half-jokingly referred to Larry as "the world's leading defender of the First Amendment."

Larry's belief that our articles could help blow the lid off this or that conspiracy kept us hopping. We seemed to run a lot of pieces asking, "Who killed John F. Kennedy?"

JFK was Larry's one true hero, a hero, it turned out, whom Larry had actually met. After being cashiered from the Army when they discovered he was only sixteen, Larry wrangled his way into the Navy. President Kennedy came aboard his ship one day to review the sailors on the aircraft carrier where young seaman Flynt was serving. Characteristically as bold a young seaman as he was a porno king, as the President walked along the deck saluting to the sailors Larry stuck out his foot and tripped his hero. "Oh, sorry there, sailor," Kennedy said and shook the red-haired young seaman's hand. That was it. Larry had been touched by greatness.

Hustler's periodic exposés about psychiatric abuses were partially aimed at some of Larry's relatives. It seems that the family, including brother Jimmy as well as wife Althea, had worried that the born-again Larry Flynt might slaughter the porn cash cow and instead start endowing Ruth Carter Stapleton. But none of us ever thought he was *that* crazy.

* * *

It was night when we landed in Las Vegas. Larry and I and a pair of gun-toting bodyguards rode in a casino limo to the Sahara Hotel, where we were going to meet other *Hustler* staffers when they arrived the next day. Larry's Dilaudid and coke injection had apparently not worn off because he seemed pain-free and talkative. He rolled through the Sahara's ground-floor casino in his gold-plated wheelchair. No one paid the slightest attention to our armed escorts brandishing automatic weapons.

When we got up to the penthouse my mouth must have dropped open when I watched as Clifton, one of the bodyguards, unlocked a red, heavy-gauge metal toolbox he'd been carrying, and dumped out half a bushel of cash. He counted each bundle: Two hundred thousand dollars!

Larry told Clifton to put ("putt") half the cash in the "cage," or casino bank, downstairs and another hundred thousand dollars over at the Silverbird Casino, where he loved to play poker. Larry also liked the Silverbird, he told me, because "they serve this sandwich they call the French dip and *Lay-ee*, it's this really good roast beef and they give you a little dish of gravy [pronounced *gry-vee*] and you can dip the sandwich in the *gry-vee*. It's real tasty."

Later, as we were driven over to the Silverbird for French dip dinner, Larry talked about his poker-playing sideline, including several sessions in the famous World Series of Poker held in Las Vegas. "It's a lot easier to make bets when you're not playing with the rent money," he assured me. I was hoping, of course, that Larry would see fit to drop a hundred or two on me to wager at the tables. He didn't. He can be tight with a dollar, let me tell you. Today, though, Larry owns the Hustler Clubs, California poker clubs that are elevated to something approaching casinos by the addition of glitz and pretty cocktail waitresses.

Later that night, tight as he might be with actual cash, he did tell Althea, who'd picked up fifty-thousand dollars shooting craps, to go back down and lose 10K back to the house. After all, he told the recalcitrant former go-go dancer who'd rather have parted with her sister than with a hundred-dollar bill, the whole *Hustler* crew was comped, staying and eating at the hotel for nothing, and it's just not polite to take all their money, too.

279

Other editors who'd been ordered up to Vegas by Larry began to trickle into the hotel from their commercial flights. Although we were supposed to have some sort of editorial confab, it turned out that Larry actually just brought us up here to have fun. He was no more interested in talking business than were any of the rest of us.

It's easy to lose track of time in Las Vegas. There are no windows in the casinos so you're never quite certain whether it's night or day. And it's difficult to keep track of time when you're boozing and abusing stimulants so you can stay awake around the clock. But sometime during the ensuing twenty-four hours I was sitting drinking in the hotel bar when one of my publishing compatriots walked up with an incredibly beautiful young woman. He introduced his date as Bunny or Brandi and told us she was a prostitute. He swore to us while she tried to blush that she was "the best lay I've ever had. You guys ought to try her."

Bunny or Brandi sat down, hoping one or more of us would open negotiations. I thought I held a trump card. I asked her whether she'd like to be a *Hustler* centerfold.

"What?" the lovely young hooker asked in utter amazement. "And ruin my reputation?"

THE WEDDING GIFT

The first *objet d'art* one noticed upon entering Larry and Althea Flynt's "mansion"—as they insisted we call their Bel Air home—was a statue of a youngish lad having sexual intercourse with a chicken. This piece of sculpture stood in the foyer of the house, which was guarded in those days by two ferocious attack dogs and several ferocious, and heavily armed, attack men. Larry proudly boasted that the artwork was an anatomically accurate depiction of his first sexual experience. Now that wondrous encounter that set the young Kentucky lad onto the road to porn aristocracy had been memorialized for the ages in this lovely piece of bronze.

Many years after Larry's assignation with the hen, when the *Hustler* editors in Columbus, Ohio, learned that the boss was going to make an honest woman, or as honest a woman as was possible, out of his companion and Hustler Club hoochy-coochy dancer Althea Leasure, top editor Bruce David came up with the perfect wedding gift for Larry: a live chicken in a box with a note reading, "In case things don't work out."

Bruce David, by the way, was as key a player in turning Larry's small, cheaply reproduced Hustler Club newsletter into a hugely profitable smut magazine as was Larry himself. Living in New York, Bruce sent Larry complaints about the newsletter with some suggestions for how to turn it into a professional-looking, glossy, big-time men's magazine. Not adverse to considering criticism, Larry hired Bruce to oversee *Hustler*'s upward mobility from the relative obscurity of a cheap newsletter for tittie bars into the national, even international, porn limelight.

Bruce David and I had our differences over the nearly two years I worked for *Hustler*. In fact he fired me for the third and final time I was let go by Larry Flynt Publications. But I still think that he and I headed the smartest group of writers and editors I've ever worked with. Bruce David is brilliant, witty and has the perfect sort of clever-but-dirty mind needed to run *Hustler*.

Knowing the story about Larry's first sexual encounter, and wondering what to buy as a gift for the boss's upcoming nuptials, David ordered one of his *Hustler* editors to go find a live chicken and buy it. David, whose once-volatile temper had evoked both fear and loathing among some of his underlings in those early *Hustler* days in Columbus, told the editor not to show his face in the office again until he'd rounded up the bird.

The editor decided the easiest way to come up with a chicken on the hoof, so to speak, was to go directly to the source, a chicken ranch on the outskirts of Columbus. Michael, as the editor was named, got in his car and drove out through the Ohio countryside.

When he got to the poultry ranch, he told me, he parked and walked over to an elderly man, the owner of the establishment, who was sitting in a rocking chair on the front porch of his rustic home.

"I'd like to purchase a chicken," he told the farmer.

"Well, Sonny," the man wondered, "what do you want it for? Roasting? Frying" Laying?"

"Fucking," Michael replied in all honesty.

The farmer shrank back into his rocker in disgust.

"Well," the old coot told Michael, "I ain't gonna help you pick out a chicken to fuck. You go get one on your own." He handed Michael a wooden crate, the kind with thin slats that lettuce and cabbage and other produce used to come in.

Michael headed out into the huge flock of chickens that roamed and squawked and pecked at the ground and one another just beyond a fence made, appropriately enough, out of chicken wire.

Now he realized that he had no idea exactly what kind of chicken Bruce David might have in mind as a potential sexual partner for Larry "in case things don't work out" on his

282

honeymoon night with Althea. But he finally picked one bird, apparently believing it looked sexy enough, and with some deft coaxing and shoving stuffed the bird into the crate, paid the farmer a couple of bucks and tossed the box and bird into the back seat of his car.

Disaster struck as Michael headed back into Columbus. The chicken, which had been screeching and kicking and batting its wings against the side of the crate, suddenly cracked one of the slats and broke out of the box. As Michael tried to keep his car on the road the hen began flying around the inside of his sedan.

"It was making a hell of a noise," Michael reported, "and it was shitting everywhere. It was like there was a shit-and-feather storm inside the car. It was a nightmare."

Trying to keep one hand on the steering wheel, Michael attempted to grab the bird with the other. He was on a busy highway and didn't want to risk pulling off the road with an enraged chicken winging its way around his head.

It took a few miles and a lot of chickenshit but he finally got a hand around the bird's neck. The chicken crapped on his lap. Enraged, Michael rolled down his window and tossed the screeching chicken out of the speeding car.

Unfortunately for all involved, the hapless chicken smacked the windshield of an oncoming truck, a big truck, an eighteen-wheeler. The bird splattered across that windshield in such a frightening and disgusting manner that the trucker, too, became enraged. He turned his Peterbilt around and began to follow Michael who, fearing mayhem, led the truck-driver on a high-speed chase along that highway, then on less-traveled roads, then on municipal streets and finally down alleyways and across front lawns and parking strips. He was sweating bullets.

Finally, Michael realized he'd ditched the angry trucker. He heaved a sigh of relief, then also realized that while he had avoided one disaster he faced another, the wrath of Bruce David, unless he brought back a live chicken to the office.

Reluctantly, he turned his car around and headed back to the country. When he got to the poultry ranch the farmer was still sitting in his rocking chair. He looked at the forlorn young man standing in front of him, coated with chicken manure and assorted feathers.

Michael almost wept as he told the farmer, "I need another chicken."

"Another one?" the farmer asked with the sort of abhorrence that only a chicken man could have for a city-slicker pervert who'd buy a bird for his own sexual gratification. "What happened to the one I already sold you?"

"Well," Michael replied timidly, a touch of shame in his voice, "something bad happened."

Bad?" the old guy wondered.

"Yeah, bad. Unfortunately, I killed it."

"Oh, sweet holy Jesus," the farmer whispered.

Then he looked at Michael and sadly informed him: "That'll be another two bucks."

ETHICS: SMUT AND TV

The questions I am most frequently asked by female friends about my stint as Executive Editor of *Hustler* magazine is, "Don't you think you were exploiting and degrading and encouraging violence against women? Don't you feel ashamed now?" The question I am most frequently asked by their husbands or boyfriends is, "Did you ever get to screw the models?"

To the first two questions, I answer, "No." To the third, I answer, "Sometimes."

Understanding that some of aspects of working conditions in the United States are regulated by various federal, state, and local laws, and realizing that matters such as sexual harassment have caused the downfall of numerous business executives as well as countless public officials, it's not easy to pinpoint just what ethical considerations there are for sexual relationships that develop in the pornography industry. Much of the business, for instance, consists of filmmakers, men for the most part, taking photos or making videos of women. In most cases these naked women are having sex with men or with other naked women. Tastes vary from pornographer to pornographer and from customer to customer, but essentially there are guys who like women with gigantic breasts, there are directors who make their livings filming blondes having oral sex with other blondes, there are filmmakers who occasionally get into the action themselves and there are guys shooting porno for niche customers such as men who pay to buy bondage films, guys who like POV, point of view, films that make it seem as though the girls are having sex with the viewer (when, in fact, it's with the cameramen) and, well, you name it. And, of course, there are gay films for gay viewers. There are sensitive women directors making porno movies for other sensitive women who find men's porn too intimidating or disgusting or exploitative. In fact, there are women directors whose videos run the hard-core porn gamut from rough and kinky all the way through blue and bawdy.

I am unaware of any sexual harassment cases that have arisen from those conditions that are an intrinsic part of the porn business—except, I guess, the late Linda Lovelace's charge that her husband forced her into pornography. Lovelace was the star of 1972's *Deep Throat*, the first well-known example of commercially successful modern smut.

But there's no doubt that men behind the cameras or in the directors' chairs have always had sex with the women they encounter in the porn business, particularly with women who were models or actresses. In many cases the episodes were filmed following a script that called for those very men to engage in sex with the women. (Al Goldstein, the late founder of the once-infamous *Screw* tabloid paper, told me that he convinced his wife that he was gay so she wouldn't get suspicious that he was having sex with women posing for his publication.)

Since I wasn't involved in the video end of the business, including Larry Flynt's video production business, I have no personal knowledge about unscrupulous men forcing themselves upon actresses hired for porn films. I suspect, however, that many of the porn actors, male and female, lead relatively normal southern California lives: Some are homebodies who get up, go to work, make a fuck film, go home, feed the dog, cook dinner, and watch TV before going to bed for the night. Others, who are by no means unusual in the San Fernando Valley, may screw for money at work and later screw for pleasure and/or money or for dinner at a nice restaurant.

I should explain how the business, at least how *Hustler*, found models when I was at the magazine. The typical model for a so-called "girl shoot" at *Hustler*'s studios was an attractive eighteen- or nineteen-year-old hick chick who had just arrived in Los Angeles hoping to break into show business. She would hear about *Hustler*'s "talent coordinator," who would ask the young woman to fill out forms that included personal employment data as well as models' releases. The talent interviewer, always a woman, would also take a set of Polaroid prints in those pre-digital camera days so the photographers and photo editors and, when she was alive and running the show, Althea Flynt, could see what the latest would-be models for *Hustler* and other Flynt magazines looked like.

Many of these young woman were the potential "Blonde on a Brass Bed." The "girl copy" we wrote to accompany the photos usually said things like "enjoys moonlit strolls on the beach, riding horses bareback, and quiet evenings in front of the fireplace." We didn't mention that she frequently enjoyed cocaine, sex with other women, and showing her naked body to men for money.

Smut-writing, by the way, is as artful a craft as, say, food-writing or literary criticism. We saw as our audience not only a million sex-starved masturbators bent over their *Hustler*s looking at what Larry called "pink," in other words, portions of female genitals previously unrevealed in publications available openly on your local newsstand; we also wrote for our peers. It turns out that most of the men, and they were mostly men, working for porn magazines in Los Angeles when I was at *Hustler* had, at one time or another, also worked for Larry Flynt—or wanted to. We knew each other and often we wrote for one another, trying to use sexual metaphors that might seem hot to guys jacking off in the privacy of their own homes, but that definitely drew giggles from our fellow pornographers. One metaphor I wrote had to do with a guy "landing his 747 of sex in her velvet runway of love."

Ben Pesta, editorial director of *Chic*, was the best. I accompanied Ben to USC one evening to speak to a night class in magazine-writing that my longtime pal John Riley was teaching. A young woman in the class asked Ben what sort of writing he was looking for to publish in his magazine.

Ben told her he was looking for writing like: "Steaming silver bullets of white-hot jism!"

"Oh," she whispered.

The potential new *Hustler* or *Chic* (Larry's supposedly slightly more-sophisticated magazine) model would almost always show up at the talent coordinator's office with her boyfriend, generally a rube from the same small town that she was fleeing in Indiana or Kansas or some other rural part of the country. The young lovers were almost always looking for first-

and last-months' rent on a crappy room in deep Hollywood. (I think *Hustler* in those days paid something like fifteen-hundred dollars for a "girl shoot," eighteen-hundred if included in the gatefold (the centerfold) and a couple of thousand dollars more if the girl were also chosen to appear on the cover. In the late 1970s that was, in fact, enough money to rent a room and get something to eat and score some cocaine—the fuel of the porn business when I was riding high at *Hustler*.

It was always clear to me, when I would see an eager young couple waiting in the lobby for a get-together with the talent person or when I'd see them at the studio—where the guys would linger to make sure no one was going to put any moves on their sweethearts—that the relationship that started somewhere out in the sticks, probably in a car parked at the Dairy Queen where they both worked, was not going to last for long in sunny, southern California. It seemed the pretty girls were always taken by the seemingly wild and adventurous lifestyles of the *Hustler* photographers or the men they'd meet when and if, and usually when, they'd move on to porn video work. I could feel it in my bones, as it were, that the hayseed trying to look tough and possessive around his lovely gal, who was by now spiced up with some glamorous studio makeup job, would be heading home alone before long and living in another crowded apartment with other single Hollywood dudes before too many weeks had passed.

When women friends, particularly from in my longtime, politically correct hometown, Santa Cruz, started griping about *Hustler* exploiting these young ladies, I argued that they applied for the work and made more money per hour by a long-shot than I did! We weren't exploiting them; they were on the make for rent money so they could begin their new life in La-La Land.

As my ex-wife Melody, herself the editor of *Playgirl* magazine when I met her, pointed out, "The ones who are really being exploited are the men who pay four bucks to buy *Hustler*." (It's worth noting here that Melody, who was acting executive editor of *Playgirl* when I met her at a publication party in Venice, was quite certain that the vast majority of the "readership" of

Playgirl magazine consisted of gay men." She later worked for *Playboy*, as an editor of its second-string magazine, *Oui*.)

I did some writing for Melody when she was editor of *Playgirl Letters*, a digest-sized publication filled with supposedly real letters from women readers asking questions about sex, or, more often, relating their own lurid tales of sexual adventure. I hate to spoil anyone's sexual fantasy, but those letters were definitely *not* real. They were written by money-grubbing pornographers. Like me.

Playgirl paid me fifty dollars for every page of copy I could turn in for the *Letters* digest. My output was usually related directly to how much I needed for my share of the house payment on the little house Melody was buying in Venice Beach. I suppose I turned out five to ten letters a month and Melody made sure I was always paid as quickly as possible—something that was unusual for most sex magazines I wrote for in those days. (I often had to argue with editors, accountants, "comptrollers," and even with publishers to get them to put money they owed me in the mail. The Flynts, among the very few porn publishers who understood and appreciated writers, always made certain ours were paid in a timely fashion, even before other creditors got their payments.)

After *Hustler*, I made some money freelancing for a few other so-called men's magazines. I also had a job as a story editor on what was possibly the worst television show in history: *That's My Line*, which featured the venerable Bob Barker as host and a pair of beautiful women sidekicks. I became friends with one, Tiiu Leek; the other was married at the time to novelist Michael Crichton. The show was owned by the pioneering television firm, Goodson-Todman, which had produced the famed *What's My Line?* in the early days of TV.

Mark Goodson, one of the original game show producers, visited our offices regularly and would meet with some of our show's executives poolside at the Beverly Hills Hotel. One producer told me that he was constantly distracted during one such meeting with the boss because the suntanned old TV macher—Yiddish for big-shot—was getting a hand-job from a beautiful young woman in a bikini. He said the rhythmic up-and-down, up-and-down handwork was obvious despite a hotel towel draped over Goodson's genital area. And this wasn't even the porn business.

Part of my job as a story editor on this awful show, which ran for about six weeks on CBS, included skimming a couple hundred newspapers every day. My fellow story editors and I were charged with finding people around the U.S. with fascinating jobs—jobs so astounding that they would be worth presenting to an amazed public on *That's My Line*.

Since this was commercial television, it soon turned out that not only did our subjects have to have incredible and unique ways of earning their livings, they had to have some tear-jerking story line to double their interest to our producers and, so the producers believed, to our viewers. Like the blind carpenter, who was featured because he was, in fact, a blind guy who ran boards through a band saw that could have taken his arm off, had he let his hand slip. I found a fellow who got paid for bringing a cannon to concerts when Tchaikovsky's "1812 Overture," which calls for some cannon-fire, was played. He was perfect, except that he had no obvious handicaps, had no sad story to tell, had not had to struggle to become a cannoneer, and was as regular and normal as the next guy. With no sob story to relate, the producers decided the cannon man would not appear on *That's My Line*.

That, by the way, was in 1980 in the early days of television reality shows. Even that long ago, I discovered when I'd try to get in touch with people for our TV show, half the people in the country seemed to already have videos of themselves performing their unbelievable ways of earning a living, Not only that, *they even had their own agents!*

As I sat in my Goodson-Todman office a block from Sunset and Vine one morning reading some of the newspapers on my desk, an intern working on the show dumped fifty-or-so more papers on the pile. This young lady was about six feet tall, had a figure that was more astounding than anyone I'd recently interviewed to be on our show, and was as beautiful as any woman I've ever seen. She was nineteen, a freshman enrolled in the UCLA radio-television department. Aside from dumping papers on my desktop every few hours, she'd never given me the time of day. I'd cracked jokes in her presence but she either hadn't understood them or wasn't disposed to crack a smile.

Later that day I heard her outside my office door talking with a secretary.

"I never read anything," she said.

I knew immediately that she was telling the truth.

"Except," she told the secretary, "sometimes I read the letters in that *Playgirl Letters* magazine." And a moment later she asked no one in particular, "I wonder if they're real? I mean, if they're not, I wonder who writes them?"

"I do," I shouted at her through my office door.

She looked in at me with a sort of disappointed glare, perhaps even a disappointed sneer. She started to turn away, then glanced back and walked a step into my office.

"Do you really write those letters?"

"Some of them," I told her. "I get fifty bucks a page."

In a voice that I could not, even as a professional pornographer, describe other than to say it was the sort of voice that makes millions in the telephone sex business, she coyly wondered, "Uh, did you write the one about the window-washer?"

I knew the instant I told her the truth—that I had no idea whether I'd written the piece about the window-washer who had, clearly, tickled her fancy—that I should have lied, I should have said, "Yes! Yes, I did." But this window-washer of porn let that golden nymph of opportunity knock.

"I don't know," I said instead. "I have no idea. I don't pay any attention to what I'm writing when I write that kind of stuff."

"Oh," she said, and opportunity walked right out the door.

The lovely intern never looked at me again, never said another word when she dropped the day's papers on my desk.

* * *

When I wrote earlier that when asked by male friends—generally when their wives or girlfriends were out of the room—whether I'd slept with *Hustler*'s models, I usually replied, "Sometimes." I also could have said, "not usually," or even, "rarely."

By the time I was Executive Editor of *Hustler* I hardly ever drove over to our Culver City photo studios from our offices at the edge of Beverly Hills. And I didn't spend much time in the talent coordinator's little office meeting prospective models for the magazine. But I did meet some and I enjoyed time away from the office with a few of them.

It was easier to meet the models before I was the top editor at the magazine. Before that I was editor of the Bits & Pieces, or "openers" section, generally a collection of visual jokes we'd come up with and then have one of the photographers shoot out at the studios. I worked then directly with models as well as with a stylist who decorated the sets, made up the models, and brought the Bits & Pieces concepts to life.

During a Bits & Pieces studio visit I noticed that a photographer shooting for a centerfold spread was taking pictures of one of the days' best-known porn models, a well-endowed, blond young lady who called herself Seka. As I stood behind the camera watching the scene for a few minutes, the photographer, who liked the red wool Pendleton cowboy shirt I was wearing, gave me a models' release to sign and told me to stand behind Seka, pointing at something off-camera. So I did. And somewhere in a 1978 *Chic* magazine, *Hustler*'s sister smut publication, there's a nice photo of Lee Quarnstrom, with a naked Seka a couple of feet away.

They never asked me to appear in the nude. But I would have.

Speaking of my job as Bits & Pieces editor, I proposed to Bruce David a little photo gag on a not-uncommon bit of bawdy philosophy, "If God didn't want man to eat pussy, why would he make it shaped like a taco?" The photographer I was working with suggested a model: "Get Maria. She'll do *any*thing!"

I hired Maria and she sat chatting with me as the studio stylist added some grated cheese, some lettuce and some salsa, mild salsa, to her appropriate part, making her genitals look, yes, quite like a taco. It was a typically almost-clever little gag and played well in Bits & Pieces.

Later, when I told my friend John about the photo shoot, he wondered whether I'd followed through with the taco joke and actually tasted the fixings when the photo session had ended. To this day, I've ever answered, though he has asked repeatedly. "Only Maria and I know," I've told him.

But I do love Mexican.

* * *

One of the reasons for *Hustler*'s success was that Larry Flynt is a genius. I've often said that had Larry decided to put his mind to curing cancer he probably would have. Don't get me wrong: Larry Flynt is *not* an angel. He can be at least as devious and cold-hearted as anyone I've ever known. He can often be extremely generous but he can also seem like a greedy, self-centered miser.

He could be cheap. I remember the day after a strong earthquake caused our forty-two-story tower in Century City to rock like a metronome—and this was not too many days after we'd been told during quake-safety training to stay away from windows during temblors because shifting desks could crash through plate glass windows and send us tumbling to our deaths on the pavement, which in our case was thirty-eight stories below. As the building rocked I walked to the lobby and told the receptionist to announce over the P.A. system that we were closing down shop for the day because of the earthquake. "Earthquake?" she shrieked. Then she fainted. I took the microphone for the public address system and told the entire Larry Flynt Publications staff that we were closing for the rest of the day and that they should file down the stairway, down thirty-eight stories, in an orderly manner, as we'd learned in our earthquake-preparedness session. Then I got on the last elevator leaving before they all shut down and went to Harry's Bar to drink and wait for my *Hustler* compatriots, who arrived up to an hour later after a nightmarish descent on the stairs.

Larry was mad as hell the next day that I'd let the entire LFP staff off for part of the afternoon when he was **paying them to work, dammit!**

But Larry did know, and knew well, that it takes money to make money. He certainly knew how to rake in millions of bucks with *Hustler* and its related enterprises, which now include, of course, retail sex emporiums and gambling casinos. And he did not depend on austerity and cost-cutting to make his millions.

Larry spared no expense in producing his pride and joy. He hired some of the best photographers available and he insisted, in those pre-digital camera days, that they use only Kodacolor film, which gave our images the most-brilliant color, the sharpest clarity, the best contrast and the warmest feeling of any of the film available in those years. Also, Larry demanded the highest production values and had his color separations, part of the color-printing process, done at an expensive lab in Switzerland and the printing itself done by a top-notch firm in Milwaukee. It was expensive but Larry believed that it takes money to make money. Most of the other smut publishers I knew cut corners wherever they could and their magazines looked like it. They looked dirty.

Larry was sincere, I know, when he told me more than once that his goal in life was to publish enough sexual stuff—call it information, call it porn—that humankind would become so familiar with sex and so knowledgeable and enlightened on the topic that, as Larry once put it, "there'll never be any need for porn any more." I've thought that a worthy goal, but frankly, I can't see it happening. The other day I saw an ex-CIA spy on television saying that the surest way to turn a North Korean government official into a U.S. spy was to give the guy some porn. I do believe that pornography is here to stay.

I have doubts that Larry or anyone else is going to enlighten humankind about sex to the point where there'll be no need or desire for pornography, especially if our readers' letters to the magazine were any indication. There was the guy who kept submitting photos of himself, his fat body stuffed into various bras and girdles and other articles of ladies' lingerie, rolls of fat bulging around his garter belt and poking from beneath his corset. In his photos, this *Hustler* reader always had an erection and his stiff penis was always inserted into the gaping, toothy mouth of a stuffed bass. How were we gonna enlighten him? Well, we weren't.

Many *Hustler* letter-writers were behind bars and I often thought to myself after opening the mail addressed to Larry, "Thank God for prisons." That was my immediate response after opening a letter from an inmate in some federal penitentiary who wondered, "Can *Hustler* run pictures of girls with nails pounded into their heads?"

I do not, however, believe that pornography causes violent sexual behavior. I believe just the opposite, that smut may well lessen or even prevent such violence.

The original presidential commission on porn and violence, appointed by President Lyndon Johnson, concluded (and thusly made itself politically irrelevant) that pornography does *not* cause violence against women. I know this is a touchy subject and I respect others' points of view. At the same time, I strongly dislike left-wing and feminist censorship as much as I dislike the religious and right-wing kind.

One finding of LBJ's commission on the subject was that prison inmates convicted of violent crimes had, as a group, first encountered pornography at a significantly later age than America's male population as a whole. I'm not willing to extrapolate anything from that; but if I were willing, I'd conclude that encountering pornography as teenagers may actually lessen the likelihood of violence by men.

Despite complaints by some feminists during my tenure with *Hustler* that the porn business is run by men and for men, there are indeed women pornographers as well as customers. Althea Flynt, of course, comes immediately to mind.

Not all of *Hustler*'s photographers were men. One leading shooter for the magazine was Suze Randall, an Englishwoman with as raw a sense of sexual imagery as you could find anywhere. Suze had shot for *Playboy* before she went to work for Larry Flynt. As a young woman she began as a model in the United Kingdom and later became an erotic model in the States. Suze then discovered she could take good pictures and became one of the world's top porn shooters.

One evening several of us from the office sat at a table *Hustler* had reserved for the annual Adult Film awards given by an industry group at the Hollywood Palladium. Suze, among others working at Larry Flynt Publications, was making videos at the time as well as taking photos for *Hustler*.

These adult video guys, many of whom looked like they were personally familiar with what the term "crime family" might mean, were taking this awards' banquet very seriously. With women who could only be described as young bimbos on their arms, these guys in their tuxedos with their flouncy-front shirts looked down their noses at us. Larry Flynt was a hillbilly as far as they were concerned, not somebody who'd made his bones in some urban racket, not someone they'd consider as an equal. And they didn't seem to take kindly to all the laughing and hooting coming from the hillbilly publisher's employees.

At one point toward the end of the evening, the emcee solemnly announced that it was time to present "the prestigious humanitarian award." Jesus, we all asked one another, is that like the Jean Hersholt Humanitarian Award they give at the Oscars?

It seems the lucky man who was to be presented with this important award by the makers of America's smut films had himself infiltrated the legitimate film industry, where he worked as an assistant director. He used a pseudonym when he made porn movies, and he'd made several; he used his real name in Hollywood.

During that previous year, the emcee informed us, this humanitarian pornographer had been asked by a famous director to help him make a movie that was basically an attack on the adult film business. It was a movie that argued that young women were forced into appearing in smut videos, that they would soon end up completely degraded, broken, abused, and abandoned. I knew from my own acquaintances how misguided this was. I knew that there were as many options open to porn models as there were to UCLA girls—except the option of ever getting their names on marquees for the legitimate film industry.

So, when the master of ceremonies sanctimoniously told us that the award winner had turned down the offer by the famous movie-maker to direct a brief "erotic" sequence in his anti-porn film, and when this master of ceremonies said proudly into the microphone that such a fine man was unique and was more than deserving of the Adult Film Humanitarian Award, and when he said that "There's only one word for a man like our award winner . . . " Suze Randall stood, and from the *Hustler* table she shouted her choice of the word to complete the emcee's sentence:

"Yeah," she yelled. "It's *'Asshole!'*"

THE GINGER MAN

Because I was *Hustler* Executive Editor emeritus at Jim Heinisch's wake, held in the back room at Harry's Bar and Grill—where I and my fellow Larry Flynt Publications editors had whiled away thousands of hours and dollars over the years—I was asked to give the toast in Jim's memory.

"I never thought," I truthfully told the half-dozen or so compatriots who joined me in the barroom following Jim's memorial services in a dingy Hollywood funeral home a couple of hours earlier, "that Heinisch would die a natural death."

God's mercy

On the wild

Ginger Man.

–J.P. Donleavy

I have never met a more desperate man that Jim Heinisch. He was a jovial but unpredictable drunk, a pathetic cocaine fiend, a self-deceived borrower of cash, an unholy debtor, even to his few close friends.

When Jim died, a few years after we'd both left *Hustler* and he'd sunk deeply into the cocaine underworld, he owed a lot of people a lot of money. There was, for instance, a Hell's Angel who had put out a fifteen-hundred dollar contract just for information about Jim's whereabouts. It seems the biker had been stiffed for several thousand dollars after accompanying Heinisch as an armed guard to a business meeting with several drug wholesalers in South Central L.A. The deal had gone sour, guns were drawn and the Angel, who had brandished his sawed-off shotgun as he'd been hired to do, expected to be paid despite the failed transaction. Then there was our Larry Flynt Publications amigo Don, who loaned money at usurious rates to his fellow porn editors out on a tear and who might need a few bucks for the rest of the evening, but who would generally repay the loan, with vigorish, the following payday. This guy, whom we called The Bank of Don, was out seven-thousand dollars plus interest with Heinisch's passing.

I pointed out, in my sad toast, that while all of us were sad at Jim's death, no one was sadder than Don. The generally good-natured proprietor of The Bank of Don stood and left Harry's Bar in an angry huff. Making fun of a Bank of Don loss was no laughing matter to the financial institution's namesake.

Heinisch had been managing editor of *Hustler* when I was promoted over him from the Bits & Pieces humor section to the top job of Executive Editor. Jim had been using the corner office as acting executive editor, so I told him to collect his stuff and put it in a smaller and less-prestigious room next door.

I quickly discovered that aside from using the grooved pencil slots in the top drawer of my new desk as storage areas for various grades of white powders, he had failed to do most of the housekeeping chores editors must do to keep themselves from being overwhelmed by crap. I'm not a particularly tidy person but the huge box of unread manuscripts in the corner of this grand office on the 38th floor of a Century City skyscraper irritated me.

So, on my first morning in this office with the magnificent view eastward over Beverly Hills toward downtown Los Angeles, I set to work emptying the box of so-called "over the transom,"— unsolicited, articles, stories, interviews, and insane attempts at pornography or literature of one sort or another. There were more than eight-hundred manuscripts that Heinisch was supposed to have read and either reject or, in the rare instances that unsolicited manuscripts are considered for purchase, pass along to the articles editor.

I rejected them all by lunchtime using a few basic criteria. I rejected any that were handwritten or single-spaced or typed in tiny or flowery fonts or were accompanied by cover letters bearing quill-pen logos indicating membership in a writers' club.

(Manuscripts accompanied by SASEs—self-addressed, stamped envelopes—were returned; those without went directly into a trash pile.) I read the first paragraph or two of the twenty-or-so documents remaining after my initial cull and was able to reject them out of hand after perusing just a few words. Sweet Jesus, what were those people thinking?

"HEINISCH," I bellowed through my open office door.

Jim came running in, still unhappy that I'd kicked him into the smaller space next door but exhibiting just the sort of friendly servility that had kept him on the payroll at LFP for the past several years. "Get this shit out of here." Always docile around anyone above him on the masthead, Jim picked up the rejects to be mailed in their SASEs and called for his assistant to get rid of the manuscripts I'd put aside for the trash.

Although Heinisch as a boss had developed somewhat of a reputation as a tyrant around Larry Flynt Publications, Inc., I found him affable, cooperative, properly deferential, and extremely bright. We became good friends.

His cocaine habit was legendary. Whenever I heard the receptionist in the LFP lobby page Jim Heinisch to pick up a manuscript I knew another drug dealer was on the premises. Heinisch was a production man, involved with scheduling and pacing the publication and getting it to the printer. He didn't have anything to do with reviewing manuscripts.

There was a production editor who worked for Jim and who did all the actual ass-kicking required to encourage editors to pass material along in a timely fashion. Because she could not stand the smell of cigarette smoke and because smoking in offices was legal three decades ago, I encouraged smoking in my office to keep the production editor from nagging visits.

Although she was generally a nice person when she wasn't nagging, as far as I could tell, she was never interested in being friends with any of the staff beyond working hours. She apparently lived with a communal group and had to leave early every few days so she could be on time to that group's weekly orgy.

Heinisch was generous with his drugs—although he did balk when he discovered that the associate publisher was using a master key to break into his office at night to snort up part of the powder supply in his top desk drawer. Heinisch solved that problem by pouring bottles of Wite-Out onto his desk, waiting for it to dry, chopping it into granules, pulverizing the tiny grains, and filling the pencil grooves in his top desk drawer with that powdered Wite-Out—instead of cocaine. As far as I knew, the associate publisher continued his nightly snorting raids on Jim's white powder supply.

One evening not long after Althea Flynt had named me Executive Editor, Heinisch, Ben Pesta, and I were doing what we always did after work: enjoying aperitifs, lots of them, at Harry's Bar. After a half-dozen or so drinks and no doubt a snootful of stimulant powder, Jim decided I'd been unfairly given the top job at the magazine when he, who'd been with the Flynts since the beginning, was the one who deserved it. One thing, like one drink, led to another, and before long Jim was drunkenly shouting, and staggering around Harry's usually decorous barroom and telling anyone who'd appear to listen that he, not I, deserved the job.

So I fired him on the spot.

Now, I'd fired him before, always at Harry's Bar, several hours after we'd started drinking. And I'd always hired him back before the evening was over. This time, however, I was pretty serious because I realized that Jim's anger was real and was going to cause problems in the office. I told him I wasn't speaking to him any more that night and that he should go home.

Heinisch got up and stumbled into the men's room, where I assumed he would snort some more drugs before returning to the table to see if I'd rehire him once again. Instead, though, he put his fist through the glass on a framed print above the urinal. He not only shattered the glass, he cut his hand badly.

Upon leaving the restroom Jim was informed by a stranger sitting at the bar that his hand was bleeding. "Fuck off," the drunken Heinisch told the Samaritan, who didn't cotton to the ingratitude and proceeded to pick up the barstool and smack it into Jim's face, fracturing his jawbone and eliminating some teeth, among other things. Heinisch staggered out into the night.

When he called a few days later, contritely seeking reappointment as managing editor, I told him he'd first have to apologize to the folks down at Harry's Bar as well as find out how much it would cost to replace the glass on the framed print.

"Ah, no problem," he assured me, "I already know."

"Great, you already checked?" I asked.

"Nah," said Heinisch, "it was twenty-seven bucks the last time I did it."

* * *

Occasionally, my job took me away from Flynt's offices and our nearby annex, Harry's Bar, to courtrooms where plaintiffs were depending on small-town local juries to squeeze some bucks out of Larry's bank account. That's why I flew into Louisville to meet Heinisch, who'd arrived on an earlier flight. He drove us across the river and up a highway to some little Indiana burg. There, we were supposed to testify in one of the endless lawsuits that private citizens, who saw Larry Flynt as a potential pot of gold, insisted on filing against *Hustler*. We usually lost those local trials because juries and judges in many of the tiny towns around America saw *Hustler* and the Flynts as disgusting merchants of filth. Actually, we were pretty proud of working, as we sometimes joked, "in the smut mines." We generally won those cases on appeal; appellate judges were more versed in First Amendment law. They probably still are.

In fact, aside from putting out a monthly magazine, one of my major responsibilities was giving depositions and testifying in libel, slander, invasion of privacy, and just plain old pornography cases.

Once I had to wait a week in sub-zero Columbus, Ohio weather to appear for the defense in an invasion-of-privacy lawsuit brought against Larry and *Hustler* by *Penthouse Magazine* publisher Bob Guccione. He was seeking six-hundred million dollars but was only awarded four-hundred million by the outraged Columbus jury, as I recall, for what he and his attorneys believed was a calculated effort on Larry Flynt's behalf to mock and demean him and his magazine. We of course denied it, although it was indeed true: Larry loved making fun of Guccione as well as *Playboy* publisher Hugh Hefner. The motto on *Hustler's* cover, "For the Rest of the World," meant we intended the magazine for readers who found *Playboy* and *Penthouse* too tame, too repressed to "show pink." Like it or not, *Hustler* was far, far more graphic than the two older men's magazines.

I remember Guccione's lawyer, the famous Norman Roy Grutman, asking me at one point during the Columbus trial whether I had written a line in a Bits & Pieces section humor gag referring to his client as "the bejewelled Guccione."

"In fact, yes, I had," I replied.

And why, thundered the lawyer, would you refer to Mr. Guccione as "bejewelled?"

Well, I told him, "As I look at Mr. Guccione sitting here in the courtroom, I can count from here on the witness stand approximately seven gold chains around his neck."

After leaving Louisville, as Heinisch and I headed north to the Hoosier burg where we were to appear in court, he had a question as we crossed the Ohio River bridge into Indiana. Jim had been sent to high school at an Indiana military academy where he'd graduated several years earlier. Halfway across the river Jim looked up at the sign stating that we were leaving Kentucky and entering the Hoosier State. "I wonder," he mused to himself, "what the statute of limitations is on inciting a riot in Indiana?"

We actually won that particular invasion-of-privacy lawsuit on the trial level. There was no jury and the judge, seeming a bit flirtatious with the two pornographers testifying in his courtroom, apparently found some of the hateful testimony from the plaintiff's side distasteful, so he ruled in our behalf.

* * *

The wake at Harry's Bar occurred after Heinisch died not once but twice. The first time, he was at Cedars of Lebanon Hospital in L.A. undergoing a biopsy when his heart stopped pumping. He was dead, he reported to me a day or two later. A heart team was summoned stat and after cracking open his chest and doing some bypass work on a random, eeny-meeny-miny-mo basis, the surgeon brought Jim back to life.

"What was it like being dead?" I asked. "Was it like people say, a long tunnel with a figure of light beckoning you toward the far end?"

"No," Heinisch told me with great sincerity. "It was more like riding the Santa Monica Boulevard bus through Hollywood in the middle of the night." I shuddered and still do at what the afterlife apparently held for my friend.

A few weeks later Jim died for good. His body, it turned out, had been riddled with cancer. I was glad that I'd had the opportunity to talk with him during his brief hiatus between deaths, and I took a day off work to attend his funeral.

With the exception of a handful of relatives who sat in the front pew in the seedy Hollywood chapel, the *Hustler* contingent was by far the most-distinguished-looking group of mourners. There was a lot of sniffling in the back of the room, but no one back there was crying. They just had the runny noses that mark many drug-users.

After the minister gave a eulogy for someone who was certainly not the Jim Heinisch we'd known and loved, Jim's sister got up to offer a homily. She spoke briefly, then said that a few months earlier Jim had sent her a letter, a letter she would cherish forever, a letter she wanted to share with us now.

After a couple of sentences about how well he was doing out here in L.A., Heinisch had written his sister something like, "At night you will look up at the stars. Where I live, everything is so small that I cannot show you where my star is to be found. It is better like that. My star will just be one of the stars for you. And so you will love to watch all the stars in the heavens. They will all be your friends . . . In one of the stars I shall be living. In one of them I shall be laughing . . . "

I turned, incredulous, to Ben Pesta. We both knew Jim had never displayed any writing talent. He could not possibly have written that note to his sister. "That doesn't sound like Heinisch," I whispered.

"It's not," Ben replied. "It's Antoine de Saint Exupéry, *The Little Prince*."

VI.

NEWSPAPERMAN

HAIL TO THE CHIEF

When a newspaper city editor assigns a veteran reporter to cover an appearance somewhere on his suburban beat by the President of the United States, most people would probably consider it an honor. Reporters, however, know better. When the *San Jose Mercury News* editor told me to drive down to Fort Ord—which was, in fact, on my Monterey Bay-region beat—I knew I wasn't being sent to the decommissioned Army base to write about whatever utterances Bill Clinton would have for the crowd. I understood that I was being assigned as the "death watch" guy, the spare reporter on the scene who could be a gofer, more or less, for our presidential correspondent in case the Chief Executive was assassinated.

I didn't mind, except that I had to wear a suit instead of the shorts and Hawaiian shirt I favored as a reporter in the *Mercury News* bureau in Santa Cruz, a surf-and-hippie-oriented university and tourist town on the coast about twenty miles west of San Jose. I'd been working in that bureau for almost fifteen years by the time of the President's visit to Fort Ord. And I'd lived in Santa Cruz for most of the previous thirty-five years. I'd been a reporter (for the *Mercury* and earlier for a small-town daily) for about the same amount of time—minus time spent at *Hustler* in Los Angeles.

Getting into the Fort Ord press parking lot for the President's visit was no piece of cake. Even though the military no longer operated the huge installation, there was plenty of security on hand. I had to show not only my usual press credentials but some special identification issued by the Secret Service for Clinton's appearance at the brand new Monterey Bay campus of the University of California system. I showed my clearances and credentials perhaps a dozen times at checkpoints manned by various soldiers, federal agents, deputy sheriffs and, at the entrance to the press parking lot, two beady-eyed, particularly suspicious young female Sea Scouts. They reluctantly let me into the parking area.

Much of the abandoned military infrastructure of the decommissioned fort still stands, including hundreds of small structures that served as bunkers, ammo dumps, sleeping huts, and command posts for U.S. Army trainees on maneuvers. Realizing I was going to be standing in a crowd for a few hours waiting for the President to arrive, to speak, and to leave, I decided I should duck into one of the abandoned shacks to take a leak while I still had the time and some privacy.

Unfortunately, after relieving myself and trying to zip up the fly of my tan poplin suit, I had a problem: a broken zipper. *Oh crap*, I thought, *this means I have to take off my jacket and then spend a few minutes trying to fit the teeth of the zipper back into the damned little gizmo that goes up and down the fly.*

I sat down on the sandy soil inside the bunker and realized almost immediately that this was not going to work. My eyesight, murky at close range because of the presbyopia that strikes most of us in middle age, was out of focus. I couldn't see the zipper clearly enough to fit it together. My crotch and the zipper were just outside the range of my 1.50-strength reading glasses but just inside the range of my vision minus the eyewear. I could not see the damned zipper with or without glasses. I was fucked.

If I were going to fix my trousers I was first going to have to take them off so I could bring the crotch of the suit pants close enough that I could see the zipper clearly through my reading glasses, which I needed to do to be able to fix the problem.

I was getting nervous. The President's speech dedicating the new campus was scheduled to get underway shortly. It was reassuring to remember that Clinton was always late, but damn, I had to be there when he arrived in case somebody shot him.

I took my suspenders off my shoulders and squatted down with my trousers around my ankles, hoping that would bring the zipper into focus so I could work on it. Meanwhile, I could see through a crack in the wall enthusiastic students and other well-wishers clustered about a hundred yards away. They were beginning to whoop it up in anticipation of Clinton's arrival.

It was then that I had a horrible realization. There were no doubt dozens of Secret Service sharpshooters stationed on rooftops and behind buildings and elsewhere around the area to protect the Chief Executive. Others, I knew, would be patrolling Fort Ord's grounds looking for potential assassins. And here I was, a guy with his pants down around his ankles, a guy acting suspiciously, as though he were about to perform some particularly odd perversity while hidden away in a decrepit old bunker less than a gunshot away from President Clinton. I could picture the headline in my own newspaper, the *Mercury News*, which would never, ever, live down the shame:

M-N JOURNALIST NABBED IN

BIZARRE SEX ACT NEAR PRESIDENT

I had to avoid getting caught with my pants down. So I quickly tugged up my trousers without fixing the busted zipper. I left the fly wide open—and this was one of those pairs of pants with a very long rise. The space between the top and bottom of the broken zipper was unfortunately huge. It was like an open window on my crotch. It caught a breeze that caused the trousers to billow out like a spinnaker on a racing yacht.

I draped my suitcoat over my left arm and held the folded jacket in front of my crotch, masking the open fly and, hopefully, maintaining my dignity. It was a warm day, so it didn't seem all that odd to carry the folded poplin coat over my arm.

Fortunately, no one shot the President.

CITY NEWS KID

I got the crap beaten out of me on my first assignment as a professional news reporter.

I was nineteen when I was hired by the venerable, and now defunct, City News Bureau of Chicago. City News, a fixture of Chicago journalism since 1890, was owned by a partnership of the four daily newspapers that were published in the Windy City in 1959. When I was hired—as a copy boy, at one dollar an hour—City News still sent "Xerographed"—sort of mimeographed—copies of its stories to those four papers, to the Associated Press, and the UPI, using a vast underground system of pneumatic tubes. Those tubes, much like the pneumatic cash payment and change systems in old, pre-credit card department stores, ranged far and wide beneath Chicago's Loop, zipping hard copies of the news to the City News owners and clients. Some never-seen workers in the basement of the office building where City News was located sat, so we were told, at a console of brass pneumatic tubes looking like they were sitting at the keyboard of a huge and mighty pipe organ.

Over the decades, City News, had trained a majority of Chicago's newspapermen (and during WWII, when men were away at war, newspaperwomen). The Bureau was basically charged with covering Chicago crime. We were assigned to police stations, local and federal criminal and civil courts, the Cook County sheriff, and the county coroner. The daily papers had reporters on some of the same beats, but the "City News kid," as each of us was invariably called by veteran journalists and the cops, was supposed to do the scut work. That meant checking each and every coroner's case and reporting any findings to our news media customers. It also meant checking out every crime that occurred anywhere in the city in case there was either a brief story worth writing or a bulletin requiring us to alert the newspapers so they could send their own reporters. We checked and updated the progress of various criminal cases as they wended their way from arrests through Cook County's generally corrupt court system. We spent our days, and our evenings, if we were on the "dog trick," as the night shift was called, phoning or visiting police stations and spending time "downtown," meaning the police administration headquarters at 12th and State Street. Day shift reporters did the same, plus they checked in at the criminal courts, the city and county building (which housed the mayor and city council, and top Cook County officials) as well as the massive and decrepit Cook County Hospital. Adjacent to that medical facility was the unforgettable and spooky Cook County Morgue, which was also part of that beat. We rubbed shoulders with cops, crooks, chaplains, medics, firefighters, lawyers (often the sort of attorneys who used to be called "mouthpieces"), and other newspapermen, a few of them local legends—including a couple who had been memorialized as characters in the famous play, *The Front Page*.

When a City News kid stumbled onto a story that might actually make the front page or some other fairly prominent part of a newspaper, we were supposed to call our editor immediately. That way, City News would get a beat (or, as it's called in fiction, a scoop) on the reporters for the daily papers.

In actual fact, however, beating a veteran reporter could prove disastrous to a young wannabe's career. So instead of calling our City News editor first we phoned around until we could find one of the reporters for the dailies. We'd tell him about the story before phoning our city editor.

We'd quickly learned that if we phoned in a story and stiffed, for instance, the reporter named Joe Morang (who could often be found drunk at a seedy South Side joint called the Midget Bar) that Joe would phone his cop pals around the city and the offending City News kid would never get anywhere trying to coax any of Joe's desk sergeant pals into tipping us to what stories might be happening in those coppers' bailiwicks.

New hires at the City News spent their first few months as copy boys. We listened to a police radio so we could notify the city editor if we heard a call (in police radio code, which we quickly memorized) about a fire or a shooting or a "man down" or an "officer in trouble." In fact, my first day on the job, as I was awaiting instructions on how to run the mimeograph machine, I suddenly heard the city editor scream "Boy! Boy! Boy, get your ass up here!" Naturally, I jumped, and ran up to the city desk, where the editor yelled, "They just broadcast a ten-twenty-two. For God's sake, are you deaf? That's a fire! When you hear about a fire, you let us know **immediately!**"

"Yessir," I said meekly. "I'm sorry, I just got here. My first day."

"I don't care," he yelled, in a slightly less-angry tone of voice. "When there's a fire, for God's sake, it could be another school. Pay attention! Do your job!" I kept yessiring when this pissed-off man would pause to catch his breath.

Then he introduced himself. His name was Mike Royko, who later became a legendary Chicago columnist. He was probably the best as well as the best-known columnist in the country for the next few decades. Royko was to leave City News Bureau a few weeks after introducing me to the important piece of journalistic information that you don't have to be nice to be a reporter or an editor, you just have to get your job done. Thoroughly.

Royko was but one of scores of City News "graduates" who gained fame in journalism or, too, in many other fields. Playwright Charles MacArthur, who included a City Press kid in his play, *The Front Page*, had worked at City News, as had novelist Kurt Vonnegut, actor Melvyn Douglas, and Pulitzer Prize-winning investigative reporter Sy Hersh, among others.

Our night editor, Arnold Dornfeld, was not that well-known in the world of newspapering, but his dictum to young reporters certainly was:

"Check it out! Check it out! If your mother says she loves you, check it out!"

After my apprenticeship as copy boy, I was seasoned enough for the editors to send me out as an actual reporter. So one spring night I was assigned to accompany an older City News guy named John Eulenberg, son of an editor at one of the daily papers.

John was known for his fascination with fires and writing about fires. Later, he got into trouble with the bosses for his lead (or, as editors spell the word for the first paragraph of a story these days, *lede*) about a fire at a church: "Holy smoke!"

John had learned about a fire that was consuming several abandoned apartment houses not far from Comiskey Park on the South Side. He and I headed south so he could watch the flames and I could gather enough facts to phone in bulletins and/or a story. This would be my first bulletin, my first story, to one of the so-called rewrite men back at the office. Rewrite men were slightly more-experienced employees who could coax the necessary facts out of young reporters, then put them in the correct order to constitute a story. They thought of reporters as almost illiterate, I think, and said so as they attempted to fashion from our breathless phone calls a no-nonsense City News Bureau story to send out to the papers, the wire services, and to radio and television newsrooms.

The rewrite men were actually great teachers, even though the accepted teaching style at the time I worked at City News was to shout and yell like Royko had at new reporters when they thought we screwed up. They also asked questions designed not only to elicit facts but to teach young reporters on the street to ask those same questions before phoning in, thusly avoiding becoming the goat of a rewrite man's ire.

Some of those questions were basic, such as, "How old was the victim of the shooting?" or "How many kids did he leave?" Others were foolish, or impossible, but they were asked just the same.

I was asked about a wino who froze to death in the hallway of a skid row flophouse. "How wide was the hallway?" the rewrite man, the late Bob Billings, questioned me. "I don't know." "Well," Billings shouted, "find out." He slammed down the phone, a rewrite man's basic teaching move.

The flophouse had no phone. The cops laughed when I asked about the width of the hallway. There were several feet of snow on the ground and I wasn't going to trudge a half-mile to some decrepit workingmen's hotel to measure the hallway. So I walked out of the pressroom at the Monroe District police station and estimated the width of the nearest hallway, then called Billings: "Forty inches," I said. "Good work," he replied, almost as though he were teaching me how to lie. I assume, though, that he was teaching me to be thorough. "Now, Quarnstrom, what did the guy do for a living?"

"He was a wino," I told Billings.

"Yeah, but what did he do before he was a wino?"

Another round of phone calls and some soul-searching finally resulted in another prevarication on my part. "He was a retired electrician."

* * *

Three or four abandoned buildings were ablaze when John Eulenberg and I reached the scene of the fire. Many of the African-American neighborhood's residents were on the sidewalks, watching the firefighters at work. The first thing John did, and I was impressed enough to do the same at subsequent scenes when I was reporting on my own, was to knock on the door of a three-flat across the street from the burning buildings and ask if we could pay to use the phone. The woman who answered the door said sure, and John gave her a fifty-cent piece to pay for our calls.

During the evening I called Dornfeld, the night city editor, four or five times, relaying to him and then to a rewrite man various newly discovered facts about the fire. The main fact was that no one had been injured in the abandoned houses, which, it turned out, had been slated for demolition to make way for an expressway. Demolition by firebug was not an unknown way of doing business in Mayor Richard J. Daley's Chicago.

Then, as I was lighting a smoke and heading back to the neighbor's home to make another call to the office, I heard someone say, "Let's get this guy's cigarettes." I didn't put it together with the fact that I had a pack of Chesterfields in my hand. I said to myself, *They're gonna get somebody's cigarettes.* Then I forgot about it.

My next thoughts were, in order:

1. *Someone just hit me over the head with a lead pipe.*

And

2. *Someone just hit me with a chain.*

I looked up and saw a dozen or so black teenage boys standing above me. I realized I was on the ground, lying in the street. I also realized that they were kicking me and smacking me with lengths of pipe and at least one length of heavy chain.

Although this happened more than fifty years ago, I can still recall distinctly my thought process as I knew in an instant that they were hurting me badly and that I might die. I knew that I had to do something to save my own life and the most-efficacious thing I could do about it was to scream at the top of my voice. Which I did.

Someone helped me to my feet. The gang of teenagers vanished into the crowd watching the fire. When I'd been lifted from the gutter to my feet and was able to stumble away toward the rented telephone, I knew I had to call for an ambulance before I called my office. I called the nearest police station where the desk sergeant told me they were too busy to get an ambulance over to pick me up.

Then I called my editor. I told him about my beating and that the police were too busy to get an ambulance for me. He told me to talk to a rewrite man while he made some calls. I gave the night rewrite man a first-person report on the beating of a reporter, a fledgling reporter, at that. I have no idea what I told him.

It turned out that the editor was also unable to get the police in that district to send anyone to rush me to the hospital. So he went to Plan B: Using a secret piece of information from a file that was only accessible to editors far above my pay rank. The editor phoned Mayor Daley at home and explained how the cops at the local station wouldn't send any help for the unfortunate young reporter beaten by a gang—and this happened not all that far from Daley's own Back of the Yards neighborhood. The mayor, in those days long before the 1968 Democratic Convention, was very chummy with the press. He told my editor not to worry about an ambulance; he'd take care of it.

I do not know what Mayor Daley said when he called the captain in charge of that police station. I do know that moments later there were three squad cars parked in the street and there were three teams of officers fighting with one another over the privilege of getting me to the emergency room. I learned later at a hospital that I was not the only white person beaten by local gangs that evening. By the time I got to the nearest hospital there were several others being treated. In fact, my cracked rib, my broken nose, my bleeding scalp, my concussion, and my swollen head, which was about the size of a head-and-a-half, were not enough during a nurse's triage to get me into the emergency room until one or two of the other victims of the night's racial violence had been treated.

My old and dear friend Julius Karpen from those City News days (and, later, from our Merry Prankster days together) harbors a decades'-long hatred of Mayor Richard J. Daley. But because he may have helped save my life, or, at least, helped me get treated before things got worse, I think the mayor was okay.

I don't remember much of the rest of the night. I do remember seeing a lot of blood on the sheet when I got off a gurney and I remember the policemen who'd rushed me to the hospital in their squad car asking me if I could identify any of the teenagers who'd attacked me. I could not. I'd gone into shock before I thought to look up to see who was trying to kill me.

Eventually, my friend John Riley, a high school pal who by then was also a City News employee, a copy boy at that time, came to the hospital to pick me up and drive me home. I got a few days off, without pay, but was back at work a week later.

Now that I was a real newspaper reporter, I was raring to go.

JULIUS

I met my lifelong friend Julius Karpen when I was copy boy on the overnight shift at the City News Bureau and he was the overnight editor. He's two years older than I but within the City News hierarchy he was king and I was peasant. However, after a few weeks we became good friends and our lives have been linked over the decades as we passed through what I guess we could call our beatnik period, our Merry Prankster era, and lately our old coot years.

For several midnight shifts I thought of Julius only as my boss, the guy who barked orders at me—to get him a cup of coffee, to run out to get the final editions or early editions of the daily papers, to send City News stories via the pneumatic tube system to those papers and to other clients. Then, at about 3 a.m. one morning, Julius gave me a few bucks and told me to go down to an all-night restaurant—the Ham'n'Egger, a couple of blocks east on Randolph Street—and pick up a five-scoop vanilla malted for him.

"What the hell is a five-scoop malt?" I needed to know.

"It's a vanilla malted milkshake, for Christ's sake, with five scoops of ice cream!"

The Ham'n'Egger, frequented at 3 a.m. by an assortment of pimps, touts, hipsters, and an occasional working girl, did have milkshakes to go, but, the guy behind the counter advised me, they did **not** make shakes with five scoops of ice cream for anybody. I pleaded my case, telling him that my boss demanded such a confection and I couldn't go back without it. The counterman demurred; he had no sympathy for my plight. So I asked if I could use the phone and I called Julius at the office and explained that even three scoops could be a problem.

"Put the manager on the phone," Julius ordered.

I couldn't make out the words but I could hear enough noise to know that my boss was shouting. I assume he was shouting something about letting the police know what kind of clientele hung out at the Ham'n'Egger in the middle of the night. When he'd hung up the phone, the counterman quietly went to his ice cream cooler, dug out five scoops of vanilla, put it and some milk and some malt powder into one of those metal cups that he stuck on the milkshake blender, then turned on the power. After a few moments of heavy grinding, the blender blades went nuts, and gobs of vanilla ice cream and milk came flying out of the metal milkshake cup.

He looked at me but never said, "See? I knew this would happen." He didn't have to.

But I did return to the office with what was left of a Ham'n'Egger five-scoop vanilla malted.

* * *

Julius left City News for United Press International, which stationed him in its Des Moines bureau, where I visited him once on my motorcycle. He and some other friends and I went to Denver, where they headed further west to San Francisco and I turned south toward Mexico.

By that time, I liked to drink but Julius was drinking a lot. His morning bottle of gin mixed with a can of grapefruit juice topped my morning intake by a substantial margin.

Three years later, when I'd moved to San Francisco, I used his pad on North Beach as my nodding-off place when I'd get too drunk to drive home to my apartment across town on the edge of what would soon become famous as the Haight-Ashbury.

Julius wasn't much of a barroom drinker. He preferred to stay home and smoke pot and drink gin and watch TV. I, on the other hand, enjoyed the conversation and companionship among the habitués of the bars along Grant Avenue and its side streets, the West Coast epicenter of the lifestyle of folks who local newspaper columnist Herb Caen nicknamed "beatniks."

I loved the occasional barroom brawl. The best I was ever involved in was in a joint called the Anxious Asp, where beatniks, artists, beat chicks, bohos, and drag queens drank elbow-to-elbow. It was one of the best North Beach joints for dancing and was where I was taught to stop dancing like a white boy by my ladyfriend Toni. It was also one of the best bars just for drinking—although Gino and Carlo's, next door, was then and remains one of the best drinking spots in the neighborhood.

The latter bar, where beat poets like Gary Snyder, Jack Spicer and even, occasionally, Allen Ginsberg, often had their own table, was too dignified a place for brawling. But the Anxious Asp would occasionally break out into one of those free-for-alls that could have come from a 1940s western movie: chairs flying through the air and punches thrown willy-nilly, not at any particular person, really, just at anyone who wasn't a close friend.

I remember such a brawl one afternoon when I saw that one of my fellow drinkers, a black man wearing a fez, noticed my friend Toni, who is black, dancing with her boyfriend and future husband Len, one of my best friends, who was white. I watched as the cat in the fez walked back to the tiny dance floor and prepared to cold-cock Len, just because he was white and dancing with a black woman, as far as I could tell. So, as he had his fist back and ready to smack Len, I hit the guy over the head with a beer bottle.

To my surprise, he turned and looked at me. I found this odd because in my experience anyone hit over the head with a long-neck beer bottle crumpled to the floor. So, as he stared at me, I hit him again. This time he did drop. Meanwhile, the entire barroom had broken into a fight. There were no sides. I mean there were no noticeable racial or any other divisions between brawlers, just a lot of men slugging each other and breaking chairs over one another's heads. I heard later that the woman behind the bar, actually a drag queen, had a rib broken in the set-to. Personally, I grabbed Len and Toni and we fled the bar for Julius's apartment.

* * *

Julius quit drinking alcohol as soon as he had his first LSD trip. I'd moved down to La Honda to join Kesey and the Pranksters and Julius took acid for the first time at my cabin in the redwoods. From that day on he stopped craving gin and has devoted his time to smoking pot.

By knowing about booze but no longer drinking it, Julius was able, after being with the Pranksters when we went on the Acid Test trail that ended in Mexico, to deal with Janis Joplin. Janis put away a lot of Southern Comfort when I was around her. That was just one of the problems Julius had to deal with when he became manager of one of the highlights of San Francisco's music scene in the late 1960s, Janis and Big Brother and the Holding Company.

But when he *was* drinking, and smoking a lot of pot at the same time, Julius knew he was having memory problems. Much like I've been doing since I turned sixty, Julius started to write himself notes so he'd remember what he had to do every day.

He even hired Len, our mutual friend, to be his memory. I remember Julius writing Len a check—worthless of course—for one million dollars just for acting as his memory and having the right answer when Julius would ask important questions such as, "Where did I put my joint?"

Julius always carried his notes, written on three-by-five note cards, in his shirt pocket. One day I noticed that while he held a joint in his right hand he had one of those note cards in the other hand. I couldn't see what was written on it.

"What's on that card?" I wondered.

Julius looked blank. He looked at the card, then chuckled and showed it to me. It read:

"Look in your shirt pocket."

POLICE REPORTER

One of the hazards of being a police reporter in a big city like Chicago is that you bump into a lot of dead people. I have seen corpses that looked almost alive, except for smudges of congealed blood that had leaked from a bullet hole or two. Or three. I've seen children burned to death in fiery tenements set ablaze by heating fires lighted in the middle of freezing living rooms, their tiny corpses looking like nothing so much as gingerbread men, flattened thin by dehydration and blackened by flames. I saw bloated, colorless bodies dragged from rivers and lakes, disgusting heaps of flesh, parts missing, devoured by fish or decomposed and disappeared. Once I even saw a body that consisted, really, of nothing but some meat and bones stuck in a pair of shoes on the floor mat of a convertible—only it wasn't really a convertible. It was a car that lost its top and everything else above the dashboard when the driver sped beneath a huge steel beam being carted on an articulated series of trailers heading from a steel mill to a new highway overpass. The roof, the car, and the upper body of the driver—everything above his ankles—had been sheared completely off and, essentially, pulverized.

Once I saw a union leader dead in the front seat of his car in an alley in a quiet Chicago neighborhood. The labor leader had one small bullet hole beneath his left ear. After the coroner removed the body, the cops tried to start the car to take it downtown to the department's auto impound lot. They turned the ignition key but the engine was apparently dead. The cops lifted the hood to find and fix the problem and instead found six sticks of dynamite wired to the ignition. I knew from my months working as a dynamiter that had it exploded, the blast would have killed me and several cops and a handful of other reporters gathered nearby. We scattered until they'd unwired the explosives and towed the car away.

That day with the dynamite, in 1961 during my second tour of duty at the City News Bureau, was the first time I'd ever worked with radio and television reporters. Until that time, they'd been unknown and invisible. But by 1961 they had already become paparazzi pushing their way ahead of print journalists so they could shove their cameras and microphones into the faces of the police officers we were interviewing. One guy with a microphone pushed it toward a cop who was giving us important details such as the name of the dead labor leader. The TV reporter asked a question that was so stupid that even a City News rewrite man would not ask it of a cub reporter. It was a question almost as mundane as, "What color socks was the victim wearing?" The *Daily News* reporter taking notes next to me calmly placed his pen in his shirt pocket and put his notebook in a pocket in his jacket. Then he cold-cocked the TV reporter, who crumpled to the ground, his hand still clutching his microphone. The *Daily News* guy took out his pen and notebook and the little press conference continued as though nothing untoward had just happened.

The first time I puked after covering a news story was when my City News editor sent me out to the southwest side of the city to a neighborhood at the southeastern edge of Midway Airport, which, in 1961, was the only major airport in Chicago. The pilot of a cargo plane trying to land on a cold, stormy day had misjudged his altitude and crashed into a row of three-flat apartment buildings across the street from the runway. The skeleton crew aboard the huge plane had been killed, as had some residents, nine, I think, in the apartment buildings.

A clutch of reporters stood inside the police barriers (no yellow plastic tape yet in 1961) watching firemen poke through the rubble looking for survivors. We knew, really, that they were seeking bodies, and they found one here, one there. A makeshift morgue was set up in a nearby vacant lot. The bodies were laid out, one by one, on a tarpaulin on the ground behind the Red Cross coffee-and-doughnut wagon that the charity always brought to scenes of terrible crimes and accidents to warm the cops and firefighters and reporters working or, like the press, waiting inside the police lines for something to happen. I found a phone I could use and called in every time another body turned up or another resident came home from work safe and sound, only to find that his apartment was gone and, perhaps, that his wife or kid had perished.

Firemen poking through the ashes with their long, hooked poles found something that immediately affected them. I could tell they were ready to cry. The other reporters and I reluctantly approached the nearby fire chief to ask what his crew had uncovered in the rubble.

Suddenly, a man pushed past the police barricades. He had a young boy on his shoulders, his son. Ignoring police orders to stand back, to return outside the barricades, the man pushed forward toward the blackened wreckage. He was pointing. I looked at the smoking remnants of apartment buildings and the huge freight airplane and saw what the firefighters had uncovered: two bodies, a woman and a child. The dead mother was clutching her dead baby to her breast in a final instinctive gesture to save her child and even without knowing it to preserve the tiny repository of her genes and the genes of the man she had chosen to be her baby's father.

The rubbernecker was shouting excitedly to the small boy perched on his shoulders. "Look! Look, Timmy, there's two bodies!" Little Timmy stared wide-eyed at the flattened, blackened bodies, then looked away. He was horrified. He began to cry. I'll bet if he's still alive today Timmy still sees the flattened, blackened bodies of that mother and child, dead as doornails, lying in the smoldering ruins of their apartment home.

Despite what you may think, and despite what news reporters like to think, it's really not possible to become desensitized to tragedy, to not feel anything when reporters—or firefighters or cops—see a dead woman grasping the charred corpse of her baby, mothering her child as her world was literally crashing down around her. Only sociopaths would not have been moved.

The man with Timmy on his shoulders continued to point and shout to his son.

Then an old photographer, a veteran shooter from the *Chicago Tribune*, lifted his camera, a large, heavy, four-by-five-inch Speed Graphic, and took a step toward the father and son. It looked as though he was angry enough to smash the man with his camera. A cop, an old Irish sergeant who looked as though he'd known the photographer for decades, grabbed the camera and shook his head, warning the photographer to calm down. He did.

Then the policeman, protected by the full authority enjoyed by Chicago cops in the days before the police riot at the '68 convention, raised his nightstick and smacked the man with the club. He hit him a hard blow to a kidney and the man dropped like a sack of manure. The boy tumbled from his dad's falling arms.

The old cop looked at me; he looked at each of the journalists. No one said anything. We all tacitly agreed that we'd seen nothing out of the ordinary. The man screamed in pain and anger. The boy scrambled to his feet and made no sound as he waited for his disabled father to get back up on his feet.

I turned away and looked again at the bodies of the mother and her baby. They were burnt, they were flat, they were human yet not human, *no longer human.* When I got home that night I puked.

* * *

One of the fabled heroes among Chicago police reporters when I was hired by City News Bureau was Walter Ryberg, the assistant city editor of City News. He was famous for his days when, as a young reporter, he acted as what was sometimes called, way back in the 1920s and 1930s, a picture-snatcher. That describes exactly what his job entailed.

One day, according to legend, Walter—truly a kind and refined elder statesman among older journalists—was assigned to get a photograph of a young man who had died in some long-forgotten tragic shooting or accident or act of God. Walter, it was said, went to the young man's house and met his parents. He asked if they had a photo of their son and they said yes, they did, and they showed him a headshot of a handsome young fellow. The photo, framed and sitting on the mantle, was, it turned out, the only picture they had of the beloved son they would never see again.

Young Walter Ryberg asked whether he could borrow the picture just long enough to take it down to whatever newspaper he was working for at the time so they could make a copy to run in the next morning's edition. The parents wisely refused. A dejected Walter Ryberg shook hands goodbye and left.

Only he didn't really leave. Instead, he waited a few minutes, then climbed a fence into the back yard, where he saw a stack of old newspapers by a trash barrel. Thinking that maybe he could frighten the parents out of their house by lighting a fire and getting some smoke to pour in through an open window, Walter stacked the papers so they'd burn, then tossed a match at them.

Oh, he did indeed smoke them out. The fire, however, also spread quickly to the house itself and burned the building to the ground.

In Chicago, we were taught to get the story, no matter what. Unlike the journalists of today, who come up with all sorts of codes of ethics and self-congratulatory restrictive procedures that have often eliminated their abilities to get the story, to get it at all cost. In my mind they've gone way too far with such nonsense. But it does allow the bureaucratic copy editors who seem to run newspaper staffs these days to pat themselves on their backs and tell one another what good jobs they've done holding their reporters to some higher standard.

But young Walter Ryberg operated under no such restrictive code of ethics. Ethics in those days, and when I was at the City News Bureau of Chicago, consisted of get the story, check it out, make sure it's accurate. But first, get the story!

So, as the grieving parents ran out the front door of their house to escape the flames that were rapidly turning the family home into a pile of ashes, Walter Ryberg ran in the back door, ran through the smoke and flames into the living room, snatched the picture from the mantelpiece and made haste to the city room where he worked. Once again, an inventive newspaperman had got the story, the picture in this case, no matter what.

* * *

One other City News bigwig, City Editor Larry Mulay, was famed in Windy City newspaper lore. Larry, a prissy fellow and the man who hired me at City News, had been the model for the character "Bensinger" in the wonderful and famous play, *The Front Page*. The play has been brought to the screen at least three times, the best and most-famous being the Rosalind Russell-Cary Grant movie, *His Girl Friday*, the only film version featuring a woman as the main character, Hildy Johnson.

Hildy Johnson had been the name of a real reporter in the heyday of Chicago newspapering. But since Mulay's character was not quite so heroic as Johnson, authors Charles MacArthur, a City News Bureau alumnus, and Ben Hecht called him Bensinger in the final version of their play.

By the time I was first hired and put on the job as copy boy on the overnight shift, my last duty of the night was based on Larry Mulay's phobia of germs. Larry held a Kleenex in front of his face when he spoke on the germ-laden phone as well as to shield himself from germs when he picked up anything left on his desk.

The desk itself was germ-free, slick as a whistle, when Larry came to work each morning. Every day, just before my shift ended at 7 a.m., my final assignment was to pour some benzene on Larry's desktop and, with a benzene-soaked rag, wipe it clean, wipe his chair clean (other editors used the chair and desk on the night and overnight shifts, some of them not exactly models of good hygiene). I would rub the benzene rag over all parts of his telephone, including particularly the dial, where possibly filthy fingers had possibly left colonies of disease-causing bugs during the night, and, of course, I cleaned the handset, to prevent germs from entering Larry's body through his mouth or his ear.

* * *

My personal tribute to Larry Mulay, one he never learned about before he died, involved my freelance writing for a variety of men's magazines in Los Angeles. After I'd left *Hustler* for good I still continued to write for it every now and then. I also wrote so-called "men's hard-boiled fiction" for several rags and turned out a few pieces of exposé journalism for a magazine Althea Flynt had started, *Gentleman's Companion*, and for a couple of other L.A.-based men's magazines. For the most part, my exposés were only new information for people who neither read newspapers nor watched the television news.

Gentleman's Companion was a vehicle for running unused "girl sets," the girlie photo sessions that somehow had not been up to *Hustler* or *Chic* standards. Some models had failed Althea Flynt's ban in *Hustler* of photos of girls with the soles of their feet dirty. Other girls looked too cheap, or too tasteful for *Hustler* but just right for *Gentlemen's Companion*. It was a crapshoot.

The editor of *Gentleman's Companion*, in immediate need of an article or a piece of fiction, would call me and tell me what she needed, usually twenty-five hundred words, and, usually, she needed it by that afternoon. If it was just fiction, I could turn it in by the end of the lunch hour. And that was in the days before computers, mind you, so I'd have to write a story, then drive the typed manuscript down to the Flynt offices from my house near the beach in Venice. I'd give the editor the piece and she'd give me a check for three-hundred dollars. It was a good deal for both of us.

How did this commemorate Larry Mulay, my editor at City News Bureau? On some of those freelance pieces I'd use the *nom de plume* "Ace Mulay" as my byline, that's how.

Besides *Hustler*, *Chic*, *Playgirl*, and *Gentleman's Companion*, I also wrote for a second-rate men's magazine called *Velvet*. Published in Hollywood by porn veteran David Zentner, *Velvet* hired some former *Hustler* editors hoping to raise their standards. They did, because they got some stuff written by me, smut-laced but literate men's fiction, under the byline of Alex Delchinko, a pun on the name of another one-time City News Bureau worker.

For the Ace Mulay exposés—like the one about dangerous cars to drive, such as the Chevy Corvair, entitled "Are You Driving a Car or a Coffin?"—I hired a researcher. I'd get three-hundred dollars for the article, which would take about an hour to write, and I'd give fifty bucks to a researcher named Bernard, who'd find me enough facts (usually three was sufficient) to write the piece and blowing the lid off whatever I was exposing.

I must say, though, that I am proud of one article I wrote, I think for *Hustler*, about global warming. This was in 1979 or 1980 and it might have been the first mass-market piece about the dangers of climate change. I'm sure it was the first such piece in a porn magazine.

* * *

Mafia guys in Chicago belonged to "the Syndicate," or "the Outfit." Local newspaper readers followed their antics—their indictments and arrests, their deaths by violence, their suspected crimes, their reputed rises and falls along the ladder of mobster success, the way people keep track of all the statistics about players on their favorite baseball teams. I wouldn't be surprised if there were today some sort of Fantasy Mafia game, where you can choose real Mafia soldiers and crew leaders and shylocks or juice guys and *capos* and a *capo di tutti capi,* or boss of bosses.

When we moved to the Chicago area, just before my eighth-grade year, our neighbor across the street in the North Shore village of Wilmette was the always-pleasant Mr. Russell, or, as I discovered a few years later, Harry "The Muscle" Russell, or, actually, Mr. Rossellini.

The Muscle had been one of the sluggers, enforcers, for Al Capone, so a newspaper story indicated. He had grown up in the Outfit with the guy who had for years, despite several reported retirements from the mob, been the boss of bosses: Anthony Accardo, called sometimes in the papers "Tony 'Big Tuna' Accardo." Frankly, I doubted that anyone ever called him Big Tuna to his face. He was, in fact, known to his fellow gangsters as J.B., for "Joe Batters," the name he'd earned as another of Capone's sluggers. Accardo was not big on publicity, but he was always atop the criminal flow charts that ran with some regularity in the daily newspapers.

Although I never encountered Accardo, I did occasionally run into some of his close underlings when I covered the police and the criminal courts.

For instance, the time the union boss was found shot to death in his car, killed with a gun after the dynamite wired to the ignition failed to explode, the police department gang unit brought in for questioning a long-time Outfit hit man, Marshall Caifano, also known as John Marshall, now the late John Marshall. Caifano was one of Accardo's early overseers of the Outfit's skim operations in Las Vegas.

After the union leader's car had been towed away, we reporters gathered at the nearest police detectives' squad room for a press conference. While we waited, the cops brought a handcuffed Caifano past us in what's now called a "perp walk."

333

As the little guy looked at the reporters and photographers, who were busily shooting his picture, he hocked a gob of spit toward us. Pissed, one reporter said something like, "We oughta get that little bastard." So, noting that the gangster almost stood on tippytoes out of his loafers, obviously hoisted by lifts, we all agreed to refer to him in our reports for the next editions of the papers as "Marshall 'Shoes' Caifano." We did and the nickname stuck, at least for a while.

I was disheartened when I learned that an older reporter I admired, a veteran journalist who'd worked for the *Chicago Tribune* for many years, had been "doing favors," as it was said, for a sadistic, mad dog killer, Outfit hit man and minor crew boss, Sam DeStefano.

The reporter, Bill Doherty, had sort of taken me under his wing when I was assigned to the North Side beat that he also covered, only for the *Trib* instead of the City News Bureau. Bill took me around to several of the police districts and introduced me to some police captains and lieutenants and, most importantly, some desk sergeants. With Bill's endorsement, these gruff sergeants, who read the teletyped reports of every crime reported in the city and knew everything going on in their particular districts, as precincts were called in Chicago, would give me tips they'd have kept under their hats had I not been introduced by the well-liked Doherty. Bill's family had sent a number of its young men through the generations into the priesthood and the police and fire departments as well as into daily newspapering. He seemed to know *every*body.

Bill even taught me how to perform the number-one job of the North Side beat reporter for the City News Bureau in those days: how to fix traffic tickets. The North reporter generally hung out at the traffic court building north of the Chicago River. There was one police district headquartered there and it was close to the busiest cop shops north of the Loop and to the Henrotin Hospital, where for some reason most of the fire, accident, boating, and every other kind of victim of any sort of mayhem was transported by city ambulances.

When I'd come into the City News each morning, on those days I was assigned to the traffic court building, there was always an envelope awaiting me. It contained the names of all the coroner's cases from the northern part of the city during the previous twelve hours, a few news clippings and copies of old City News mimeographed stories about court cases that needed follow-up coverage, and a stack of traffic and parking citations held together with a rubber band. My primary duty was to take those tickets in to the office of the clerk of the traffic court and make sure he understood that they were from City News reporters and editors and needed to be fixed immediately. They always were; fixed, I mean.

In those days, anyone who could flash a police department reporter's ID card was essentially immune from a ticket or an arrest by a member of the Chicago P.D. The cops and the press were, simply, in bed together, at least part of the time. (A few years later, in 1968, when I watched squads of helmeted Chicago police officers on television banging their nightsticks over the heads of journalists with press credentials pinned to their shirts or coats, I knew those halcyon days of cozy accommodation between the coppers and the press were over.)

Was there something wrong with getting tickets fixed? Of course there was. Aside from the fact that it was just plain illegal and wrong, it led to situations where reporters looked the other way when they saw cops breaking the law or doing something unethical. And that lead to situations like that of my mentor Bill Doherty, the *Tribune* reporter who, like all of us, would be tipped off by cops so we'd be ready to go when some big police operation was planned. Only Bill, sad to say, might not call only his city editor to let him know a big raid or a major arrest was planned. He might also call Sam DeStefano.

I learned of Bill's close ties with the gangster after I'd left Chicago. Had I still been a police reporter in the Windy City I don't know how I would have responded to the disclosure that Bill Doherty was bent. Everything in Chicago was a little bent, I think, and I suspect that the City News reporter on the North Side beat still took parking tickets up to the clerk of the traffic court every morning to make sure the fix was in.

When I first went out on the street as a City News Bureau reporter—after the requisite training as a copy boy—I was warned by veteran reporters, out of the hearing of my editors, to keep stories about police brutality under my hat.

One evening not long after being put on the street as a reporter I watched a desk sergeant at the old Hyde Park district turn a fire hose on a black prisoner as the copper was washing some crap, probably literally crap, out of the cells. The prisoner had been shouting about something; prisoners were often shouting or puking or fighting. This guy made the mistake of shouting while a cop was nearby and manning a high-pressure fire hose. I was dialing my office to ask what I should do about it when one of the old reporters, a veteran with one of the dailies, told me to keep my mouth shut. "No need to stir up a load of shit," he told me.

At a South Side detective squad late one night the dicks, as they were called, were doing their best to amuse me by asking a very large black detective called Moose to show me his service pistol, the model which every officer was required to carry. Moose pulled out a .45-caliber Colt Army automatic, a small, .22-caliber handgun, some other sidearm, a few knives, a sap, or blackjack, and some brass knuckles before he finally, acting as though he'd forgotten where he'd put it, found his .38 police special tucked into the back of his belt, hidden beneath his coat.

Later that night, when I asked to go along with the detectives when they went to "arrest" a man suspected of raping a little girl, they told me to stay put, that they'd be back soon. Even before they returned I knew they were going to shoot the guy in the back for "resisting arrest."

Yes, I did do some youthful introspection when I watched cops rough up a suspect. Today I guess I'm ashamed to admit I never complained about any of it, neither to my editors nor to the cops themselves.

But there were times, I believe, as I look back a half-century, when I saw nothing wrong with what today would be outrageous police brutality and fifty years ago was doing what was necessary to get the story, some future story, by keeping the lid on activities that should have been reported to the public and to a grand jury.

* * *

Rainbow Beach was a South Side park on the shore of Lake Michigan. In the late summer of 1960 some black youngsters decided to hold a "wade-in" to integrate the previously all-white beach. As you'd expect, they were met with abuse, pelted with rocks, and threatened with worse violence if they didn't mind their own business, stay away from where they were not wanted—by whites, of course.

The following summer the wade-ins continued and the police sent officers daily to keep violence to a minimum. One day when I was assigned as the cop reporter in police headquarters at Eleventh and State Streets, a lieutenant came to the press room and asked if any of us wanted to go with him to Rainbow Beach.

"We're going to integrate it today," he said.

When we asked how, he just said to accompany him.

I couldn't leave the pressroom so I called my City News editor and told him what the lieutenant had said. The editor told me to stay put and that they'd try to send a bulletin to the four dailies and also see if they could send a reporter out from the City News office.

What transpired, I later learned, was that as usual, when the first group of brave black teenagers arrived for their daily wade-in at Rainbow Beach, some white kid threatened the black invaders and picked up a stone to throw. The police lieutenant, unwilling to keep his officers at the beach every day for the rest of the summer, walked over to the white kid, grabbed his arm, twisted it until the boy dropped the stone, then somehow used his billy club to smack the young man on his forearm, breaking it. The kid fell to the ground screaming in pain.

"Okay," he said to the rest of the white guys waiting for their daily attacks on the wade-in group, "anyone else here opposed to letting these black citizens share this beach?"

The angry crowd demurred. They left the beach, as did the police. From that point on, Rainbow Beach was open to all races—but essentially it became a beach for black Chicagoans. White sunbathers went elsewhere.

I saw something similar when a race riot threatened to break out on the city's West Side. I got a tip that white demonstrators were gathering in front of some homes in a block that had no black residents.

The pattern in those days, known as "block-busting," was that real-estate sharpies would buy a home in the name of a black family, then spread the word that blacks were moving in and immediately get For Sale listings from the rest of the white neighbors—*and* not only get commissions on those sales, and the purchases by black families anxious to find housing, but would also make commissions when they steered the fleeing white homeowners to houses for sale in other parts of town.

I got to the scene to find hundreds of white men, women, and children milling in the street as white residents stood on their porches and steps shouting their hatred at a few policemen who were on the scene to keep order. Then a police captain with a megaphone began to announce, "Everybody, get back in your houses and clear the streets." The other reporters and I kept our press passes visible as the cops tried with little success to get the residents back in their homes and to get outsiders who'd come to cause trouble to leave.

Suddenly, a phalanx of three-wheeled police department motorcycles came roaring around a corner. Helmeted members of the police tactical squad, obviously called in by Mayor Daley to prevent a riot, began walking down the middle of the street. Nightsticks in their mitts, the coppers began methodically to swing their batons at anyone who refused to disperse. Men went down, the cops marched. Whites yelled at the mostly white detachment that they were "nigger lovers," only to receive a smash across the arm or shoulder with a cop's billy club.

Squadrols (you can't call them paddy wagons in a city where Irish-Americans hold the power; and yes, that's where the term "paddy wagon came from, a vehicle to haul drunken "paddies" to jail) were called to haul would-be rioters off to the hoosegow.

Within minutes the street was clear, the neighbors were back inside their homes (no doubt calling the realtors who'd left their cards and their warnings earlier in the day) and the tac squad and the press were gone.

I was twenty-one. That's not an excuse, that's the reason I wasn't clear-headed, politically aware, or hip enough at the time to realize that the mayor's approach to the impending race riot had been similar to tactics used by fascists to create and maintain order. It did seem all right to me at the time, I must admit.

I phoned in the facts to a City News rewrite man. My employer, though, had a policy at the time of not reporting race riots, or impending race riots, until they were over because once word got out via the radio, the television or the latest edition of one of the daily newspapers, supporters of both sides would flock to the scene to make things even worse.

* * *

Borders between the interests of some cops and some reporters were blurred to the point that my roommates in an Old Town apartment and I—we were all City News reporters—bought our marijuana from a cop. He'd confiscated the pot from some dealers and, when one of us would call, he'd come over to sell us a lid or two. In those days, a lid meant an ounce.

However, my housemates and I really didn't trust that particular cop and finally we told him we'd all stopped using marijuana. *Ah, he asked, could he still visit once in a while so he could keep tabs on the Cuban revolutionaries who lived and plotted Castro's overthrow in the second-floor apartment beneath us?* No, no, we thought not, at least for a while.

* * *

One evening, I awoke, or came to, I guess, is the better word, finding myself in the emergency room of the Henrotin Hospital. As I slowly opened my eyes and glanced around to see where I was, I noticed one of my apartment-mates, Bonny, making out in a nearby corner with a young doctor. Bonny saw that I was awakening and signaled me with her eyes and a slight head gesture to stop coming to and to act like I was still passed out.

Oh, yeah, I remembered: I'd been hauled away from the North Avenue Beach on Lake Michigan in an ambulance. That was after I'd jumped, knowing I can't swim, into the lake off the end of a jetty that hooked out into the lake. I'd jumped to impress a pretty girl who used to sit in the third-floor window of her apartment and make eyes at me across Wells Avenue while I sat in the window of the third-floor apartment I shared with my good City News friend George Murray, with George's girlfriend Bonny, and with a couple of other fellow City News reporters. The neighbor girl had accompanied us as we took a nighttime stroll down to Lake Michigan.

As soon as I'd hit the water I'd called out to George that I couldn't swim. Rather than come back to help me, George, who was nuts, shouted that he would swim in to shore, perhaps seventy-five yards away, and send someone out to help.

"Man," I shouted, swallowing a cup or two of water, *"I can't swim! I can't swim!"*

George found someone on the beach willing to help save his friend from drowning. Before long, two drunken young men swam up and considered what to do with me. Meanwhile, I was, as they say, going down for the third time. I thought I was a goner.

"I know what to do," one of the drunks told the other. "I'll slug him and knock him out and you grab his hair and drag him in." This was some sort of life-saving method they'd picked up from a wax-paper cartoon strip in a Fleer's Double-Bubble gum pack.

I fought off the guy who was going to knock me out and dog-paddled away from the one who was going to pull me to safety by my hair. I was apparently headed toward the beach because I suddenly discovered that my feet could touch bottom and I could walk ashore. It was a miracle! I *could* swim.

By this time, a city fire department and rescue squad ambulance had pulled up on the sand. I had flopped down on the beach, exhausted. As one of the ambulance attendants looked down at me, I vomited up a few cups of Lake Michigan plus the spaghetti dinner I'd eaten an hour earlier.

"Look out," someone shouted, "he's puking his guts out. Stand back! Give him air!" Now *that*, I realized as I lay there in the mess, is foolish; there's plenty of air, no matter how close anyone is standing. Yet it was comforting to see the pack of gawkers pull back so I could puke without having to apologize for splashing it on anyone.

So as Bonny signaled me with her eyes, and as I wondered why she would let this emergency room doctor put his hand inside her blouse and undo her bra while I was strapped to a gurney, possibly near death, I saw that she'd been messaging me by pointing her eyes over toward a medicine cabinet. There, my co-worker and her boyfriend George, stood peering at the labels of each of the dozens of bottles, jars, ampules, and vials in the cupboard. When he spotted one containing some useful drug we might all find handy back at the Wells Avenue apartment, such as various small bottles of codeine and other opiates and some diet pills, he'd slip it into his pocket.

I got the picture, closed my eyes and continued resting in my apparent near-death coma. Bonny continued to allow the medic to plunge his hand and wrist farther into her blouse. And George, once he'd picked the medicine cabinet clean of everything we might use, nodded at Bonny and at me, then left the emergency room. I groaned and tried to sit up. Bonny rushed to my side and unstrapped me from the gurney. The medic just stood there, his erection showing through his white doctor's coat.

I gathered later that the girl across the street had been impressed, at first, with my bold decision-making when I leapt off the end of the jetty. However, when she learned that I couldn't swim she'd been less impressed with my judgment. When George and Bonny had followed my ambulance to the Henrotin, she walked home alone.

POLITICIANS

Most of the politicians I encountered during my long career in the newspaper business weren't worth, as John Nance Garner, once America's vice president famously said, "a warm bucket of piss." Because newspapers, even to this day, have never been able to let themselves use words like "piss," Cactus Jack Garner's quote has always, when it's appeared on newsprint, been "a warm bucket of spit." But because Garner was not a typically mealy-mouthed pol, he said piss because he meant piss.

And that's the damn trouble with politicians! And with newspaper editors.

Over the years I came upon two distinctly different types of politicians whom I admired, both a small minority of the general breed of political hacks who occupy city halls, county courthouses, state capitols, and the federal buildings in Washington, D.C.

First were the totally decent men and women who actually ran for office to benefit their communities and to serve their local constituents as well as their city or county or special district or nation at large.

Also admirable, in my book, were a few politicians who really understood not only that they had power but figured out how to use it, usually to good ends, but not always. I was often, during my newspaper reporting years, disappointed, even angry, as the "liberals" or the "progressives" with whom I usually agreed suddenly got cold feet when they realized that they could wield their political power to some good end; often, instead, unfamiliar with the possibility of being on the winning side, they would freeze up and let some Republican minority not trembling at the thought of using power run right over them, thwarting yet again the possibility of seeing some bit of governmental good prevail.

I'm not talking here about Democrats who suddenly start voting like right-wingers because they're afraid of the National Rifle Association or of some perceived streak of conservatism back home in the district. I'm talking more about pols like

President Obama, who at almost two-thirds of the way through his two terms as head of state, seems to have been afraid to knock heads and smack down rivals and use his voter mandate to do exactly what his opponents were certainly trying to do to him since he first appeared on the national scene.

I cannot tell you of the number of times I've heard some recent winner of an election suddenly explain to his supporters that "we have to support the other side's point of view just for a little while so we can win in the long run." No, sir or madam, you don't ever let the other side win now so you can gain some tactical advantage somewhere down the road. It just never turns out that way: You *never* win that next battle because your opponents realize how weak you are and because your supporters are already jumping ship and looking for someone to replace you.

On the one day that I was sent by my City News Bureau editor to cover a Chicago city council meeting I watched in amazement as one alderman attempted to memorialize some recently dead ward-heeler by speaking the dead precinct captain's remarkable accomplishments into the record. Meanwhile, not one of his fellow council members was listening, not even the Mayor, the first Mayor Richard Daley, who was chatting with some underling up at the podium while the alderman droned on and on about the dead guy. Everyone in the large council chamber was talking with someone else.

Suddenly, exasperated, the speaker pleaded loudly with the mayor. "Your Honor," he shouted, "please, could you call the council to order while I talk about this man who did so much for the Democratic Party in Chicago and Cook County!"

Mayor Daley looked up and out across the room, which was abuzz with chatter. He pounded his gavel once and yelled, "Shut up!"

Everybody did as they were told and the alderman who had the floor continued with his paean to his beloved precinct boss.

When I covered the Santa Cruz County board of supervisors while working for the Pulitzer Prize-winning

Watsonville Register-Pajaronian, I grew to know and admire our local, Watsonville-area supervisor, Henry Mello. Henry went on to the State Assembly and retired as one of the Democratic Party leaders in the State Senate. He was a small-town boy but he could play hardball with the bigwigs in the state capitol.

In the early 1970s, UFWOC—the United Farm Workers Organizing Committee—came to town to organize the mostly Mexican men and women who harvested lettuce and other row crops in the fertile Pajaro Valley surrounding Watsonville. UFWOC's entry into the farm labor scene meant boycotts, like the successful table grape boycott stemming from United Farm Worker organizing efforts in the San Joaquin Valley, were going to be in play. It meant the anticipated arrival of scores of farmworker organizers and hundreds or even thousands of college-age students to provide the bodies needed to keep UFWOC's efforts going.

I remember the thrill of driving north on Highway 1 one day in 1970 and seeing a procession of men and women carrying large red banners featuring the United Farm Workers black eagle on their centers. The union members marched along the highway south of the Pajaro Valley, near the mouth of the Salinas River. Union organizers were also signing up farmworkers in the Salinas Valley, just over the hill from the Pajaro River. I was reminded of the pilgrimages and processions I'd seen in rural Mexico, with dozens of family members carrying banners and statues of *La Virgen de Guadalupe* as they marched along narrow roadways going to small chapels, distant cemeteries, and God knows where else.

As UFW organizers began to trickle into Watsonville, Henry Mello called a meeting in his office at the county courthouse in Santa Cruz. He invited me to attend, and to watch, as he sat at a table with representatives of the growers, the United Farm Workers Organizing Committee, and with the county sheriff. Mello asked each to tell the rest of the group what they wanted from the county and from one another.

The representative of the growers said his group didn't want union representatives to interfere with the harvest of lettuce and other crops in the valley stretching north and south of the Pajaro River. He also said they didn't want any violence.

The UFWOC organizers said they wanted the opportunity to talk with the men and women chopping the lettuce and cabbage and other row crops. And they didn't want any violence.

Sheriff Doug James, now the late Sheriff James, unusually sober for a post-lunch get-together, said he didn't want any violence.

Supervisor Mello listened, then thought for a few seconds, then spoke to his small congregation.

"I want you to allow union organizers on your fields to talk to the workers during lunch as well as during morning and afternoon breaks," he told the grower—who nodded but was obviously put off by the fact that Mello was referring to work breaks that, while mandated by law, were not actually allowed by farmers nor taken by workers.

Turning to the UFWOC men, Mello demanded: "I want you to let trucks on and off the fields without pickets blocking them so the workers can keep working and the growers can get their produce to market." The union guys nodded their assent.

Then Mello turned to the sheriff, a shirt-tail relative-in-law and, Mello feared, the leader of a huge squad of deputies, who could turn out to be the source of any violence that might occur.

"And if I hear," Mello roared at the sheriff, "of one deputy sheriff hitting or roughing up even just one union organizer or member, when next June's county budget hearings roll around, you and your department are not going to get one fucking dollar, not one fucking new squad car, not one fucking bullet!"

Well, everyone got just what they'd said they'd wanted, so everyone stood up, shook hands and left. I sat there a while sort of dumbfounded. I had seen a politician use the power that he possessed (and, to tell the truth, even more than he possessed) and I was fucking impressed.

* * *

The Pacific Gas and Electric Co. let us know in the 1970s that it was going to build a nuclear power plant on the coast at the tiny community of Davenport, about ten miles north of the Santa Cruz city limits. The idea was greeted with hardly any approval and with an extraordinary bit of disapproval and anger by residents of Santa Cruz—where a new University of California campus had brought to town sufficient numbers of students and professors to change the town's political leanings from the conservative business-oriented voters who left things in the hands of the Rotary Club and the Chamber of Commerce to lefty young people who knew they had the power and were set to use it.

To make a longer story shorter, all local appeals to stop approval of the Davenport nuclear generating plant fell on deaf ears. We learned that the county had no jurisdiction; location decisions for atomic power plants were made by the federal government—and in those days the feds loved nukes.

A very bright county supervisor whose district included the university campus and most of the City of Santa Cruz was one of the leaders of the opposition to the PG&E proposal. Gary Patton had a good track record on environmental issues and he was as smart as they come in the world of local politics. But like most of the rest of Santa Cruzans, Patton was frustrated by the county's lack of jurisdiction over the proposed nuclear generating facility.

Then one day Patton had a brainstorm. It turns out that while the county had no say-so over the site where the electric company wanted to build the plant at the edge of the seacliffs at Davenport, the county *did* still have its power to zone the land surrounding that site. So Patton quickly drew up a proposal to strengthen the forestland zoning on all sides except that side that was beneath the surf of the Pacific Ocean. The zoning, approved by his colleagues on the board of supervisors, banned the construction or installation of high-tension electrical power transmission lines.

That meant that while the power company was able to build its nuclear plant with no restrictions, it would not be able to transmit any electricity generated there off the site. It could not be connected to the state's electrical grid because no transmission lines would be allowed to connect it.

The nuclear plant was never built and faded into distant memory.

* * *

In a car with former State Senator Fred Farr, a Carmel Democrat now running for an Assembly seat during a special election, I asked all the usual questions for profiles I'd been assigned to write about him and his Republican opponent, who won the run-off a few weeks later. "Senator," (you always call a politician by the highest position he ever held, the way President Clinton will always be referred to as President Clinton, ditto Governor Schwarzenegger, etc.) I asked him, "what was your greatest accomplishment in the California Legislature?"

I expected some political bullshit about sheltering the poor or feeding the hungry or educating the little children. Or, in Senator Farr's case, some propaganda about his successful efforts to save Highway 1, the Coast Highway through Big Sur, often called the most-scenic stretch of road anywhere, from widening into a four- or six-lane freeway. Ladybird Johnson led the national effort to declare that beautiful stretch of coastline as a wild and scenic highway—and that, I believe, helped slow the inevitable march of Los Angelenos into Big Sur.

Instead, Fred Farr thought for a few seconds, then looked up and out across the artichoke fields that seemed to go on for a mile or more in every direction. He pointed to some portable latrines parked here and there across the fields.

"There," said Fred Farr, "is what I'm most proud of as a state legislator. I wrote the legislation that requires that Porta Potties be placed throughout the fields, close enough that workers can get to them when they need to."

It turns out that before Farr's bill was passed and then signed into law by some governor, farmworkers had to squat between the rows of whatever crop they were trimming or cutting when they had to pee or to take a crap. That, in turn, led, I later learned, to women being hassled and observed and even abused while doing what we all have to do but what we mostly are able to do in private.

I looked at Farr, whose son Sam was subsequently elected and served for years representing the Monterey Bay region in the U.S. House of Representatives. I realized as I stared at him, at former Senator Fred Farr, that I was looking at a great man.

* * *

Tom Bradley, the first black mayor of Los Angeles, gave little evidence of being a man willing to rock the boat. He seemed to be a go-along, get-along sort of politician, a mayor who listened to what the big power brokers had to say before agreeing with them.

I was not expecting to have much of an opinion one way or the other when the *San Jose Mercury News* sent me to Los Angeles to cover Democratic headquarters the night that Bradley expected to get elected governor and former Governor Jerry Brown hoped to get elected to the U.S. Senate. When I went to sleep long after the polls had closed, it was clear that Brown was not going to join the Senate; but Bradley seemed to be squeaking by.

I awoke early in my tiny room at the Biltmore Hotel, the party's headquarters on election night, and headed down to a 7 a.m. press conference with, I expected, governor-elect Bradley.

But as I walked along a corridor toward the press conference I saw that Bradley, whom I hadn't realized was taller than my six-foot, four inches, was walking beside me, tears in his eyes, sad tears, not tears of joy. He had lost when the final precinct counts were tallied.

So, I felt sorry for a while for Tom Bradley but I never had much good to say, or think, until I went back south to Los Angeles in 1985 to do an article on the city twenty years after the so-called Watts Riots. The first thing I learned was that in Watts and the other black communities surrounding it, the events were known as The Revolution.

While a *Mercury News* photographer took pictures showing what had been built back since The Revolution and what had not, I talked with neighbors, just plain folks as well as so-called community leaders. I wanted to talk to Tom Bradley but he was out of town. I did, however, spend an hour or so with a man who had served as one of Bradley's assistant mayors. I got off on the wrong foot by suggesting that many observers had pegged Bradley as a feckless person, both as a politician and as a man. His old friend, whose name I've forgotten, did his best to disabuse me of that notion.

When it came time to rebuild Watts, he told me, Bradley took the lead in coaxing the owners of burned-out businesses to return to their storefronts. He helped them find the money to rebuild, or at least to fix up their damaged properties.

Yeah, so? Isn't that what any mayor would do?

Then he told me about a piece of property right in the heart of Watts, just down the street from new low-income townhouses (with addresses painted on the rooftops to make it easier for cops—he said for fire-fighters—to identify each residence when "necessary" during emergencies).

Mayor Bradley, his associate assured me, found small businesses whose owners were willing to lease space in the small shopping center planned on the property in question. He told me that the owner of a dry-cleaning chain had signed a lease, as had a few other business operators. But there was a hang-up: The plans called for a supermarket to be the anchor business in the little neighborhood mall—and no supermarket owners were willing to risk building and stocking a store right in the center of the hotspot that sparked the Watts fires.

Rather than twiddle his thumbs and pat supermarket owners on their backs and tell them that he understood, Mayor Bradley, his vice-mayor told me, used some old-time roughneck politics to get a grocery chain to open a market in Watts. What he did, I was told, was to call the owner of one of the main chains of grocers then operating in Los Angeles after learning that the owners had plans to open several more stores around town.

The mayor's conversation with the chain owners, so I was told, went something like this:

"This is Mayor Tom Bradley. I'm calling to ask you to join in our rebuilding effort and open a new market in a project we're putting together down in South Central."

"You mean that project in Watts?"

"Yes."

"Well, Mayor, my partners and I have no intention of putting one of our markets on that site."

"How many markets do you have in L.A., sir?"

"We have …" I think the number was around a dozen.

"And," asked Mayor Bradley, "how many more do you hope to open around town?"

Again, the number was a few, let's say five.

"Well," said a grim and determined Bradley, if I can believe his friend and assistant, "if you want to open even one more damned market in this city you're going to have to open this one in South Central first! I mean it!"

And they did and I'm glad Tom Bradley knew that there are times in the world of politics when shaking a stick is more effective than shaking a hand.

* * *

I want to mention two more politicians, both of them are men I got to know and admire and befriend because of their basic human decency. Both have passed away.

One is my longtime pal John Vasconcellos, an Assemblyman, then State Senator, from what came to be known during his legislative tenure as Silicon Valley. John successfully promoted the concept of nourishing students' self-esteem as a way of integrating them into society as creative, thoughtful, productive, and just plain decent citizens. And after term limits forced John to leave the State Senate, he continued working with a small staff promoting the concept of decency in government as his legacy to the state he served for many decades.

The other is the late Ralph Sanson, a Santa Cruz County supervisor who often found himself, along with Henry Mello, in a two-man liberal minority on a five-member board. The board was dominated by politicians who believed that the "highest and best use" for any piece of land was to develop it as intensely as possible, whether that meant building condos on endangered wetlands or putting housing developments in redwood forests or covering the Pajaro Valley, some of the most-productive soil in the country, with houses and strip malls.

One afternoon the board of supervisors was scheduled to hear a presentation by Governor Reagan's appointees to Cal-Trans, the state department of transportation up in Sacramento. These guys were fresh off a similar presentation to the Santa Clara County board over in San Jose.

Now it happens to be that Santa Cruz and San Jose are linked by one of the most-dangerous stretches of twisty mountain road anywhere in the state of California. Much of Highway 17 is not only a series of dangerous curves, it is dark and often damp, even when it's not raining, beneath huge redwoods that stand along either side of the old highway, which was designed back when it was only a dirt road. And of course it's dark and winding up there. That's the summit of the Santa Cruz Mountains that motorists have to cross to get from one side of the hill to the other.

The Cal-Trans engineers had a gift, or gift horse, in their pockets: a new freeway that would be a straight shot between San Jose and Santa Cruz. It would not only have as many as a dozen lanes for automobiles but would include space down the middle for some sort of public transit, be it buses or even some sort of railroad.

This road-builders' dream would be expensive, but it would not cost the county anything. All the money would come from Sacramento and Washington, D.C. In short, it would, the transportation engineers assured everyone, be the greatest thing since the invention of the automobile.

Right away everyone in Santa Cruz realized that widening and straightening Highway 17 would mean the death of our town and our county as we knew it.

Sure, we all knew that the highway was dangerous. Most of us thought our friends and neighbors who commuted to San Jose were nuts. We knew, of course, that the new superhighway would attract commuters unwilling to negotiate the existing dangerous highway. It would make it easy for them to live near the ocean in Santa Cruz and to speed to work over the hill in the then fledgling Silicon Valley. Our main local nightmare was that we'd wake up some morning to discover that Highway 17 had been replaced by an expressway and that all the forests had been cut down and all the farms abandoned and all the beaches bulldozed so thousands and thousands of townhouses and apartments could be built for a new horde of people who worked on the other side of the hill.

The five county supervisors listened with apparent interest as the Cal-Trans guys made their spiel. They looked at slides and charts and architects' elevations showing new bridges and roadways and other glorious amenities that would make the commute a thing of beauty. All that was needed was an order by the Santa Cruz County board of supervisors designating Highway 17 as an official freeway.

When the presentation was finished, the supervisors looked at one another. Finally, Ralph Sanson spoke.

"I move," he said, "that we designate all lanes of Highway 17 as a one-way road *out* of Santa Cruz County." With no lanes leading into the county, he further explained.

"I second that motion," said Supervisor Mello.

The motion failed on a two-to-three vote. But a motion to take no action on the Cal-Trans idea passed unanimously.

Not quite knowing what had happened to them, but knowing that something very unusual was going on down in the hippie neighborhoods of Santa Cruz, the bureaucrats packed up their roadshow and headed back to Sacramento. They would have had to drive over Highway 17 to get there.

VII.

BRIDEGROOM:
THE SEVENTH TIME IS THE BEST

SONGBIRD,

OR

ANOTHER FABLE WITHOUT A MORAL?

In my house in Santa Cruz, in a sun-porch sort of space I called the Fish Lounge, there were two bird cages, a hearty ficus benjamina tree, an ivy plant that sent vines around most of the windows and walls, some other miscellaneous houseplants and a fifty-five-gallon aquarium that gave the room its name. The large Oscars and Jack Dempseys and other cichlids in the fish tank competed for attention with a proliferation of colorful finches in one cage and a somewhat dull-colored canary in the other.

After the canary had lived as my guest for several months without whistling any musical tones whatsoever, a call to the breeder where I'd purchased the bird provided me with the information that I'd bought a female and that only males sing. In other words, this bird was a complete waste of money, music-wise. I needed to bring her a mate.

A visit to a local feed-and-seed store that had a sideline in birds resulted in my introduction into the female canary's cage of a bright-yellow male, a lovely little guy, a true singer, the salesperson at the feed store assured me.

Nonetheless, the musical drought continued.

It wasn't long before I discovered one morning that the pair had fallen in canary love: A broken egg lay beneath one of the perches, smashed evidence on the cage bottom of avian romance in the air. A bit of reading convinced me to provide materials for a nest. I hoped the female canary would take advantage of it when she felt it was time to bring offspring into this environment—a cage made safe by closely spaced metal bars that kept out a world fraught with dangers, including a cat. (Cats can learn to leave caged birds alone. One teaches a cat not to make aggressive moves on such birds by holding the feline in one hand and a spray bottle filled with water in the other. The cat is positioned so its head is adjacent to the cage. Then the concerned householder starts screaming "No! No! No!" at the animal while simultaneously spraying it with the water bottle. This method has such a deleterious effect on a cat's instinctual need to attack birds it usually keeps the feline out of the room completely.)

Still there was no singing.

My female canary eschewed the little reed nest. Instead, she continued to drop her eggs from the considerable height of the perch, always with the same result: a broken egg splattered on the newspaper-lined cage bottom.

Meanwhile, the male canary was a complete bust as a crooner. Despite the promises of the feed-and-seed folks, the bird steadfastly refused to whistle even one dull note.

Later I learned that males sing only when they're lonely and horny and want to attract a mate. He had a mate. So, I decided, he would never sing.

Then one day as I sat in the nearby living room reading a newspaper I heard my male canary break out in glorious song. It was magnificent! It was as though the tiny, feathered Trapp Family Birds had gathered in the Fish Lounge and were treating me to a symphony of song.

I walked into the Fish Lounge so I could see my bright-yellow male canary serenading his mate—and sharing his song with the finches in the other cage, with the fish (even though they can't, as far as I know, hear birdsong), and with me, his owner and master. Only this canary was not singing to his mate at all. In the previous minute or two she had breathed her last and had fallen off the perch, landing dead as a doornail on the *San Jose Mercury News* on the bottom of the brass-wire cage. She was no more. The male was a widower.

There he was, on a perch above his dearly departed, singing his little bird heart out. And it was anything but a sad or plaintive tune that the little guy was warbling. It was as though he were singing, "Oh, What a Beautiful Morning..." and was at the part where "the corn is as high as an elephant's eye..." and he could hardly wait to get on to the next glorious musical score in his repertoire.

As I said, I learned from a canary book that males do sing, but they only sing to attract females. If they have a female canary, any female canary, it turns out, the males figure there's no need to waste a grand aria, no reason to croon a snappy melody, no damned reason to be chirpy at all. If the mate dies, that's a whole different kettle of fish.

* * *

My friend Riley calls me a "serial monogamist." That's not really true. I feel as though I've been more like a serial lover, in the sense of being in love or wanting and trying to be in love constantly.

I *have* been married seven times (and divorced six) and I do like weddings, at least my own weddings, and I am convinced that my present marriage, to Claire Christine Hultman Quarnstrom, is my ultimate, final connubial relationship.

Chris and I met at our fortieth high school reunion, as mentioned above. We had lived near one another, just a few blocks apart, in a Chicago suburb for the four years that we attended New Trier High School. But since I had come out of St. Joseph's Catholic School and she from a public junior high, we had never met. Even after we both matriculated at New Trier, we still never met nor even shared a class or study hall at the high school.

More about Chris later. First, though, I want to note that I am nothing like the male canary that broke into song like a ham actor in a local little musical theater when his mate bit the dust. Rather, I see myself as a sensitive guy, often wounded in love, who luckily stumbled through a gauntlet of often angry, occasionally sad, girlfriends, women-friends with benefits, live-in lovers, wives and exes, and mistresses unknown, at least for a while, to some of the various women mentioned earlier in this sentence.

Also, and this becomes more and more apparent as I grow older and find that some marriages which have lasted for decades are suddenly on the rocks, I realize that the concept of marriage was invented when people died of old age before they were thirty! Modern medicine and knowledge about what to eat and especially what not to eat are among the advances that have prolonged marriage far beyond the shelf life envisioned by earlier arbiters of morality. Some cultures, or many cultures, actually, don't limit loving couples to either monogamy or permanence. After all, nothing lasts, as Kesey said. Nothing created by mankind, as the Buddha pointed out, can avoid falling apart. Don't expect that the industrious, helpful, handsome man you married forty years ago is still any of those things. Odds are that he has changed so much you would no longer recognize him were you at the age when he was courting you. Ditto for the men regarding the gorgeous, accommodating, loving, intensely sexual young woman you got hitched to all those decades ago.

My advice: Keep in mind that your marriage is what it is and that's not necessarily something that you bargained for. If you want to move on, tell your spouse, get a lawyer if you must, then split. Otherwise, figure out a way to live with it.

Actually, many (or at least some) of the women I've lived with remain my friends, good friends. Others would no doubt run me down with their fuel-efficient little cars were they to see me standing on the street in front of them. Others I would avoid, were I to see them, by wearing fake dreadlocks and long, fake beards, if necessary, or by running in the other direction down dark and dangerous alleyways.

My first former wife died of cancer not long after our son was shot to death. The second, whom I married at a rock-and-roll dance at the old, original Fillmore Auditorium in San Francisco, later married another friend, then lived with yet another close pal of mine, then dropped almost out of sight, although I know she's still in touch with mutual acquaintances. The third, whom I understand was relocated once by the federal witness protection folks, lives out of state; the fourth never remarried and stays in touch via the Internet. My fifth ex-wife, also married to a good pal of mine, is friendly and visited Chris and me two or three years ago. The less said about my sixth wife the better, and that goes for each of us.

Nonetheless, there are some things I should mention about each of these women and a few others, and about a lesson I finally learned, although I'm not always able to put this particular insight into practice:

It is better not to be an asshole when dealing with a wife or a lover.

That is not always as easy as it sounds.

CRUSH

When I was a skinny teenager with absolutely no experience whatsoever with girls other than to think about them when I masturbated and to act like a frightened geek if I actually bumped into one, I had a crush on a girl a year or so younger than I. Let me call her Sandra, although that is nothing at all like her real name. And while I guess I could describe her as a busty blonde that, too, would be very far from the truth.

I know I'd had crushes on other girls as I'd grown up. One, for instance, was a little girl in my early elementary school classes. I remember virtually nothing about her other than I used to think sweet thoughts about her when I was a schoolboy. I was fascinated to learn from an old class photo my father sent me many years later, as he was cleaning out the attic of our family home, that this particular little girl was black. In fact, she was the only black student in the class picture and may well have been one of the few black children in Longview. The only other "Negro," as African Americans were known in the 1940s, whom I can recall was the man who swept out the downtown barber shops. He went from shop to shop, sweeping each for a while before continuing on his janitorial circuit among the five or six places where men and boys, could go to get their ears lowered, as wits put it in those times. By the time he'd return to the first shop there was another accumulation of men's hair on the floor around the barbers' chairs.

I believe I took Sandra to a dance when I was a sophomore, perhaps to what was called a sock-hop—where we danced on the polished gym floor wearing no shoes, just socks. I don't recall kissing her at the end of our evening together and I can't even remember how we got to the dance; perhaps our parents brought us separately and dropped us off so we could meet before heading into the school gymnasium. Whether we again went out, or even met up when we were out, is doubtful. I knew she was beautiful and I still think she is beautiful.

When I saw Sandra on an up escalator as I was on the opposing down escalator almost three decades later and two-thousand miles away from that school gym, I recognized her immediately. She hadn't changed. She was still as beautiful as I remembered, with her bobbed hair still dark, her figure still trim and her eyes still exotic, the only word I can think of to describe Sandra's eyes.

I called her name, her maiden name, and when she'd reached the top of the escalator she turned and I waved. I rode back up to her level and introduced myself. I didn't look the same. I was not still the tall, skinny boy with the nerdy haircut who'd danced the bop and the bunny-hop and the hokey-pokey with her all those years before. She recognized me, though, and remembered our brief relationship, if one date and making googly eyes at her in the school cafeteria might constitute a relationship.

Amazingly, Sandra not only looked exactly like the beautiful girl I'd known and had wished I'd known better in high school—she was wearing braces!

Sandra said it had been a long time since anyone had used her maiden name. She'd been married for almost a quarter-century and, to my immediate delight, said she and her husband had just separated. At that time I was, as I often was, recently divorced.

Would she care to go out sometime for a cup of coffee or a drink or for dinner? Dinner, Sandra said, would be wonderful and I could pick her up at her house. She gave me the particulars and we parted knowing we'd soon have what would be, I figured, our second date.

Sandra and her children lived comfortably. She said, when I arrived to pick her up for our dinner date, that the kids were with their grandparents for the weekend.

I was hot and I was fascinated. This seemed to be one of those fantasy situations in the men's magazines I was writing for, very close to the run-of-the-mill cheerleader fantasies but even sexier and better because this was the first girl I'd ever asked on a date and physically *she had not changed one bit* since that awkward evening in the high school gym all those years before.

We had an enjoyable dinner, a couple of drinks, and a nice chat about high school friends we'd had in common. Then Sandra suggested we go back to her place. I couldn't argue with that.

Once we were at her house, it didn't take long to get to the tearing-the-clothes-off-one-another stage. Soon we were in her bed. I was thanking my lucky stars as our groping and exploring, feeling, kissing and touching with hands and with fingers and with mouths had us both ready for what I knew had to come next:

Sandra looked into my blue eyes with her beautiful, exotic, dark eyes and in a sexy, throaty whisper spoke softly into my ear.

"Lee," she murmured, "I like to take it up the butt."

IN-LAWS

It didn't take too many sips of beer to get my Filipino father-in-law Gene drunk. In fact, Gene was so short and wiry that one can of Safeway's Brown Derby beer would knock him for a loop.

That's why I trust the drunken version of Gene's Pearl Harbor Day story instead of the sanitized version he told me several times when he was more or less sober.

In that version, Gene said that he and "some Pilipino boys," as the word is pronounced in English by first-generation immigrants from the Philippines, "went looking for some Japanese," after they'd learned that part of their homeland was bombed on December 7, 1941. Gene didn't learn for a year that his family on the island of Luzon had been killed in the Japanese bombing.

Gene's American family, like that of many Filipinos who were encouraged to emigrate to the U.S. in the 1920s and 1930s, was a product of America's immigration policy at the time. Farmers who needed workers to do the actual labor involved in raising fruits and vegetables wanted men, not women, to work in their fields. So, depending on local policies, anywhere between eighty and ninety percent of the farm laborers imported from the Philippines were males. That meant there weren't enough Filipina women available for the men to marry and that meant that relationships developed between the Filipino men and Latinas, women who for the most part were from Mexico.

There were, of course, white women who fell for the Filipino farm laborers and that became a bone of contention in America's Southwest, including California, the way black-white relationships were troublesome for white racists in the South (and elsewhere) in the USA.

Lupe, my third wife, was the child of a Filipino father and a Mexican mother. She was raised by her father's brother, Gene, and her mother's cousin, Gene's Mexican wife. She was brought up thinking of them as her real parents and she didn't learn until she was twelve that a man she had thought of as her uncle was in fact her biological father. The same day that her real dad told her the truth about her real parents was a sad day for Lupe: Hours later, after Gene and his wife had driven Lupe home—to her home, their home—her true father's pickup truck stalled on some railroad tracks and he was killed when a freight train barreled through the crossing.

We went to visit her real mother, her birth mother, one day. She was estranged from the rest of the family, apparently for having had Lupe out of wedlock, something unforgiveable to her Catholic cousins. Lupe said she felt little affection for her real mom and continued to consider Gene and his wife as her parents.

I liked her folks—hell, I've always liked all of my in-laws! I must say, however, that there are few accents more difficult to understand than the English spoken by someone raised speaking Ilocano, the Filipino dialect Gene used until he came to America. It was particularly difficult to understand Gene if he'd had more than a half-can of beer and it was really hard if he'd also gulped down a shot or two of the brandy or whiskey or tequila that some of the sturdier, larger Mexican in-laws would bring for holiday dinners or birthday celebrations.

Speaking of celebrations, my good friend Bill Kelsay—who served as a judge in Santa Cruz for many years and who performed four of my seven marriages—said the reception after the ceremony joining Lupe and me as partners for life, or for a year or two, was one of the best parties ever. We had a Mexican band singing traditional songs as well as playing salsa-flavored rock-and-roll. We had a lot of booze. We had a score of drunken Filipino in-laws, in a tradition I'd not known about until a wad of money was tossed in my face, throwing money at Lupe and me as we danced. And we had some drunken politician pals playing their own dance music when the *mariachis* took a break.

We had a daughter, Lupe and I, but she was very premature and died a half-hour after she was born. I never saw her. When she awoke, Lupe asked me, "Where's my baby?" I had to tell her that she had almost died from the loss of blood before we got to the hospital and that the baby had not made it. It was the saddest and the hardest thing I've ever had to tell someone.

A nun at the hospital told me she had baptized the infant before she died. I figured, and tried to convince Lupe, that the baby had needed just that half-hour of attention and baptism this time around through the endless cycles of living and dying. I don't think that impressed her.

We buried our daughter, whom we named Yolanda, in Pioneer Cemetery on the outskirts of Watsonville, where I worked on the daily paper.

There were many sad aspects to my wife Guadalupe's life, and not just the tale of learning about her real parents only to have her dad die hours later, but I don't think it is my place to reveal stories that others whom I have loved might want to keep secret.

Gene's story, however, need not be kept under wraps.

Out of their minds with anger (and probably with alcohol) the "Pilipino boys" of Tempe, Arizona—where Gene was working in the tomato fields, he said—went "looking for Japs." Why? To avenge their Luzon countrymen who had been victims of Japanese bombs that same day that much of America's Pacific fleet was destroyed by Japanese bombs at Pearl Harbor.

The angry gang of young Filipino farm laborers ran into the Tempe town constable, Gene told me. The constable, clearly disturbed at the thought of enraged, drunken Filipinos raging through his bailiwick, told Gene and his cronies not to give him any details. He didn't want to know what they were planning and he didn't want to know afterward what they'd done. No matter what it was, of course, it wasn't going to be something pretty.

The first three times Gene told me this story, three times when he was relatively sober, he said they'd searched through Tempe's bars and hotels where Japanese farmworkers usually gathered. There was none to be found—except one poor working stiff they found asleep in a flophouse. Gene believed the local Japanese had been warned in advance to go underground on

December 7 so they could avoid lynch mobs such as his. (Gene told me once that he'd been urged by some mysterious Japanese secret agent to attend an anti-American rally "in a big tent" near Tempe. There was a large Rising Sun flag in the tent, according to my father-in-law. Gene said the Japanese man was trying to recruit Filipinos to join in some pan-Asian attempt to sabotage farm equipment when Japan went to war with the United States. Gene said he stalked out of the rally, as did his Filipino companions.)

Those first three times I heard the tale of Pearl Harbor day, Gene and his companions beat the crap out of that one and only Japanese man unlucky or unwitting enough not to go into hiding.

The fourth time Gene told me the story it had a slightly different ending.

"So we found this Japanese man in the hotel," he mumbled as I tried to decipher his alcohol-enhanced Ilocano accent, "and Lee, we all had our knives and we stabbed him and we killed him."

Gene paused for a moment and I thought his story, his new and true version with the fatal ending, was done. Then he jerked his head up and looked into my eyes with an intensity that can only be generated by the severely inebriated.

"But you know what, Lee?" he asked, rhetorically, "I think he was a Chinese."

WEDDINGS AND MORE ABOUT THOMAS PYNCHON

How could I have known that very first time my bride and I tied the knot that it and several other marital knots would be tied and would unravel over the years, over several decades?

Getting married, you know, is a way of getting high. There is that moment, after you've recited whatever vows you may have chosen, and when the officiating minister or judge says the formulaic words, "I now pronounce you husband and wife," when you look into the eyes of your beloved, your new spouse, and you feel a flash of ecstasy that is just about as high as it's possible to experience with or without some artificial or spiritual stimulant. Only a girl- or boyfriend telling you for the first time, "I love you," or the birth of your own child, is, as far as I'm concerned, as powerful. I am hoping the moment of death might be, as well.

But is that a reason to keep getting married? Probably not, but perhaps. Maybe that's why Brigham Young and his cronies had so many wives: so they could keep getting that natural nuptial high.

My first wedding had no ceremony but it did have that exquisite moment of transcendence when the judge, some Seattle jurist whose name I promptly forgot by the time we left his chambers, pronounced Judy and me wife and husband.

My mother happened to be in Seattle from Chicago to visit her mom, my grandmother, Mayme. I didn't find out until years later that my mother also took advantage of these family visits to rifle through the medicine cabinets of my aunts and uncles and cousins looking for any sedatives that might help knock her out. I did know, though, that she had begun to drink sweet wine (which my dad, when he was some kind of bigwig at the Chicago Council on Alcoholism, referred to as "fortified wine," as in, "Your mother is at her fortified wine again tonight"). She'd begun to drink a lot of fortified wine, also known as port.

During an adulthood that must have degenerated into a continuing and depressing series of clandestine trips to the liquor store, my mother became a less and less pleasant person to be around—or even to speak with on the telephone. She and my father lived in a dry Chicago suburb, Wilmette. The nearest liquor store wasn't that far away as the crow flies, but a mid-morning trip to Schaefer's Liquors generally meant that you were a secret drinker who lived in one of the handful of dry communities north of the Chicago city limits.

My mother had a few friends, but her unhappiness, her drinking, her slurring of repetitious put-downs of my dad, her tendency to be a mean drunk, and her unwavering hewing to the most-repressive forms of Roman Catholicism made her unbearable, at least to my brother and me. I've wondered for years why my father stayed married to her and now it's too late to ask. Gordon had a series of girlfriends and mistresses during my folks' years as a married couple. I can only conclude that neither of them was ready to split up and lose their relatively comfortable way of life in their comfortable suburban house—comfortable, that is, if you don't count all the miserable, booze-induced moments of bitterness about his cheating.

So here she was, my mother, in Seattle, the same day Judy and I were heading to the courthouse for a quickie wedding in the judge's chambers. Judy and her daughter Susan and I gathered at my grandmother Mayme's house, where my mom was staying during her visit.

When the time came for us to drive down to the courthouse, my mother suddenly announced that she couldn't possibly attend the heathen (i.e., not Catholic) wedding. That was not, actually, because there was no priest involved. No, it was because Judy had been previously married and divorced.

My grandmother looked at her middle-aged daughter, shook her head, and in the exasperated voice of a mother reaching the limits of her tolerance, that voice moms use to round up the kids when they're having tantrums in the cereal aisle at the supermarket, demanded:

"Lenore, get in the car!"

Lenore did as ordered. We got to the courthouse with no further maternal outbursts. Before the few minutes it took the judge to say all the things the law required him to say, my mother had taken Susie by the hand and retired to a far corner of his chambers. While the judge intoned the official marriage lingo of the State of Washington, little Susan, fascinated at these new surroundings, gaped at shelves packed with law books and at a wall decorated with a plentitude of diplomas, certificates, awards, and photos of the judge with people who looked as though they could be important. Neither Susan nor her new grandmother Lenore listened to a word the judge or Judy and I said. Susie had a reason. She was only a toddler.

I felt that cosmic flash, even in the grim company of my mother, when the judge told Judy and me that we were wife and husband. What I didn't know at the time but learned any way, was that weddings without fun are no fun. Weddings should be big whoopdeedoos, parties, bacchanalias, fiestas! Yes, a wedding's purpose is to join together two people, man and woman (man and man, or woman and woman), whose relationship has evolved into a marriage. And I am a firm believer in marriage—and in parties!

No need to reiterate the story of that marriage's end a year-and-a-half later, the move south from Seattle to Oakland of my soon-to-be ex-wife Judy and my stepdaughter Susan and my six-month-old son, Eric, on that same day that John F. Kennedy's life ended in Dallas.

I understand that some men actually think of themselves as bachelors. I had no such self-image during the three years that followed, years spent, for a while, in Seattle but for the most part in Bay Area beatnik bars and beds and browsing in bookstores and mostly getting laid. My friend Toni Frazer, a beautiful Chicago woman I met at my brother's pad in the Haight-Ashbury before it was the Haight-Ashbury, taught me how to dance, how to dance like big city rock-and-rollers, like she did, instead of the embarrassing suburban white-boy shuffle I'd picked up somewhere along the way.

My San Francisco pals included some old friends from the Windy City, including my City News amigo Julius Karpen. We all drank enormous amounts of booze. We learned that Carlo Rossi's Red Mountain Wine, at a dollar-forty-nine a gallon, might cost twenty cents a jug more than Mountain Castle red, the cheap house brand wine at the Safeway store, but it was worth it because it didn't stain the carpets as badly when spilled.

I moved with Toni to an apartment across the street from the Panhandle of Golden Gate Park. Then her old boyfriend Len arrived from Chicago and Toni was gone. But Len turned out to be a good friend, someone to drink and eat Bennies and yammer and smoke pot with. Later, much later, Len lived with my second ex-wife, Space Daisy. Then he became one of my first peers to die, one of my first good friends whose body just gave out after too many years of too-hard living.

But I still remember the thrills riding behind him on his bright red, 650-cc motorcycle, neither of us yet twenty-five years old, zipping up and down San Francisco's hills, Twin Peaks, Bernal Heights, Diamond Heights, Potrero Hill. It was like riding in a car with Neal Cassady at the wheel: neither Len nor I nor Toni had any fear. I knew I was safe no matter how fast Len drove his bike, no matter how many corners he took at speed, no matter how many cars and trucks and streetcars he danced the machine between and around, no matter how high or how stoned or how drunk he or I might be. It was magic. We were all each other's guardian angels.

I understood immediately why Toni had left me for Len. He was a good-looking guy to boot—tall, thin, brooding. I think of Len and I think of my son when I read those E. E. Cummings lines that begin, "Buffalo Bill's/defunct..." and end, "how do you like your blueeyed boy/Mister Death[?]"

Those very early days when I lived in what would soon be known as the Haight-Ashbury were powerful reminders to each of us beatniks/hippies/longhairs that we were not alone. I remember one day walking along the edge of the panhandle of Golden Gate Park and seeing, perhaps a block-and-a-half away, another guy my age, who, like me, had hair down over his collar. From that far away we each smiled at one another and when we met, and before we passed, we had goofy grins on our faces as we both recognized a comrade-in-arms. I thought of the Dylan song and thought to myself, "Yes, we *do* know what's happening, don't we, Mr. Jones?"

One of my roommates in my apartment near the Panhandle of Golden Gate Park was Bruce Barton, a fellow drinker—only Bruce was not the same kind of drinker I was. He got loud and boisterous and, eventually, pugnacious when he was drinking. I enjoyed some of the drama during his stay in that apartment, but I was just as happy when he moved out.

The drama generally centered on debts owed to the telephone company. Bruce was at the time listed in the Bell Telephone white pages as d'Artagnan Pig. In those days nobody I knew was listed under his or her own name. It was too easy to come up with a funny name and too easy to skip out on an overdue phone bill and to get a new phone under a new funny name.

Early one morning I heard Bruce shouting into the phone in his room, "Pig? Pig? I'm French, you idiot! It's Pige!"—pronounced with a soft "g." He slammed down the phone and went back to sleep. The next morning Bruce's phone again rang very early. A moment after he picked it up he again began to shout: "Pige? Pige? It's Pig! Pig! Are you afraid to say *Pig*?" He hung up and returned to sleep.

Later that day Bruce called the phone company and said he was moving and was terminating his service. Then he waited a day and called again, describing himself as a new resident who wanted telephone service. And what, they asked, is your name?

From then on, at least for a while, Bruce was listed in the San Francisco telephone directory as Monroe Sweetmeat.

* * *

My friends and I spent much of our time in joints along Grant Avenue, San Francisco's bohemian enclave in North Beach, an Italian neighborhood with beatnik bars, coffee houses, and little restaurants where locals took dates to dinner. A typical clientele in some of those Italian holes in the wall might include a writer and artist or two, a couple out with their children, a painter, a poet, and a Mafioso. The food was delicious.

One day some friends who lived on Russian Hill called and asked if I could come to dinner and meet their other guest, Thomas Pynchon. Of course! I loved Thomas Pynchon. I still love Thomas Pynchon. He may be the single most-important American writer as far as my contemporaries go. He is to me what young people call "a God."

That afternoon, sitting in a bar drinking and contemplating breaking bread with Thomas Pynchon that evening, I noticed that Slow Walkin' Jackson had come in and was sitting nearby. Slow Walkin' Jackson was a North Beach habitué and pimp who had recently been shot in the leg in front of the Coffee Gallery.

Between us was a truly beautiful young Chinese lady who was his protégé. She and I got to talking and, as things turned out, we made a date to get together for dinner after her shift working for Slow Walkin' Jackson had ended for the day. I told her I'd drive her to her parents' home down on the Peninsula, where I was working for the time as a reporter for the *San Mateo Times*.

I had made one of those snap decisions: I could meet Thomas Pynchon any time, I thought, or I could make love with a gorgeous Chinese woman. Obviously, I chose sex with the Asian lady. Who wouldn't?

Unfortunately, after I'd dropped her at her house in the middle of the night and had driven to the *San Mateo Times,* where I slept on my desk, and after I'd gone home after my shift at the *Times* and after I'd slept that night with a woman who was what they call today a "friend with benefits," I learned, in an angry phone call from that friend, that while enjoying the benefits I had given her the crabs! Damn, I had to have gotten them from the Asian beauty. I needed Sta-Dee Dusting Powder.

Banned after the discovery that DDT was killing rare and endangered species of birds, Sta-Dee Dusting Powder was the crab-killer of choice in my circle. You just sprinkled the stuff liberally on the affected areas, anywhere that hosted pubic hair. By the next day the crab lice and their "nits," which I guess were unhatched eggs, were dead as doornails.

This was no consolation to my friend with crabs, and definitely not a benefit. She had a date that night with a rich guy on whom she had some sort of designs and, as she screamed down the phone lines, **I had fucked the whole thing up.** She wasn't even consoled when I offered to stop by the Rexall drug store on Columbus Avenue and pick up a bottle of Sta-Dee to bring over to her pad.

* * *

My beatnik buddies and I drank and danced at beatnik bars like the Coffee Gallery and the Anxious Asp and old-timer Italian hangouts like Gino and Carlo's bar, a place with the best rock-and-roll jukebox on North Beach. It was a neighborhood joint where younger beats and older Italians shot 8-ball pool, at a quarter a game, the prize a drink, usually a beer—or some grappa if the winner was an elderly Italian man, drinks purchased by the loser. By the time anyone had won, or lost, a few games—it made no difference—one was well on the way to being blind drunk.

I literally thank whomever it is when we say we're thanking "our lucky stars" that I never killed anybody driving home drunk—and I drove home drunk way, way too many times: from North Beach to my place to the Haight-Ashbury; from Harry's Bar in Los Angeles where I'd drink (a lot) nightly with my *Hustler* friends, then drive out to my place near Venice Beach night after night after night; and from anyplace else, and there are plenty of such places around Chicago and around California, to places I lived or hung out or crashed for a night. I did get pulled over just once but that was the night I was celebrating the resignation of President Richard M. Nixon, and who didn't celebrate that day?

Getting stopped for a DUI wasn't the reason I stopped drinking and driving. Rather, I was lucky enough many years ago to lose my taste for alcohol. This wasn't like my friend Julius, who quit drinking after his first LSD trip. It was just something that happened for no particular reason. I used to love drinking and getting drunk. Now I rarely drink, never have more than one, and would almost rather get one of those pokes in the eye with a sharp stick than suffer through a hangover.

* * *

The fifteen-hundred or so hippies who attended my second wedding had no idea they were going to be guests at my nuptials with Space Daisy. They were at the Fillmore Auditorium for a rock-and-roll dance. One of San Francisco's premier psychedelic rock bands, Quicksilver Messenger Service, was on the bill that night. The band played, everybody danced and Space Daisy—Judith Washburn—and I were wed. Afterward, Bill Graham, who operated the Fillmore and was becoming the top dog in the emerging Bay Area rock scene, threw us a reception in a small back room, upstairs and off the main dance floor.

The third wedding reception was, as my friend Judge Bill Kelsay noted, the best: Filipinos drunk out of their minds, enthusiastic mariachis, good food, guests passed out in the rain out in the parking lot of the rural Salsipuedes Community Hall in the Pajaro Valley east of Watsonville, where I was working for the daily paper, the *Watsonville Register-Pajaronian*. Lupe was a lovely bride. My mother would have loved this wedding. It was in a Catholic church. Lupe had never been married or divorced.

Uncle Jacinto, who'd come from the Philippines the same time as Lupe's dad, was among the guests at the wedding. He promised to come down to our rural home outside Watsonville someday soon and butcher a pig for a "real Filipino barbecue."

As barbecue day approached I found where I could buy a pig, a young pig, just the right size for our family cookout. My friend Jon Sagen, who was living in the shed next to our garage, accompanied me when we drove an old Plymouth, borrowed from my brother, out to the pig ranch to pick up our little porker. We put him in the trunk of the car and slowly made our way back home, where Lupe's family was gathering for the roast pig feast.

(As an aside, my brother Dean always had an old Plymouth in those days; he favored the sturdy Chrysler Corp. vehicles of the 1949 to 1953 era and would sometimes follow old people behind the wheels of such cars to their homes, where he was often successful at convincing them they should sell him their run-down vehicle before it broke down somewhere, stranding them on a freeway or in a bad neighborhood. He was known to his fellow old-car enthusiasts in Berkeley as "Sleazy Dean.")

While Uncle Jacinto and I led the pig around to the back of the house, where a barbecue pit sat alongside my quarter-acre garden, Jon set to work cleaning out the trunk of Dean's Plymouth. The trunk was coated with pig shit, pig shit everywhere: on the floor mat of the trunk, on the spare tire, on the rear of the back seat, and on the inside of the trunk lid. It was about as bad a mess as anyone would ever want to see. (Later, while the pig was roasting, I went out to see how Jon's clean-up job was coming along. I found him bent over the edge of a fifty-five gallon drum I used as a garbage can. He was puking.)

With one of his sons at his side, Uncle Jacinto killed the pig. He spoke something in his Ilocano tongue as he slowly, very slowly, stuck a foot-long stick down the animal's throat. The hog didn't complain. Then Jacinto, using a special knife he'd brought with him, sliced the pig's throat and began collecting its blood in a pail he put beneath its head. He said the animal had to bleed to death gently so no adrenaline would get into the animal's blood.

That, he said, would cause the blood to curdle. Uncle Jacinto's wife and my mother-in-law took the pail and the blood into the house where they mixed it with vinegar and mint, turning it into "Filipino gravy" to use as a sauce on the meat. Actually, it was pretty tasty.)

Jacinto shaved the bristles from the hide of the hog, then sliced it into pieces for the barbecue. As the butcher, he got to keep the head, which he stuck in the freezer and took home with him as a reward for doing the day's dirty work. Lupe told me the "face meat" from the pig's cheeks was considered the tastiest part of the animal.

Finally, after we'd watched Jacinto cut the carcass into pieces, he cut the asshole out of the animal and told us not to watch as he took it to the rear of my property and buried it. He said all of the bad energy resulting from the pig's death accumulated in the anus and that it had to be buried secretly so no one could dig it up and use it for evil purposes. Of course!

The barbecued pork was delicious and the family gathering was a success and Uncle Jacinto had passed along to his teenage son some of the tribal secrets he had brought to America from the jungles back home on the Island of Luzon.

* * *

Wedding number four, to Karen Smith, tall and blond and beautiful, was slightly more subdued than its predecessors. That marriage lasted only three or four months, and while Karen and I are still good friends, those three or four months are not worth mentioning.

When Melody Sharp and I got married we did it at our little house on Pacific Avenue, in Venice, just a block south of Santa Monica and a block from the beach and the famous Venice Ocean Front Walk. This was during a cocaine blitz in Los Angeles and I think almost all the guests spent some of their time at the reception in the bathroom or in the back yard snorting coke—or passed out in their cars in the rear parking lot, near an intersection where a squad of local street-walkers patrolled the border of Santa Monica and Venice so they could move from one jurisdiction to the other when cops might decide to hassle them.

Although I cannot believe that anyone can "remain friends" with a former spouse in the immediate wake of a divorce, it is clearly possible to renew friendships once the anger, bitterness, jealousy, or whatever other negative emotions fueled the fires of splitting up have passed or been forgotten. Melody and I are again friendly. Her late husband Jon Sägen, an artist and sculptor, had been a good friend since I met him hours before my wedding at the Fillmore Auditorium. He had been Space Daisy's first husband's closest friend and had welded a lovely tiara for Space Daisy, Judith, to wear during our rock-and-roll wedding.

I see in photos that Gene Anthony took at the Fillmore wedding and published in a book called *The Summer of Love: Haight-Ashbury at its Highest*, that Space Daisy is wearing something that I assume is the tiara at the moment that we were pronounced husband and wife—but it's missing in a subsequent photograph of us dancing, although my wide-wale corduroy suit with bell-bottom pants shows up nicely. My pals and best men for that wedding, Julius Karpen and Len Frazier, are in some of the pictures in the book.

* * *

My Santa Cruz front porch was the scene for my wedding to Denise. I think the day soured for her when my former girlfriend Donna Blakemore introduced herself as "wife number three-and-a-half." But who cares? It was great to see Donna and to see some old high school newspaper friends who'd come from Chicago and L.A. and even from Florida to see me wed.

Actually, the whole relationship might have soured the day I met Denise's folks. Her dad was a few days younger than I! We got along well, I guess. But as Denise and I left for home, her father cringed when I asked, as we were going out the door, "Do you mind if I call you Dad?"

No, there were other reasons that marriage soured and I take all the blame. But there was one happy result of this unpleasant relationship.

Denise insisted that I accompany her to a marriage counselor. I know she thought the therapist would see through me and finally pin the blame for our unpleasant and occasionally nearly violent relationship entirely on me. I did, too, although I also suspected that any counselor worth her salt would rely on the old adage that "it takes two to tango" and somehow find both of us responsible for fixing things if we wished to stay together.

We did focus on me for the first few sessions. The counselor picked apart my psyche, helping me to admit, much like a POW being held in North Korea would admit way back then that he was a capitalist aggressor, that yes, I was an asshole.

One afternoon the therapist said something like, "Denise, let's talk next about your role in this situation." Denise got up and stomped out, leaving me to make one of those "Well, what can I do?" shrugs. So Lori the therapist asked if I wanted to work on my own emotional wellbeing. I said, "Sure."

Lori used something called eye-movement desensitization as a therapeutic tool. This consists of the therapist wagging a finger back and forth in front of the patient while I, the patient, kept my head still and followed her finger with my eyes. Then she would ask, "What are you feeling right now?" I'd answer and she'd go back to moving her finger back and forth, back and forth. Then she'd ask again about what I was feeling.

Often, I'd say I was thinking about the death of my son, the absence of my son. What was I feeling? Alone. Abandoned.

I don't know how the eye-movement deal works, but it did. I figured that it must be connected somehow to REM sleep, rapid-eye-movement sleep, the time when dreams arise.

After a few sessions, to my amazement, those dreams about my son, those happy dreams that Eric was still alive, those dreams with the depressing realization upon waking that he was still dead, those dreams went away, apparently forever. I have not dreamed of Eric since.

But I do think of him often. And often, I weep when I do.

* * *

And finally—and I mean that—Chris and I were wed in the Whittier backyard of her son Tony, who became my stepson when the minister pronounced Chris and me as husband and wife. Whittier is the next town west of La Habra, where Chris and I and our two Welsh corgis now reside. It's a nice house, Chris is a wonderful friend and helpmate and her sons, daughter, and grandchildren have become the family that I never really had. Yes, I could call, for instance, the Merry Pranksters "family"—but no Prankster ever sent me a Fathers Day card!

Chris says she was warned, when we were first introduced at our fortieth high school reunion in Winnetka, north of Chicago, that I was some sort of lothario who'd been married, and divorced, six times already. But each of us knew within minutes of that introduction that we were falling in love and that we were meant for one another. I thought about this incredible, beautiful, bright woman for every moment of a long, storm-tossed flight back to California from that high school reunion. And Chris, when she returned a call that I'd left on her Southern California answering machine, told me, when I asked how she was doing, "I'm floating."

Chris's family learned about my six previous marriages from an early television reality show, *Love Chronicles*, taped not long after we were wed. The show's "The Marrying Kind" episode featured Chris and me holding hands, being the loving couple that we were and are, and exploring my former marriages. At one point Chris was asked if she was concerned about being Wife Number Seven.

No, she replied, we'd already had fabulous times together and no matter how our relationship turned out, no one could take memories of those times away from her.

* * *

No one ever asks me for any advice about getting married, so I don't know whether I'd have any to offer. I do have lots of advice for anyone who wishes to *stay* married, but no one has asked for my thoughts about that, either. And not even a stepson and a stepdaughter, each trying to get out of troubled marriages, have asked me about one topic that I know well and have a wealth of advice to give, if only someone would ask: getting divorced.

All in all, though, I guess my advice on keeping a marriage together boils down to "Don't be an asshole," and my advice on getting divorced is, essentially, "Get a good lawyer, and, there are a lot of other fish in the sea!"

VIII.

SO IT'S COME TO THIS?

A GUN, BUDDHA AND *LA VIRGEN DE GUADALUPE*

My writing room is painted a deep red. It overlooks the backyard citrus trees they tell us are doomed to fall prey to a tiny bug that carries the fatal and incurable "yellow dragon disease." It is a small room and the darkest of the 3BR advertised when we bought our southern California place in 2001. The room is cramped. Besides a huge roll-top desk littered with notes, scraps of paper, news clippings and similar crap, there's a futon awaiting overnight visits from friends and family.

I've heard that you can tell everything worth knowing about a woman simply by dumping her purse on the table and looking through its contents. I've believed for years that one can determine the state of a woman's mind by looking in the back seat of her car: Is it clean and neat or is it filled halfway up the backseat with empty Diet Coke cans and job applications and dirty laundry and stuff she hasn't unpacked from the last time she moved?

I know you could tell a lot about me just by looking around the red writing room.

Starting directly ahead of the chair I use when writing, let me describe this cluttered red space:

The wall I face, beyond the large monitor I need because my eyes aren't up to reading my own output or emails or Google search results on my Mac laptop, has three pieces of art affixed. There is a sweet, framed photo of my wife Chris. There is a large painting and a small lithograph, each by my painter friend, Stanley Fullerton. The painting is of a faceless Catholic cardinal wearing his red biretta and gown tugging or stroking the ear of a basset hound. The dog is Fred, who was my companion for a few years when I first lived in the Santa Cruz area. The smaller drawing is a self-portrait of Stan, the artist, listening to his muse, an angel disguised in a bizarre mask with a long, beak-like nose. Stan has a palette in one hand, a large brush in the other. He listens to his muse for inspiration but stares straight ahead, toward me.

Also on that wall, high enough that the grandchildren can't reach it (even though it's permanently disabled) is a beautiful, century-old .22-caliber rifle. It once belonged to my dad's brother Reuben, an uncle I never met. The gun has a heavy, octagon-shaped barrel, a pump-action, like a shotgun, and a wooden stock that makes the rifle look like a cowboy weapon from a Randolph Scott western. The rifle was made sometime before World War I by the Meriden Arms Co., and possibly sold by Sears, Roebuck; a similar weapon is listed in a 1916 Sears catalog for twelve dollars and ninety-five cents. Were it in working condition Uncle Reuben's rifle might be worth, so I discovered on Google, about a hundred bucks these days.

I keep this rifle not only because it's the *only* Quarnstrom family heirloom, as far as I know, but because I almost killed someone with it when I was young. I was at my Uncle George's house on a tidal bay outside Bremerton, which is across Puget Sound from Seattle. As the tide came rushing in one day when I was eleven or twelve I took some shots at debris floating up the bay. A few minutes later an angry man who lived across Mud Bay, about a quarter-mile away, drove around to my uncle's place and said one of the bullets had zipped past his head close enough that he could hear it.

I apologized, of course, and my uncle took his late brother's rifle to his workshop above the garage. I was mortified. But after the guy left, Uncle George gave me back the gun and said I could keep it. He pointed out, though, that he'd taken the firing-pin mechanism out of the rifle and smashed it.

My Uncle George's small bayside home was my favorite place when I was a boy. He made spears with old broom handles tipped with nails pounded and shaped into barbed hooks for me and for some neighborhood boys. When the tide came in my friends and I would stand in the oncoming flood, until it got too deep, and spear flounders that swam in and out of the bay with the tide. We'd each get one or two before the water reached our shins—and one time I accidentally speared my own foot, which resembled a flounder, I guess, beneath the roiling water of the incoming tide. I yanked the barbed tip out of the foot and the saltwater and the adrenalin cleaned the wound and kept it from hurting.

After a successful spearing expedition my friends and I would take our flounders over to a decrepit house trailer and sell them to Flannery the Wino for a nickel apiece. Flannery's trailer was parked next to some huge iron rings embedded in cement and dug into the ground. During World War II the Navy had moored blimps to the rings. The blimps had floated above Puget Sound to look for enemy submarines that might stalk vessels going to and from the Bremerton Navy Yard, where hundreds of Navy ships were maintained or repaired by civilian workers, including my Uncle George.

Continuing this tour of my writing room, in front of the wall with my wife's photograph, the Stan Fullerton art and the rifle is a narrow table that supports two computer printers: mine, which only does black-and-white documents, and Chris's combination printer-fax-scanner, the latter two features rarely used.

The wall to the left has a bookcase close to the corner. These books are generally about Western Americana, American Indians, Washington State, and my hometown of Longview—as well as the Gold Rush-era *bandido* Joaquin Murieta. Joaquin may or may not have actually existed. He may just be a myth who has, at times, been a hero to California Chicanos. He might be a composite of a number of bad men, a composite created by California gold miners who grouped a bunch of bandits named Joaquin under the Murieta (or Murrieta or Murrietta or Murietta) rubric.

Above the bookcase is an old and kitschy painting of a tent next to a lake on a moonlit night. In front of the painting, atop the bookcase, is a statue of la Virgen de Guadalupe, a votive candle with an image of the Mexican virgin, three old packs of chewing gum—Beeman's Blackjack and Clove—a tiny photo of my third-grade classmates at Kessler School in Longview, a Barry Bonds bobble-head, a folk art goddess doll I found somewhere, a small photo of Muhammad Ali, "The Greatest," standing triumphant over Sonny Liston, prone on the canvas, and, hanging from a nail on the bookcase, a Tibetan Buddhist mala, or rosary, and a tiny, white pair of baby shoes that I wore so long ago.

Almost in front of the bookcase is a hat-rack. It's about six-feet tall and holds, among other headgear, a couple of Panama hats, a New Trier High School golfing cap, a beat-up red felt hat like those that used to be worn by loggers and hunters who wanted to stand out from the crowd if gun-toting deer hunters were about, a gray fedora, and a fez.

Above the futon, folded usually as a sofa and serving as well as another place to store pieces of paper, is a Stan Fullerton painting of an Egyptian dancing woman, a sheep and a glorious, crazy sunset. Stan called the painting "Who's Leading Whom to Slaughter?" Also on that wall are a late-'60s poster for a Santa Cruz art exhibit featuring sculptures by my late friend Ron Boise and a Maya-based painting by another friend, Joe Lysowski. There is an old, long-and-narrow-framed picture of Crater Lake, a Tibetan thangka depicting a multitude of Buddhas and bodhisattvas ensconced around a larger central Buddha Sakyamuni, and, finally, two precious items made by my son, my late son, Eric. One is a bas-relief print of his tiny nursery-school hand, pushed into in clay, which was glazed. The other is a framed drawing Eric did just before his second birthday, his sister Susan tells me, a drawing that looks at first like a balloon with two strings attached but was, Eric told his family, Charlie Brown, the "Peanuts" cartoon character. And yes, the balloon does have a tiny nose and two oddly offset eyes and a mouth, as well as a few strands of hair! It's a remarkable piece of art considering that it was drawn by a one-year-old boy!

Proceeding to the next wall, the one behind me as I write, and mostly dominated by mirrored sliding doors for the closet, there is a small alcove with three items on the wall: a very old engraving of angels surrounding a saint who is baptizing someone with the blood that is spurting from a crucified Jesus; a magnificent piece of artwork by a friend, Lana Rose, depicting several animals in party outfits, including a dog in a clown suit and a white rabbit watching the fun; and a poster given to me by

Hunter Thompson during his 1970 unsuccessful campaign for sheriff of the Colorado county surrounding Aspen. The poster features a clenched, red-tinted hand, with two thumbs, holding a green peyote button.

On a narrow wall on the left side of the alcove a bookcase holds dozens of volumes of Tibetan Buddhism as well as a few books about California history. I realize that I should find new homes for all the Buddhist stuff—as my friend Stephen Levine noted yesterday in an email with an attachment containing a dharma poster he'd recently made, attachment is "an odd term yes for Buddhist stuff"—the dharma, of course, teaching the necessity of giving up attachments. Maybe I'll get around to getting rid of a lot of books and other doodads, knickknacks, and memorabilia one of these days. Maybe not.

My dad started to mail even more-useless or unwanted stuff from the family home right after my mother died. He would send envelopes to me or to my brother with, perhaps, a pair of socks inside. It went from his house to my house to the Goodwill or the trash. One day I called my brother to tell him that I'd just received an envelope containing nothing but lint.

Around the corner from the Buddhist books, on a tiny strip of red-painted wall just before the mirrored closed doors, hang three old fishing lures, a painted tin Virgin of Guadalupe medallion, and a framed quote of Moliere's thoughts about his craft:

"Writing is like prostitution. First you do it for the love of it. Then you do it for a few friends. And finally, you do it for money."

Above the mirrored closet doors and even stuck to those doors are some documents and bumper stickers, including one with a motto developed in the 1960s by litter-conscious Santa Cruz surfers: "Pack your trash."

Now, the wall with the roll-top desk taking up so much space, besides another Stan Fullerton etching, there are:

* A framed copy of the Pulitzer Prize certificate we reporters and editors received for the *San Jose Mercury News*' coverage of the 1989 Loma Prieta earthquake. That quake destroyed hundreds of old masonry buildings throughout the San Francisco Bay Area, took down half of downtown Santa Cruz, including the building where I worked in the local bureau of the *Mercury News*, and did thirty-thousand dollars' worth of damage to my home. It also eliminated earthquakes as sources of thrills and instead made me afraid, afraid for the rest of my life, of jolts and shakes. It completely wiped out my belief in so-called terra firma.

* A souvenir fake copy of the *Mercury News*' front page, presented to me when I retired and prepared to move away from Santa Cruz. The fake banner headline, noting elements of my past, including the wonderful times I've spent in Hawaii, reads,

ALOHA, HOPHEAD.

* Above the desk a window obscured, to some degree, by some old, inexpensive stained glass.

* Above the window, several hats hanging on hooks. They include more Panamas, a cowboy hat, and a cap with a "Beatnik" (some surfing outfit) logo.

* My desk, with too much stuff to describe, so I'll just mention a few: a Camus quote about beauty, limits, and Nemesis that I clipped out of the Sunday paper forty years or so ago; a beat-up pair of huge volumes that make up the compact edition of the *Oxford English Dictionary*; and a Polaroid fortieth birthday photo Hunter Thompson sent me many years ago showing Hunter in dark glasses, bare-chested except for the straps of a shoulder-holster holding a black automatic pistol and with a bandaged hand. On the back Hunter wrote:

"Lee—here's my official birthday foto—Owl Farm, July 18, 1977—don't let this happen to *you*. HST"

Past the desk, before a chest of drawers in the corner (with a Buddhist altar on its top, with a couple of bronze Buddhas, a Virgin of Guadalupe, and a Kwan-Yin, a female version of the bodhisattva Avalokiteshvara) are a photograph of Ram Dass and a Mexican tin *ex voto* depicting the Virgin appearing to a woman and saving her beleaguered *niña,* who was drowning in a river. The primitive, sacred artwork, itself a prayer of thanks, was painted on the scrap of tin by the grateful mother, as she noted, a few days before Christmas, 1948.

Above the *ex voto* is a framed eight-by-ten glossy photograph of a young Richard Alpert in Bermuda shorts about to drive a golf ball down a fairway that is probably on the estate of his railroad tycoon father. I found it among a bunch of junk that Richard, Ram Dass, left behind when he moved out of a house in Santa Cruz that he rented from my brother Dean. Richard told Dean to toss out all the junk; he didn't want any of those old photos and other detritus from his youth. Dean asked if I wanted to paw through the photos and I said I did.

I have a happy if hazy recollection from those days of Ram Dass and me lying on the bed in the house I shared with Space Daisy under a thick canopy of redwood trees in the forests of Zayante, the canyon a few miles north of Santa Cruz. He and I talked for hours, fueled by nothing but a friendly desire to share stories. Richard, for he was both Richard Alpert and Ram Dass to friends at the time, complained about having spent much of his adult life in the shadow of Tim Leary, his notorious Harvard co-investigator of psychedelia. He didn't resent Tim, he said, so much as he resented having to play second-fiddle to a guy who was indeed the acid guru he was made out to be but was also, at rock bottom, a bullshitter and attention-grabber. I told him of my relationship with Ken Kesey, not complaining and certainly not feeling like I'd ever been in his shadow. But I noted that Kesey had a habit of bristling, I thought, when he was around other big men. I was not big in those days but I was tall, six-feet, four-inches tall. And I did feel that sometimes Kesey hunched up his shoulders in a sort of alpha-dog manner when tall or big men were nearby, not consciously, maybe, but just assuring everybody, himself included, that he was The Man and that the big newcomer was not. Ram Dass said he knew what I meant, although he'd never seen Kesey in such a macho mood.

My brother Dean was not only Ram Dass's landlord, he'd been his front man, setting up appearances in college towns during his heyday as a guru, speaker, and Wise Man. I found the photo one day as Dean was about to dump it in the garbage.

It is a wonderful picture of a wonderful man at a time of his life we've known little or nothing about, back before Richard Alpert had gone to Harvard, hooked up in early LSD experiments with Tim Leary, before Richard had gone to India and met his guru and adopted a new name to go with his new consciousness. For a while he favored flowing white robes of a Hindu holy man and used the honorific "Baba" before his name, Baba Ram Dass.

(One day in San Francisco some friends and I picked Ram Dass up near a Haight-Ashbury apartment where he'd been visiting. I can't remember where we were all going, but we'd arranged to take him with us. Looking very preppy, he was wearing, instead of his Indian white robes, a salmon-colored V-neck sweater and tan chino pants. When he got in the car I said, "Ram Dass, you're beginning to look like Richard Alpert." He grinned, put his hand on his heart and told me "Richard Alpert is still inside here, you know.")

I treasure the photo of this old friend about to swing his driver. I call it, "Ram Dass Addresses the Ball.

MY MOTHER GOES CRAZY AND DIES

AND

I DISCOVER THAT I HAVE A LITTLE SISTER

At some point my mother decided that my dad was cheating on her. He was, of course. Who wouldn't?

In fact, as proof of his years of infidelity, I learned a few years ago that I have a previously unknown sibling. I received a call from a woman in New York City several years ago, a woman who turns out to be a half-sister whom my brother and I'd never heard of. She was born, and put up for adoption, when I was a senior in high school—and living in the suburban Chicago village of Wilmette.

I don't know when Lenore figured out that my father had a girlfriend, or, as it turns out, one in a series of girlfriends. She handled the revelation that her husband had a mistress by drinking to excess. I figure it was about the time that I was in my mid to late-thirties. That's when I noticed that she got drunk, unpleasantly drunk, on a regular basis. It was about then that she began talking about "the shit bitch," a generic term that covered any and all Other Women. Actually, I don't know if she thought there was only one shit bitch or whether she realized there were a number of them over the years.

During one of those extremely uncomfortable conversations that no man ever wants to have with his mother, she let me know on the phone one day that she thought her and my father's sex life, or lack of it, was behind my dad's cheating with the shit bitch. She blamed the pope, actually all the popes, particularly the beloved John Paul. Oh, she hated the Polish pope.

(In Chicago and environs, people of her generation think, or thought of, people according to their ethnicity. My mother, in her later years, hired a cleaning woman and always, always referred to her as "a nice Polish woman." That didn't necessarily mean the cleaning lady was from Poland; it meant that someone, possibly her parents or grandparents, had come from Poland. Nor, really, did it mean the cleaning woman was nice; it just meant she wasn't rude or a complainer.) Pope John Paul was behind my parents' sad, unpleasant marriage, my mother revealed to me, because he refused to loosen the church's prohibition of birth-control devices. Therefore, she opined, finding the church-approved rhythm method unreliable and unacceptable, my dad needed to look elsewhere for sex. Yes, previous popes had also given the thumbs down to condoms, IUDs, diaphragms, and The Pill, but now it was Modern Times and the goddamned pope still wouldn't come around! So no more sex with my dad.

Hence, the need for the shit bitches.

The last of the Other Women in my dad's life became his second wife, Connie. After what he believed was a respectable time following my mother's death he sold his house in Wilmette and moved in with Connie in Austin, Texas. They met when each was a travel writer and they established a business putting together "camera-ready copy" that newspapers large and small and even tiny could plunk right down and publish in the pre-digital days of photo-offset printing. I liked Connie a lot.

It took but one drink for my mother to turn from a well-spoken if narrow-minded nice Catholic lady into a mean-spirited harridan griping about her husband and his shit bitch. It reached a point, when I was about forty, that I not only quit hearing what she was saying, I hung up on her when she'd start in on what would have been a further recital of her sad story, or sad had Lenore been a sympathetic character—but wasn't because she wasn't. I always gave her fair warning when she'd call. If she wanted to have a normal conversation filled with the usual uninteresting details about some cousin or about a trip she was planning—or even about the latest Catholic priest she'd met—I was willing to listen. But as soon as I'd hear the words "shit bitch" I'd tell her I had to go and would hang up the phone.

I remember a trip she made to Santa Cruz in her later years. She stayed with my brother Dean and his wife and their daughter Anne, who was an infant. She took us out for brunch one Sunday and she hadn't even finished her first mimosa before she started in about Gordon and the shit bitch. I told my wife Melody that we were leaving and we walked out of a fine restaurant on a hill overlooking the Monterey Bay. That evening Melody and I went to Dean's house to try an amateurish "intervention," but Dean chickened out and it was left to me to intervene and to Dean's wife Gloria to back me up. It went nowhere.

As she aged, my mother began to look more and more like her father's sister, Aunt Mae, an unpleasant little woman whom I met when we moved to the Chicago area. Aunt Mae was short, hunched over, and had nothing good to say about anyone. She's the one who explained why we should avoid the Loop in downtown Chicago on Mondays because that was the day that "the fat Negro ladies jostle white people on the street and in the subway."

Mae, whose married name was Cross, was so short you couldn't see the top of her head through the front windshield when she came driving up the street on her annual visit to the Quarnstrom home. I believe she would have come more often had we allowed her to. On those annual visits she would always finish dinner by pitching forward into the peas and mashed potatoes with gravy and my mother would have to mop her face off before pushing her back into her car for her drive back to Hyde Park, on Chicago's South Side, where she lived with two little dogs who had milky clouds of cataracts covering their eyes. For a while she'd had a younger, sixtyish, gigolo living with her but none of us liked him especially when he offered to take me to a White Sox game when I was already a Cubs' fan.

Despite her drinking, my mother did have a small group of friends who would gather from time to time to sympathize with her about her husband's travel-writing trips abroad with the shit bitch, or the shit bitches. I knew they were no doubt as tired of her incessant rap as I was, but somehow they stuck in there. Perhaps they all were in unhappy marriages and shared their own sad tales with one another.

I got to meet this unpleasant group of friends at my mother's funeral. She, by the way, had dropped dead at the house one day when my dad was in France or somewhere, probably with Connie.

My brother and his wife and daughter flew to Chicago for the funeral, as did I. When I got to the family home in my rented car my dad gave me a check. He told me to go down to the Catholic cemetery on the Evanston-Chicago border, buy a gravesite for my mom, and to tell the cemetery guys to dig a grave in time for the Saturday funeral. This cemetery, which runs from the El eastward to the road along Lake Michigan, was notable on the North Shore because of a game played by all kids growing up in those suburbs. They would hold their breath as their parents' car drove the half-mile or so past the cemetery en route to and from Chicago. I didn't know until I visited my mother's grave a few years later that there are deer in that huge cemetery.

The guy at the cemetery office asked what kind of a plot I was looking to buy.

"How much is your cheapest one?" I wondered.

"Oh," he told me, "she wouldn't want to be buried over there."

"How much?"

"She wouldn't ... "

"How much?"

"Eight hundred dollars, but I'm telling you, she wouldn't want to be buried *over there!*"

I asked to be taken "over there" and discovered that what the Catholic cemetery guy meant was that there were apartment buildings on the other side of the graveyard wall and those apartments were inhabited by black people. I told him she'd do just fine in the eight-hundred dollar grave and would have preferred to spend eternity "over there."

After the funeral service, highlighted by my little niece Anne waving at her grandmother's reposing body in its casket and telling her Grandma, "Nighty-night," we went to the cemetery. As that little ritual came to an end my mother's friends, who had, as far as my dad and I knew, spent the previous quarter-century hearing my mother gripe about him and the shit bitch, approached. They asked if my dad was going to have people over to the house, in other words, was there going to be a post-funeral gathering?

"No," my dad said solemnly. Looking at my brother and me he continued, "This is the first time my whole family has been here together for a long, long time and I think we're just going to go home and spend some quiet time together."

Once we were back in my rental car I asked my dad, "Some quiet time together?" He actually had tears in his eyes, but he was able to smile. "Nah, I just didn't want to spend any time with those shrews," he said.

When we got back to the family home we all went our separate ways.

* * *

A couple of months later, when my dad and a friend were cleaning out the house so he could put it on the market, they stumbled across a sign of my mother's mental state in her dresser drawers.

In the years before she died my mother had done some things that were more than the result of drinking and taking pills. They were crazy, as well. For instance, she had once run into the street in front of the house, a fairly busy street, while naked. She had screamed, "He's trying to kill me!" There was no one else home at the time. The doctor across the street calmed her down and got her some help.

Anyway, as my dad went through a chest of drawers he came upon a drawer packed with old Simplicity sewing patterns.

Now, my mother had never been able to sew. However, she kept, from a time before I was born, an old treadle-operated Singer sewing machine. She kept it at the ready. But she had told herself somewhere along the way that she couldn't sew, so of course she couldn't. Strangely, there was a drawer full of patterns anyway. It was packed with hundreds of sheets of that flimsy tissue that they print dress-making patterns on. Fortunately, my dad thought to poke through the patterns before tossing them into the recycling. And he found, secreted away between two sheets of tissue, a Social Security check made out to Lenore L. Quarnstrom. Then he found another and another.

This had been my mother's equivalent of hiding money beneath the mattress or burying it in a coffee can in the back yard (although she might have done that, too, I guess). She had been saving for a rainy day, the day, I imagine, that her husband ran away with the shit bitch—or the day that she found them together and killed them both.

* * *

My half-sister:

For a few weeks, when I was sixty-eight or sixty-nine, we got a lot of late-night phone calls that turned out to be hang-ups. I worried that my wife would think it was a girlfriend calling and hanging up when she heard Chris's voice.

Then, one evening, I answered the phone and a woman's voice asked timidly if I were Lee Quarnstrom? Was I from the Chicago area? Yes, yes. And yes, I was the son of Gordon M. Quarnstrom.

"Well," she said, "I think I'm your half-sister."

I know now that she expected me to react angrily, to slam the phone down. But of course I didn't do that. This was exciting news! She took a lot of reassuring, but I think she finally understood I was sincerely pleased to discover at that late age that I had a baby sister, even if she *was* almost fifty years old.

Her name is Tracey. She had spent years, after her Jewish parents in a New York suburb told her that she was adopted, trying to track down her birth parents. She traced her birth back to a home for unwed mothers in Evanston, the next town to Wilmette, where the Quarnstrom family lived at that time. She'd been born at a nearby hospital.

After her folks died, Tracey put a lot of energy and a lot of online research time into trying to find out her birth mother's name. When she did, she called the woman, who lived near Minneapolis, and introduced herself. I gather that her mother, a former shit bitch, you might say, was less-than-pleased to hear from the baby girl she'd given up almost a half-century earlier. (She had never married but apparently still lived in a part of Minnesota where admitting to an affair, let alone a baby out of wedlock, could sully if not devastate a nice lady's reputation.)

Tracey and her mother established a stand-offish relationship, so she explained. The woman would never reveal the name of Tracey's father and said that she would stop allowing her daughter to communicate or visit with her if she asked again.

Then Marie, her mother, a woman of one hundred percent Norwegian heritage, died. Tracey was not invited to the funeral—no one knew about Tracey. But she found out about it and rushed to Minneapolis. Tracey's appearance at the funeral and her revelation that she was Marie's daughter caused quite a bit of hubbub at the service, but Tracey didn't care. She wanted to get back to Marie's house and break into a room that her mother had kept locked, off-limits, every time Tracey had visited. She knew there was information about her father in that room.

What she found, locked in a drawer, was a bunch of postcards from cities around the world, all from GMQ, or Gordon. She found a few photos of her mother with a man she assumed

401

was her father (he was, indeed, Gordon Quarnstrom). She found itineraries for trips Marie had taken with Gordon. And she found some papers with enough information that, using the Internet, led her to me.

It turned out that Tracey was not Jewish at all. Her mother was Norwegian on both sides and Gordon was Swedish and Norwegian.

There'd been no provision for her in Marie's will and Tracey didn't have any interest in pursuing the matter. She just wanted to find out who she was, like anybody would.

We tried a DNA test but the results were inconclusive. It's not easy, they told her when they sent her the results, to tell if half-siblings are related when one's male, the other female, and the parent in common is the father and he is no longer around to give a blood sample. But from all the information we've swapped since we first spoke, we are each convinced that we are sister and brother.

So far, it's been several years since I first heard from Tracey and we've not yet met. I'm not able to get around easily enough to fly to New York on my own and Tracey has had some health problems and some financial problems that have kept her from coming to California to meet her two half-brothers. I hope, of course, that I get to meet my half-sister one of these days. I'm not sure if I can fill the role of being her big brother. I'm way too old to beat up any guys who try to have their way with her

WHAT HAVE I LEARNED? ANYTHING?

When I was eleven years old and my family was driving eastward through southern California near the Arizona state line I yelled that I had to stop to pee *right now!* My dad pulled over to the side of the two-lane highway and he and my younger brother and I walked a few feet from the 1949 Chrysler and urinated onto the desert sand. As I was relieving myself I saw near my feet one of those "stubby" Olympia beer bottles lying on the ground at the edge of the blacktop. There was something inside.

As I peed and stared at the beer bottle I realized that the thing inside the brown glass container was a dead mouse. Clearly, the tiny rodent had climbed inside the beckoning bottle to lap up the tasty last dregs of Oly that were left inside when someone had tossed it from a passing car. The mouse apparently found enough beer to fill itself to the point that it was incapable of getting back to safety through the bottle's narrow neck.

Now, as I pissed and stared at the swollen dead mouse I knew there was a lesson to be learned here, that this dead mouse, bloated from excessive drinking, was a metaphor for something important. I just couldn't quite put my finger on it.

Today, more than six decades later, I can picture that beer bottle and that dead mouse as though I'd seen it this morning. I can see the tiny critter's girth, too thick to escape the trap that had provided a sip, perhaps, of beer before it became its coffin. And I still believe that the dead little mouse-in-a-bottle tableau was a metaphor for something important, a fable with a moral worthy of a tale by Aesop, a lesson for me and for all.

But to this day, dammit, I still can't figure out what the hell it was.

* * *

Over the years I did manage to learn a lot of what falls under the rubric of Useless Shit.

I learned, for instance, that when Queen Elizabeth visited Yosemite Park in 1983 and stayed in a suite atop the Ahwahnee Hotel, that she brought her own toilet seat, which replaced for the duration the usual seat on the commode. That way, I gather, the monarch did not have to put her bottom onto any surface that might previously have touched the ass of a commoner.

I learned from my golf teacher Grant Rodgers, then at the Pasatiempo course near Santa Cruz but lately at a club on the Oregon coast, that it's better to be lucky than to be good. "Anybody can learn to be good," he said. "But not everyone can be lucky."

Ken Kesey taught me not to try to "save" people from themselves or to rescue them from situations where we think they don't belong. "Everybody," Kesey said, "is doing what he wants to be doing."

I also learned from Kesey two important concepts that I've already mentioned and that bear repetition:

First, Nothing Lasts! This becomes more and more clear as the years go by. People die. Stuff rots, rusts, disintegrates, decays. Relationships end. Peace is fleeting. Stars explode and vanish. Prophets come and go. Glaciers melt. Pets pass away.

And, Never Trust a Prankster! I don't!

I've learned so much from Stephen Levine that I could never put half of it into words. Mainly, though, Stephen has taught me that love, joy, calm abiding, and pure light will shine from within when we allow it to.

Wavy Gravy taught me that self-respect is a prayer to the universal life we all share.

My mid-1990s girlfriend Cina, half Mexican, half Chinook Indian, told me that all men in her tribe need an eagle feather for spiritual power—but that some of those men were too impatient to wait until they found such a talisman "on the trail," as she put it. Rather, she said, some young Indian men climb the high-tension power lines leading away from Bonneville and other dams along the Columbia River and toss a hunk of raw meat out onto the wires. They wait for a hungry eagle to grab the raw meat and to touch the wire and electrocute itself and fall to earth, where the young men can pluck a feather from the fallen bird. Cina thought this was shameful.

I learned as a second or third-grader, as I sat thinking about my little classmate Kay Johnson, that there was a direct connection between thinking about girls and hard-ons.

Zonker taught me that even sweet people can be mean. Once, as he and I sat in his San Jose pad, a girl we'd both slept with came in the front door and announced that she'd changed her name to Flower. "F-L-O-U-R?" Zonker asked. She fled in tears.

An uncle of my girlfriend Donna taught me that if you own a mink ranch in the San Joaquin Valley you can drive a truck down to Turlock and pick up a load of turkey heads for feed. And my wife Melody told me about her aunt who jumped off a Rhode Island bridge in an unsuccessful suicide attempt. She leapt in her mink coat so everyone would know she'd been prosperous.

That truck loaded with turkey heads must have resembled a cloud of flies moving up Highway 99. My sixth wife's grandfather, a Merchant Marine during World War II, told me that as his ship approached Iwo Jima with a load of supplies, he could see a huge gray cloud around the embattled South Pacific island. As they drew near, he and his shipmates realized that what they saw was a huge cloud of flies swarming around the dead.

I learned that *all* of us who attended events like the Human Be-in in Golden Gate Park, in January 1967, really did believe that we were well on the way to changing things, to making things better, to expanding consciousness around the world. Did we? It doesn't seem as though we did. But I'm willing to be proven wrong. I never did learn whether Owsley made his own LSD or whether his wife did. This was a topic of great speculation in the Haight-Asbury and elsewhere in California in the 1960s. It was called Owsley Acid and he took credit for it but some of us who knew him harbored just a tiny suspicion that his wife, a chemist, brewed up the stuff. My brother, who had a close working relationship with Owsley for a while, thinks that Owsley made his own stuff.

Another laboratory man, the Mad Chemist, showed up frequently at Kesey's La Honda place, usually with a pocketful of LSD tabs or some new mix of speed or ampules of Dolophine, as methadone was originally called. Unlike Augustus Owsley Stanley, or just plain Owsley, I don't think the Mad Chemist made a bundle with his drugs; but he did manage to stay high. Owsley, of course—before he pulled up stakes and headed to Australia—made enough money with his acid to bankroll the Grateful Dead before that band had the money rolling in. Owsley also helped wire up the Dead's outrageously huge sound systems, which he'd also helped purchase with his LSD profits.

One thing I never learned, and surely we would have heard about this by now, is whether LSD causes brain damage, neurological damage, genetic damage. Yes, a few acidheads did go crazy, but that's true of the general population, as well. Some died of disease at a young age, but that, too, is generally true in the world at large. I know a number of LSD users, some of whom still take it, who are eighty years old or approaching eighty. I think all of those warnings about acid causing long-term damage were bullshit!

* * *

Some of us learn from our elders not to touch, as an example, a hot stove. Others question that warning which most children hear from parents or teachers or older brothers or sisters. These people end up with more scars and scabs than those who learn by paying attention to advice because they test the "wisdom" of older sages who relate the perils of touching hot stoves, jumping from the roof of the barn, stirring up wasps' nests with long sticks, playing with B-B guns, smoking, putting tongues on frozen metal poles, putting heads in elevator shafts, not looking before crossing the street, flushing too much toilet paper, lighting firecrackers, and a hundred or a thousand other activities that, we are all warned, will maim us terribly, perhaps kill us and, of course, go on our permanent records.

The only advice my father gave me, as far as I can recall, was to meet a woman's mother before marrying the young lady. He told me this one afternoon when I was about eight and we noticed a fat girl of about the same age sitting with her extremely overweight mother. Until then I had not considered that I might some day take a wife or that there were apparently standards of beauty and desirability that influenced adults' marital choices and behavior.

Sure, my parents gave me all the usual warnings about B-B guns (every parent knew of at least one boy who'd lost an eye to a Daisy Red Ryder-model B-B rifle) and bees' nests (I didn't need a parental warning to avoid poking sticks into places where hornets, wasps, or bees had set up shop), and tongues sticking to metal poles. I even was warned of the deadly possibilities of putting a penny on a railroad track to get it flattened by a passing freight train. (Instead of flattening the copper coin, I was told, putting the penny on the track usually causes the coin to shoot out and cut through the skull of the nearest boy, killing him instantly! When I learned from personal experience that this was not, in fact, true, how was I later in life supposed to believe that smoking marijuana would lead to the use of hard drugs?)

So, any lessons I may have picked up over my lifetime do not constitute a list of things *not* to do. In fact, I think I've learned very little in the way of life lessons that I could pass on to my son, if I still had a son. I do have five fine stepchildren, all now in or approaching middle age, and they're no more likely to respect those life lessons than I was when I was young.

What I learned from the death of my son Eric and from observing relationships between parents and their offspring in my own family and among my friends and acquaintances is that *everyone* loses their kids but almost always gets them back—although not as the same people they were when they wandered away.

You know what I'm talking about: teenagers get lost, at least that's the way it seems to parents, when they "rebel" and discover drugs or join new religions or announce a different sexuality or fall in love with and/or run off with the "wrong" partner. They find a different politics; they may join the service or they may unfurl disturbing banners for disturbing causes and call their folks greedheads or warmongers or heathens. Some may go crazy and those sons and daughters, unfortunately, almost always remain among the lost, along with those killed in war or, like Eric, dead on the street.

But most of the rest who seem to moms and dads to have gone down some wormhole into unspeakably different dimensions come out the other end ready and able to resume lives as sons and daughters who can, if they wish, provide grandchildren, become "productive" members of the community, come to dinner on holidays, and phone every once in a while to say hello.

If I might break the Grandparents' Code of Silence, let me reveal that old people can get tired of the cute little boys and girls who will occasionally interrupt their television and texting to pull on Grandpa's shirt and make some unsavory demand that requires too much energy. That's when grandparents often say, with no quibbling among themselves, "Grandpa's tired now and we have to go home" or "we have to take a nap."

* * *

I have learned that coincidence is the nature of the universe. Or at least it seems that way.

One evening in 1960, I met an interesting couple at a party in Mexico City. After a three-day drive that began the next morning, some friends and I got to New York, where I bumped into the same couple that same day walking along Fifth Avenue. That was the first time it occurred to me that all of this—**all** of it—might just be some sort of coincidence.

Then, about three years later, when I was living in Seattle and working for the Associated Press, I got a phone call in the middle of the night from the mother of my oldest friend, Ned Piper. We'd been close since we were both just one year of age (and still, in our seventies, remain close). Jane Piper was calling from the family home in Longview.

She told me my brother, who had been driving from San Francisco to Seattle with his wife and two friends had been in a serious accident on the highway just outside of town. Dean was in the hospital in Longview; his wife, Wendy, was in a hospital in Portland; another woman in the car who had been at the wheel at the time of the crash was being treated in Portland, as well; and the fourth passenger in Dean's VW bus, a young woman who had been in the front seat next to the driver, had been killed when a sudden gust of wind off the Columbia River had caused the top-heavy vehicle to overturn into upcoming traffic—which consisted, disastrously, of a huge truck hauling livestock.

Somehow, although he was barely conscious, Dean had mentioned the Pipers to a highway patrolman who had recognized the name and had made the late-night call to my friend's mom. Somehow she had found my Seattle phone number and called to tell me the sketchy facts she'd gotten from the patrolman.

To this day, the fact that Dean's accident had occurred just a few miles from our boyhood home—when his San Francisco to Seattle journey was hundreds of miles long—is a coincidence of major proportions.

I drove to Longview to see Dean, who had a broken back and was in the same hospital where I'd been born. He had long hair, much longer than anyone in Longview had ever seen on a man, and was arguing with a nun who said they intended to trim his locks. He angrily insisted he needed the long hair for his job. "What job?" the sister wondered. "I," Dean proudly whispered to her, "am a buffalo hunter!"

Wendy's coma lasted for several weeks and when she finally came to, she had mentally regressed to childhood. When she and Dean returned to their San Francisco home she still needed constant monitoring—not so much for medical problems, my brother told me, but for a childish tendency to not look both ways when crossing a busy street, to use one example. Thank goodness, she eventually recovered. Dean and she later divorced and my brother is now married to his sixth wife, a fine woman who had been his first high school girlfriend.

I drove out to the highway to see the site of the accident that had so badly injured three young people and taken the life of a fourth. Just a hundred yards or so before the crash scene was a billboard that had sat beside that highway for many years. It had been placed there by a local religious group and was perhaps the last thing the woman in the passenger seat had seen before she died. In huge gothic lettering it read:

"Prepare To Meet Thine Maker!"

* * *

I have learned just a handful of other lessons.

I have learned, for instance, that I've been invisible to young women and girls for at least twenty years. I have heard women complain that men don't look at them any more because, they say, they are just too old to attract attention. That may be true, but if so they are merely being ignored; they are not invisible. And when I say invisible I mean that I can walk through a clique of high school girls at the mall and they literally do not see that I am there. I could no doubt walk into a girls' locker room and be unnoticed. So, I have learned, I am invisible because younger women neither want nor need to see old men. So they don't. I'm amused when men my age suck in their stomachs when they see an attractive young woman up ahead.

I've previously mentioned that I have learned that marriage was never intended to last for many decades. People used to die of the plague or the sword or infections when they were relatively young. Marriage was intended to last until old age, which was about age thirty.

I have learned that the mind is a wondrous thing and that the more you look at it the more amazing it becomes.

On a fairly simple level, I learned that when I am writing, and probably when I am thinking, my mind works differently than those of young people. That's because I didn't learn to write on a computer.

One day fifteen or twenty years ago, when I was a reporter and columnist in the Santa Cruz bureau of the *San Jose Mercury News*, the "systems" manager of the paper brought over some new software for my computer. He explained that this new software would allow me to move paragraphs around, to write a sentence here, a sentence there, then another here, etc.

"But I don't want to move paragraphs around," I told him. "I start at the beginning of a story, I write it and then I finish it and I'm done."

"Oh," he replied, disdain obvious in his voice, "you learned to write on a *typewriter!*"

I began to watch my much younger office partner and sure enough, he did write a sentence, then go back and write a paragraph before it, then move a sentence down below it. My God. It had never occurred to him that one could write a linear story straight through from the lede to the final sentence.

Of course, unless you were willing to use a lot of Wite Out or use a pair of scissors and a pot of glue, it was much easier to write a story from beginning to end on a typewriter than to move words and sentences and paragraphs around like tiles on a game board.

I think I've learned that our minds don't need to operate in a linear manner unless we want them to. At a concert the other day, as the orchestra was tuning up and my wife was standing with her chorale group ready to sing, I closed my eyes and listened to what always seems to an audience like cacophony. The string instrumentalists were making certain each was in harmony with the others. Someone was softly beating the kettle drums, making tiny adjustments to assure compatibility with the rest of the orchestra. The brass players seemed each to be playing a unique glissando, no two horns playing the same notes. Odd sounds came from the oboes.

Closing my eyes, trying to listen at first to each musician bring the instrument into tune first to his or her own ear, then to the communal ear of the ensemble, my mind tried to meld the sounds into one harmonious piece of music. I knew that our minds are capable of finding harmony within apparent chaos. I knew, from my days at Kesey's place in La Honda, that we could fiddle with his color TV so the tints and hues were skewed and we could make the sky red and the grass blue and the people green and we could mute the sound and listen to the sounds coming from another black-and-white television set tuned to another channel. I knew that our minds are able to blend all this input into one interesting, often humorous, gestalt. Watching a cowboy movie with the colors distorted and just plain unnatural, juxtaposed with the voice of a football announcer blaring from another black-and-white TV with a burnt-out picture tube, was not the annoying confusion of atonal, ugly, dissonance that you might imagine. With some training, such as experience with LSD or other psychedelic drugs, that whole tintinnabulation can evolve from mental anarchy into psychic harmony.

Ditto, I determined, from the sounds of an orchestra tuning up.

* * *

Writing these memoirs, bringing to mind these memories, has been challenging as well as satisfying. I learned a long time ago, as a young newspaper reporter, that every old coot is correct when he tells you, as they/we all tend to insist, that, "I've got a great story to tell." They do. Most and probably all human lives are interesting on one level or another. The thing is, not so many people write their stories or even find anyone willing to listen to them.

In a way, recalling incidents from many decades past is like what I've imagined psychoanalysis to be, dredging up people and places and activities that are not always pleasant to handle once they've been brought to the surface. But whether they're rediscovered and retold or revealed, the memories nonetheless are real and are stuck somewhere in the mind. It's even possible that one or more of those guys who wrote all those memoirs with titles like *I Rode with Jesse James* actually did ride with Jesse James.

Paging through old *Life* magazines from the year I was born, 1939, I happened upon a feature about the great ballet dancer, Vaslaw Nijinsky. Now middle-aged, he was confined in a Swiss insane asylum. He had put on a suit and tie to welcome a visitor, another well-known dancer, Serge Lihar. According to the caption, Carl Maria von Weber's "Invitation to the Dance" was playing on a nearby phonograph while the "mad Nijinsky" greeted his guest.

As attendants watched in the background and a *Life* photographer shot pictures, Nijinsky seemed "strangely moved" as Lihar tried to coax him into a ballet position, according to the *Life* photo caption.

Suddenly, in a magnificent photo that the magazine reproduced several times over the years, Nijinksy leaped into the air, performing, so we read, an *entrechat*, a difficult move that he could once perform with "flawless grace."

Here too, it seems to me, the mad dancer has suspended himself, for his guest and for the photographer, a foot or more off the ground—with flawless grace. His leather oxfords hover above the asylum floor, his arms, constrained by his suit jacket, seem like angel wings that have lifted Nijinsky into that same space where he made his fame and fortune as a youth known far and wide as the finest male dancer in the world.

Here is one more lesson I hope I have learned, this time from a mad ballet dancer who could launch himself above his psychosis and above us all to pose for an instant in mid-air. We may be able, given the right circumstances, the right audience, to float again for a moment in familiar spaces where we have flown before.

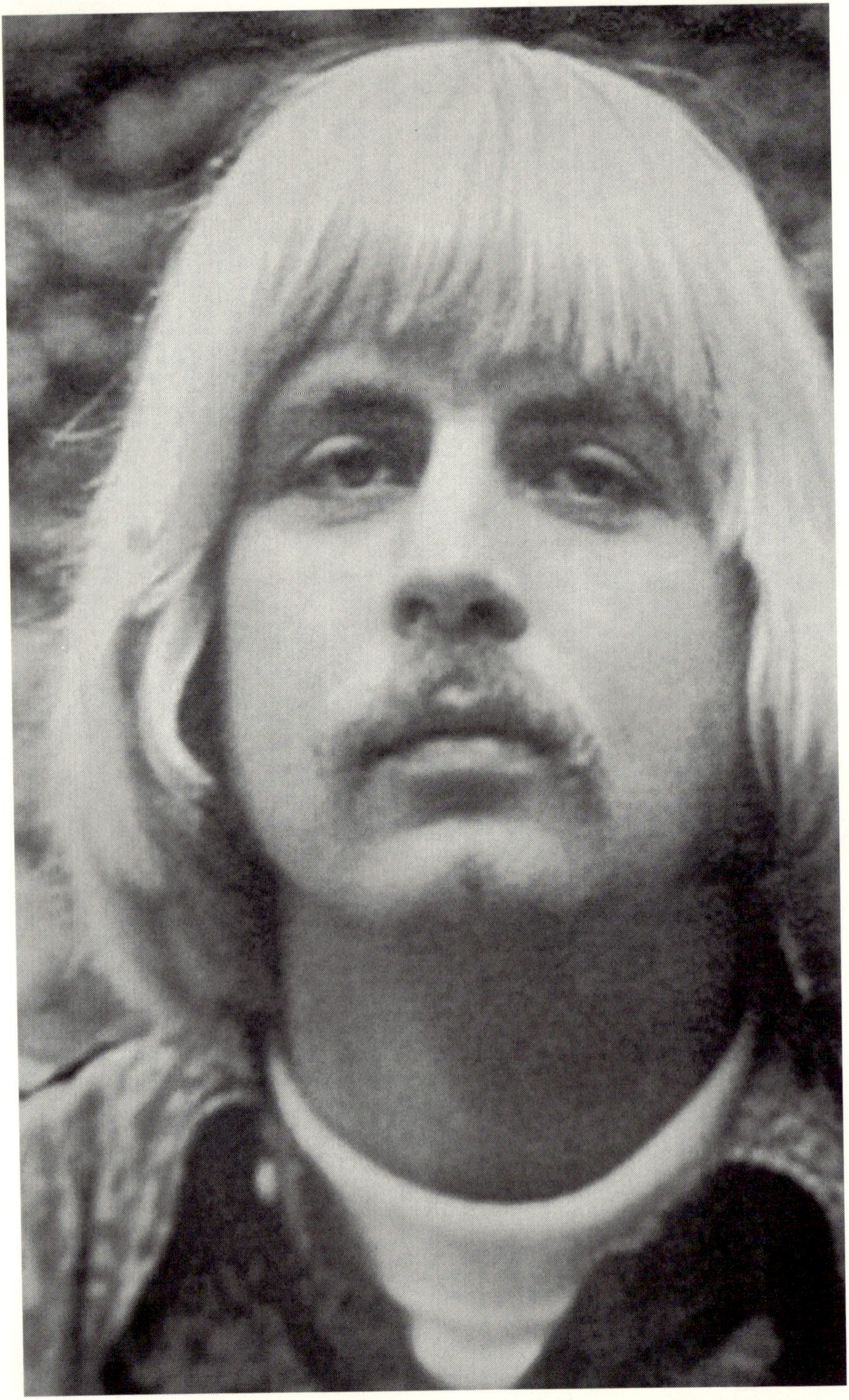

Acknowledgements

Mystery writers always acknowledge the help they've received from various coppers, coroners, criminologists and cutthroats, experts who've revealed some of the tricks of their trades. In my case, most of the people who've helped me revealed nothing; instead, they pointed me in one direction or another and told me to turn over stones until something revealed itself. "Come this way and help us look for the cosmos," Ken Kesey said to me, and I thank him. "Nothing ever happens in a newspaper office, go out and get a story," I was instructed by Ward Bushee, and he was oh, so correct. "You're a handsome boy," my parents told me, and I took advantage of that whenever I could.

Shira Tarrant listened to one of my stories and urged me to write them all down. I thank her for that kick in the pants and I thank her especially for her invaluable insight and help in editing this manuscript. I thank Iris Berry and A. Razor at Punk Hostage for their respect.

I thank my brother Dean and closest friends: John, Wendy, Ann, Madeline, Joe and Karen, my buddies since our days on the *New Trier News*; Ned and Don, two Longview pals since the 1940s; Ben, who died as I was writing this memoir; all the women who've married me, even those who left me behind, or vice versa; and Bill, whom I still love although we're no longer on speaking terms.

And I especially thank my wife Chris Quarnstrom for her love and enthusiasm and for keeping poetry in my life.

Lee Quarnstrom has asked his wife to order just one memorial word on his gravestone – **Beatnik**.

Born in a small Washington lumber mill town and raised for the most part there and in Chicago, Quarnstrom moved to the Bay Area in the mid-1960s in time to join the Merry Band of Pranksters, the acid-fueled crew aboard author Ken Kesey's psychedelically painted bus with "Further" as its destination and a warning across its rear: "Caution, Weird Load." With the musical Grateful Dead in tow, the Pranksters brought psychedelia to the west coast with their famed Acid Tests!

Prior to his move to California, Quarnstrom was a young Chicago newspaperman in the final days of the Windy City's old-time, *Front Page* journalism. Lucky enough to have read Jack Kerouac's *On the Road before* freeways replaced two-lane blacktop roads, he began years of wandering by sticking out his thumb and hitching rides back and forth and up and down around the country. Stops along the way included New York City, Mexico City, Seattle, a remote redwood canyon in the Santa Cruz Mountains, nearby Santa Cruz, and Los Angeles, where he was Executive Editor of the notorious smut magazine, Hustler.

Quarnstrom did, in fact, spend one summer felling tall trees and blasting boulders as Assistant Dynamiter on an Olympic National Park trail crew. And the woman he's asked to describe him on that tombstone is indeed his seventh wife.

More about Lee Quarnstrom –

"Although Lee Quarnstrom graduated from the Beat Generation to Ken Kesey's acid-fueled Band of Merry Pranksters, this book is not a trick, it's a treat. So gird your literary loins and enjoy his dynamite sense of humor as he morphs his way along a unique path – from a respected newspaper journalist to writing a column, 'Fables Without Morals' for my notorious magazine, The Realist, to becoming an editor for Larry Flynt's pink-revealing Hustler -- all while managing to get married seven times. Otherwise you'll never know what fun you missed."

Paul Krassner, author of CONFESSIONS OF A RAVING, UNCONFINED NUT: Misadventures in the Counterculture.

"WHEN I WAS A DYNAMITER explodes off the page in great chunks of uber extra awesome. Read all about it!"

Wavy Gravy, cosmic clown, saint, Merry Prankster, Hogfarm Commune father figure, poet, star of film, *"Saint Misbehavin'!"*

"Lee Quarnstrom is a historian of merit. He has a gift for actively clearing minds of the predictable: a dynamiter, like old Socrates, of old ways. Q is a living history, haggard and torn by time, a shining light at the center of the mandala of awakening. A bit of the real magic that historically unfolded. His great true story of the whole retinue of the retinal circus in full bloom relates ages past and coming of rapid light, blinding insight, and the realignment that once beckoned us to stand up and now calls us to reach out acknowledging each other's new age. A phenomenal read."

Stephen Levine, poet, author, death and dying counselor, teacher of Buddhist loving-kindness, traveller.

"Lee Quarnstrom's explosive memoir begins with the tragic murder of his son at age 18 then segues down his on the road beatnik days, his Ken Kesey Merry Prankster days, his Hustler magazine executive editor days, his Chicago journalist days, his acclaimed newspaper writing days and ends up with his reports on his seven wives! Boy, does Lee have a story to tell!"

Jerry Kamstra, author of *WEED*, a tale of smuggling dope over the Mexican border, and *THE FRISCO KID*, a novel set in San Francisco's Beat Generation center, North Beach.

"When you think about the mad 60's, think Lee Quarnstrom. Nobody lived through that era quite like he did."

Page Stegner, whose novels include *THE EDGE* and *SPORTSCAR MENOPAUSE*, co-wrote *AMERICAN PLACES* with his father, Wallace Stegner, and photographer Eliot Porter. His other books include *ISLANDS OF THE WEST*, a Sierra Club book, and OUTPOSTS OF EDEN: a Curmudgeon at Large in the American West.

"Lee is an old hand in the writing biz. He was a professional journalist all his working life, for many years a reporter and columnist for the San Jose Mercury. He was also a Chicago beatnik, an Original Prankster (got busted with Kesey in '65), executive editor of Hustler. He lives up to all the other superhuman claims (including marital) that he makes for himself. Lee is a sharp, funny writer with a reporter's eye for the telling detail and an appropriately wry, skeptical, wise-guy reportorial voice – and he knows, or knew ... well, everybody: Kesey, Bill Graham, Stewart Brand, Herb Alpert, the Grateful Dead, the Hells Angels, Tiny Tim, Wavy Gravy, Larry and Althea Flynt, Paul Krassner. A terrific find!"

Ed McClanahan, author of *THE NATURAL MAN* and *FAMOUS PEOPLE I HAVE KNOWN*, is a well-known Kentucky writer and a Merry Prankster. His latest book is *I JUST HITCHED IN FROM THE COAST*: The Ed McClanahan Reader.

"Lee Quarnstrom is my favorite Merry Prankster and all-around raconteur. Lee's memoirs come from a tender and witty hurricane's eye of the 1960s counter-culture and its discontents."

Susie Bright, writer, speaker, teacher, audio-show host, and performer, all on the subject of sexuality and one of the first writer/activists referred to as a sex-positive feminist.

"Lee Quarnstrom is a wondrous observer and liver of life, writ large. He spins his tales with a magic wand."

State Sen. John Vasconcellos, D-Silicon Valley, retired, the late author of California's famed self-esteem education standards and creator of The Vasconcellos Project, helping citizens bring integrity, authenticity and trust to government and politics.

OTHER PUNK HOSTAGE PRESS BOOKS

FRACTURED (2012) by Danny Baker

BETTER THAN A GUN IN A KNIFE FIGHT (2012) by A. Razor

THE DAUGHTERS OF BASTARDS (2012) by Iris Berry

DRAWN BLOOD: COLLECTED WORKS FROM D.B.P.LTD., 1985-1995 (2012) by A. Razor

IMPRESS (2012) by C.V. Auchterlonie

TOMORROW, YVONNE - POETRY & PROSE FOR SUICIDAL EGOISTS (2012) by Yvonne De la Vega

BEATEN UP BEATEN DOWN (2012) by A. Razor

MIRACLES OF THE BLOG: A SERIES (2012) by Carolyn Srygley--Moore

8TH & AGONY (2012) by Rich Ferguson

SMALL CATASTROPHES IN A BIG WORLD (2012) by A. Razor

UNTAMED (2013) by Jack Grisham

MOTH WING TEA (2013) by Dennis Cruz

HALF-CENTURY STATUS (2013) by A. Razor

SHOWGIRL CONFIDENTIAL (2013) by Pleasant Gehman

BLOOD MUSIC (2013) by Frank Reardon

I WILL ALWAYS BE YOUR WHORE/LOVE SONGS for Billy Corgan (2014) by Alexandra Naughton

A HISTORY OF BROKEN LOVE THINGS (2014) by SB Stokes

YEAH, WELL... (2014) by Joel Landmine

DREAMS GONE MAD WITH HOPE (2014) by S.A. Griffin

CODE BLUE: A LOVE STORY (2014) by Jack Grisham

HOW TO TAKE A BULLET AND OTHER SURVIVAL POEMS (2014) by Hollie Hardy

DEAD LIONS (2014) by A.D. Winans

SCARS (2014) by Nadia Bruce-Rawlings

STEALING THE MIDNIGHT FROM A HANDFUL OF DAYS (2014) by Michele McDannold

FORTHCOMING BOOKS ON PUNK HOSTAGE PRESS

WHERE THE ROAD LEADS (2014) by Diana Rose

SHOOTING FOR THE STARS IN KEVLAR (2015)
by Iris Berry

LONGWINDED TALES OF A LOW PLAINS DRIFTER (2014)
by A. Razor

EVERYTHING IS RADIANT BETWEEN THE HATES (2014)
Rich Ferguson

GOOD GIRLS GO TO HEAVEN, BAD GIRLS GO EVERYWHERE by Pleasant Gehman (2015)

BOULEVARD OF SPOKEN DREAMS (2014) by Iris Berry

DANGEROUS INTERSECTIONS (2014) by Annette Cruz

DRIVING ALL OF THE HORSES AT ONCE (2015)
by Richard Modiano

DISGRACELAND (2015)
by Iris Berry & Pleasant Gehman

AND THEN THE ACID KICKED IN (2015)
by Carlye Archibeque

BODIES: BRILLIANT SHAPES (2014) by Kate Menzies

THUGNESS IS A VIRTUE (2014) by Hannah Wehr

BORROWING SUGAR (2015) by Susan Hayden

BASTARD SONS OF ALPHABET CITY (2015) by Jon Hess

THE REDHOOK GIRAFFE & OTHER BROOKLYN TALES (2015) by James A. Tropeano III

IN THE SHADOW OF THE HOLLYWOOD SIGN (2015) by Iris Berry

PURO PURISMO (2015) by A. Razor

SIRENS (2015) by Larry Jaffe

Made in the USA
Lexington, KY
22 December 2014